Confronting the Curse

The Economics and Geopolitics of Natural Resource Governance

Cullen S. Hendrix and Marcus Noland

Peterson Institute for International Economics
Washington, DC
May 2014

D1114114

Cullen S. Hendrix, nonresident senior fellow at the Peterson Institute for International Economics, is assistant professor at the Josef Korbel School of International Studies at the University of Denver. He has published widely on the relationships between international markets, natural resources, and conflict, as well as the economic and security implications of climate change. He has consulted for the US Department of Defense, Food and Agriculture Organization, Political Instability Task Force, World Food Programme, and Asian Development Bank. His research has been funded by the US Department of Defense Minerva Initiative and the National Science Foundation.

Marcus Noland, executive vice president and director of studies at the Peterson Institute for International Economics, has been associated with the Institute since 1985. He is also senior fellow at the East-West Center. He was a senior economist at the Council of Economic Advisers in the Executive Office of the President of the United States. He has held research or teaching positions at Yale University, the Johns Hopkins University, the University of Southern California, Tokyo University, Saitama University (now the National Graduate Institute for Policy Studies), the University of Ghana, and the Korea Development Institute. He won the 2000–01 Ohira Memorial Award for his book *Avoiding the Apocalypse: The Future of the Two Koreas*. His other books include *The Arab Economies in a Changing World*, second edition (2011), *Witness to Transformation: Refugee Insights into North Korea* (2011), and *Famine in North Korea: Markets, Aid, and Reform* (2007).

PETERSON INSTITUTE FOR INTERNATIONAL ECONOMICS
1750 Massachusetts Avenue, NW
Washington, DC 20036-1903
(202) 328-9000   FAX: (202) 659-3225
www.piie.com

Adam S. Posen, *President*
Steven R. Weisman, *Vice President for Publications and Communications*

Chapters typeset by Kevin A. Wilson, Upper Case Textual Services, Lawrence, Massachusetts
Graphics typeset by Susann Luetjen
Cover photo by © Henri Bureau/Sygma/Corbis
Printing by Versa Press, Inc.

Printed in the United States of America
16   15   14   5   4   3   2   1

Library of Congress Cataloging-in-Publication Data
Noland, Marcus, 1959–
  Confronting the curse : the economics and geopolitics of natural resource governance / Marcus Noland and Cullen S. Hendrix.
    pages cm
  Includes bibliographical references.
  ISBN 978-0-88132-676-5
  1. Natural resources—Management. 2. Natural resources—Political aspects. I. Hendrix, Cullen S. II. Title.
  HC85.N65 2014
  333.7—dc23
                                    2014003825

This publication has been subjected to a prepublication peer review intended to ensure analytical quality. The views expressed are those of the authors. This publication is part of the overall program of the Peterson Institute for International Economics, as endorsed by its Board of Directors, but it does not necessarily reflect the views of individual members of the Board or of the Institute's staff or management. The Peterson Institute for International Economics is a private, nonprofit institution for the rigorous, open, and intellectually honest study and discussion of international economic policy. Its purpose is to identify and analyze important issues to making globalization beneficial and sustainable for the people of the United States and the world and then to develop and communicate practical new approaches for dealing with them. Its work is made possible by financial support from a highly diverse group of philanthropic foundations, private corporations, and interested individuals, as well as by income on its capital fund. For a list of Institute supporters, please see www.piie.com/supporters.cfm.

Contents

Figures

Boxes

Preface

The past decade's boom in prices for globally traded commodities like oil, gold, and other precious minerals would seem to have presented a bonanza for countries in Asia, the Middle East, and Africa, and the potential market from ongoing growth in China and elsewhere gave more reason to take a long view. Yet, instead of seizing the opportunities derived from their resource abundance, one country after another has turned its resource blessings into a curse. This ground-breaking and powerfully argued interdisciplinary study by Cullen Hendrix and Marcus Noland provides an innovative empirical analysis of that phenomenon and offers policy insights into how to avoid that curse.

Bringing together economic data and real-world cases, *Confronting the Curse: The Economics and Geopolitics of Natural Resource Governance* explores the economics and politics, internal and external, of natural resource dependence. The study highlights the often tragic ways that commodity wealth has weakened domestic institutions, undermined democratic governance, produced corruption and enrichment of elites, and finally led in many cases to devastating violence and war.

Even worse, the authors say, the effects of these problems are not confined within the borders of each country. The resource curse—particularly the production of oil—emboldens producers to adopt more confrontational foreign policies and causes them to spurn institutions of global governance, creating a threat to the liberal international order and to democratic values more generally. China's emergence as a major importer of raw materials and investor in extraction, and its perceived willingness to accommodate authoritarian producers, may exacerbate the problem (although the authors find little evidence of Chinese exceptionalism compared with other international investors to date).

The authors do caution, on the other hand, that it is too simple to say resources cause problems. The relationship between natural resource abundance, economic performance, and political authoritarianism remains poorly understood. The cause-and-effect implications are obviously the greatest for the commodity producers themselves. They face multiple challenges for macroeconomic management, resisting pressures towards political authoritarianism, and in the extreme, preventing outbreak of violent civil conflict. The resource curse also presents long-term challenges for US foreign and economic policy as it seeks to cope with weak states, terrorism, drug trafficking, human trafficking, and other unwanted transborder consequences of failed governance. Another problem for the US and global order addressed innovatively in their study is the more assertive behavior by Russia, Iran, and other countries with power enhanced by their resource wealth.

Hendrix and Noland cover a remarkable amount of territory in this book. They start by addressing the economics and politics of the resource curse, mining a vast academic literature for practical insights. The book goes on to break new ground by extending our understanding of the resource curse to cross-border spillovers and the impact on the international scene. Their study also demonstrates how oil exporter status shapes the foreign policies of producer countries, providing new evidence that high prices embolden exporting countries to engage in more bellicose behavior. A separate chapter addresses the role of China in Africa and the conventional wisdom that Chinese aid, arms, and investment are blindly resource-seeking and different from other investors' (including US) behavior there.

Ultimately, for new resource producers to avoid the curse, there is a need for new kinds of supportive international policies. In the concluding section of their book, Hendrix and Noland deliver the first assessment of the effectiveness of three initiatives: the Kimberley Certification Process Scheme for diamonds; the Extractive Industries Transparency Initiative as applied to oil and gas, mining, and even forestry; and the Conflict Minerals Trade Act, an attempt to bring a Kimberley-like process to bear on the "conflict minerals" problem in the Central African conflict region. They clearly assess these initiatives' performance and prescribe policies, ranging from exchange rate management to the use of sovereign wealth funds. They also address the issue of ownership structure, concluding that public-private partnerships offer the best chance of mitigating the pernicious effects of natural resource wealth. The curse can be avoided—Botswana and Trinidad and Tobago are evidence of this—but the path is not easy, and the rest of the world has a stake in making it easier.

The Peterson Institute for International Economics is a private, nonprofit institution for rigorous, intellectually open, and honest study and discussion of international economic policy. Its purpose is to identify and analyze important issues to making globalization beneficial and sustainable for the people of the United States and the world and then to develop and communicate practical new approaches for dealing with them. The Institute is completely nonpartisan.

The Institute's work is funded by a highly diverse group of philanthropic foundations, private corporations, and interested individuals, as well as income on its capital fund. About 35 percent of the Institute's resources in our latest fiscal year were provided by contributors from outside the United States. The Smith Richardson Foundation provided generous support for this study. Interested readers may access the data underlying Institute books by searching titles at http://bookstore.piie.com.

The Executive Committee of the Institute's Board of Directors bears overall responsibility for the Institute's direction, gives general guidance and approval to its research program, and evaluates its performance in pursuit of its mission. The Institute's President is responsible for the identification of topics that are likely to become important over the medium term (one to three years) that should be addressed by Institute scholars. This rolling agenda is set in close consultation with the Institute's research staff, Board of Directors, and other stakeholders.

The President makes the final decision to publish any individual Institute study, following independent internal and external review of the work.

The Institute hopes that its research and other activities will contribute to building a stronger foundation for international economic policy around the world. We invite readers of these publications to let us know how they think we can best accomplish this objective.

ADAM S. POSEN
President
April 2014

Acknowledgments

In his classic work *How Europe Underdeveloped Africa*, the late Guyanese historian Walter Rodney wrote, "Contrary to the fashion in most prefaces, I will not add that 'all mistakes and shortcomings are entirely my responsibility.' That is sheer bourgeois subjectivism. Responsibility in matters of these sorts is always collective, especially with regard to the remedying of shortcomings." We would respectfully disagree, at least in part.

This book would not exist without Kevin Stahler, who provided extensive research assistance, and Meghan Mooney, who generated the map in chapter 3. We benefited enormously from the extensive comments of seminar participants at the Peterson Institute, particularly William Cline, Nicholas Cook, Joseph Gagnon, Barbara Kotschwar, Ted Moran, Ted Truman, and Nicolas Véron. Peer reviewers Rabah Arezki, Robert Lawrence, and Erik Voeten were extremely helpful in focusing our arguments and helping us bridge the divides between both economics and political science and scholar and practitioner. Discussions with Jeff Colgan, Michael Ross, and Joe Young left an imprint as well.

We would like to thank Barbara Karni, Madona Devasahayam, Susann Luetjen, and Steve Weisman for turning our manuscript into the actual book you have in your hands.

Cullen Hendrix wishes to thank the College of William & Mary for the academic leave he needed to jumpstart this manuscript and for providing somewhat subsidized housing during his semester sabbatical in Washington, DC. He thanks his mother, father, and stepmother for the twin gifts of curiosity and tenacity and his brother and sister for their support and encouragement. He wishes to thank his sometimes coauthor and perpetual soulmate, Sarah Glaser, for her love, support, and help during this process. Cullen's contributions to this manuscript were authored across five time zones and four continents, and she was right there with him—figuratively and (mostly) literally—through all of it. Finally, he wishes to thank his coauthor, Marcus Noland. Climbing the mountain is easier when you climb with someone who knows the way and how to make the trip a pleasure.

Marcus Noland would like to thank the Peterson Institute and his family for allowing periodic retreats from management and parenting, respectively, which made his contribution to this book possible. He also thanks his coauthor, Cullen Hendrix, for indulging geezerdom.

We would also like to thank Fred Bergsten and Adam Posen. This project straddled the transition between their presidencies of the Institute and would not have been possible without the encouragement and guidance both provided. Cullen wishes to thank Fred in particular for having gambled and brought an untenured political scientist from a directional school in Texas into the PIIE fold. He hopes the gamble has paid off.

Last and certainly not least we would like to thank Allan Song and the Smith Richardson Foundation for financial support, which made writing this book possible.

With all this assistance, and at the risk of being labeled bourgeois subjectivists, we depart from Walter Rodney and accept that any remaining shortcomings are ours and ours alone.

1

Introduction

In 2007, significant offshore oil discoveries were made off the coast of Ghana, a West African nation of 25 million that had just graduated out of low-income status. Ghana's then-president, John Kufuor, was ebullient, remarking, "Even without oil, we are doing so well, already. Now, with oil as a shot in the arm, we're going to fly."[1] But the dinner table conversation between one of the authors and his Ghanaian wife was less "we're in the money!" than "oh, no."

This doubting response to a development that will surely bring income and wealth to Ghana exemplifies the increasing ambivalence with which citizens regard major commodity discoveries. In the case of Ghana, the question is whether its economic and political institutions are capable of successfully managing the sudden influx of income and wealth that the production of oil is likely to bring—or whether the oil wealth will complicate macroeconomic management to the detriment of traditional industries and encourage a reversal of the country's steady yet still fragile evolution into a mature democracy. It is an open question.

How did we arrive at such pessimism, and is it warranted? How is it that valuable natural resources are not considered an unqualified blessing for the countries that find them? Intuitively, one would assume that more valuable resources would lead to better development outcomes—that finding oil, gold, or other precious minerals would amount to receiving manna from heaven. In fact, for many countries, resource wealth has come to be viewed as a curse. Even one of the principal architects of the Organization of Petroleum Exporting Countries (OPEC), former Venezuelan Minister of Mines and Hydrocarbons

---

1. "UK's Tullow Uncovers Oil in Ghana," BBC News, June 18, 2007.

1

Juan Pablo Pérez Alfonso, referred to his country's oil wealth as "the devil's excrement"—and that was when Venezuela was the most prosperous, democratic country in South America.

This book is about one of the more curious findings/nonfindings in the history of economics: that valuable natural resources, such as oil, natural gas, and other mined commodities are not, in the main, associated with better development outcomes and may even retard long-run rates of economic growth and discourage political development. Economists have long argued over the impact of resource endowments on economic performance. Common sense would seem to suggest that if one finds oneself sitting on a gold mine, then one should mine gold (or drill oil, as in the example above). But countries that have specialized in the production of extractive or "point-source" resources, such as mined commodities like gold, diamonds, and oil, tend to be poor, creating a nagging sense that specialization in extraction is a losing proposition in the global division of labor, condemning countries to be "hewers of wood and drawers of water." This finding is true despite the fact that their primary exports are some of the most valuable commodities on earth and that their value has been growing particularly rapidly of late.

The 21st century commodity boom, during which real prices for most globally traded commodities more than doubled (figure 1.1), catalyzed a gold rush–like frenzy of exploration effort, resulting in radical upward revisions of proven oil and/or natural gas reserves and mineral deposits in many "legacy" (long-time) exporters (Iraq, Saudi Arabia, and Venezuela) as well as discoveries by much smaller and/or nonlegacy exporters. Countries across West Africa (Côte d'Ivoire, Ghana, and Liberia), East and Southern Africa (Kenya, Mozambique, and Uganda), and Southeast Asia (Cambodia, Myanmar, and Vietnam) have seen their proven energy and mineral reserves increase significantly. In recent years, Mongolia has emerged as one of the world's fastest-growing economies, driven by surging output from huge copper, gold, and coal mining projects. Even Afghanistan, a minor trader whose most lucrative export is fruits and nuts, is now estimated to have more than a trillion dollars' worth of mineral deposits. Where these deposits are found, massive inflows of investment capital typically follow. More often than not, however, this investment capital and the vast natural resources it exploits do not catalyze broad-based, inclusive growth.

Over the years, concerns about the role of resources and development have been sharpened in a number of ways. They concern the possibility that despite recent trends, natural resource products have experienced long-term declines in price; that the prices of these commodities are unusually volatile, complicating planning and giving rise to boom-bust cycles; and that by drawing in money and attention, temporary booms may undermine, perhaps irreparably, other segments of the economy. What these propositions, all of which are debatable, suggest is that countries in which resource extraction plays a central role in economic life are effectively running uphill, at a long-term relative disadvan-

Figure 1.1 Oil and metal prices, 1980–2013

price index (2005 = 100)

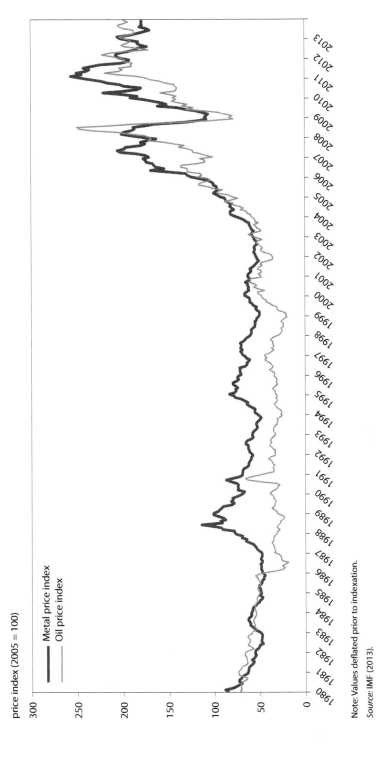

Note: Values deflated prior to indexation.

Source: IMF (2013).

3

tage in terms of economic performance in relation to more diverse, balanced economies.

It is not just that the focus on resource extraction may put these countries on a disadvantageous long-term economic trajectory. As a group, their political histories are disproportionately characterized by instability and conflict. One possible explanation for this phenomenon is that the presence of "contestable" resources heightens competition for control of the state or enables the continuation of less than best practices with respect to governance. Another is that weak political institutions have retarded the development of more complex forms of transactions and forced an implicit reliance on extraction in economic life.

In either case, the potentially deleterious impact of natural resources on development is captured in the phrase "the resource curse." The implications are greatest for the commodity producers themselves, ranging from complications for macroeconomic management to the potential encouragement of political authoritarianism and, in the extreme, the precipitation of violent civil conflict. It was in Libya—where minerals and fuels account for 97 percent of exports and more than half of GDP (Center for International Development 2010)—that the mostly peaceful Arab Spring uprising first turned violent, leading ultimately to intervention by the North Atlantic Treaty Organization. For outsiders, the resource curse presents long-term challenges with respect to coping with violence in exporting states and its facilitation of unwanted transborder phenomena, including terrorism, drug trafficking, and illegal migration and human trafficking.

Major powers may become entangled in these weaker states in an effort to block these undesirable spillovers. Such entanglement was underscored by the trial in the Hague of former Liberian president Charles Taylor for crimes against humanity committed during the diamond-fueled civil wars of Liberia and neighboring Sierra Leone—which, apart from the immediate destruction, were exploited by al Qaeda and other terrorist groups to evade anti–money laundering and terrorist finance efforts and eventually required the intervention of British troops and US-supported multinational forces.

But great power involvement may not always be so defensive or altruistic in nature. From Allende in copper-exporting Chile to Lumumba in copper- and uranium-rich Zaire (now the Democratic Republic of the Congo), the historical record is littered with US and Western involvement in or support of coups against elected leaders whose political platforms threatened Western business interests. The combination of valuable resources and weak institutions, which may encourage violent domestic conflict, may attract the attention of outside powers with less lofty motives. In contemporary times, among the shifting justifications for the US invasion of Iraq (and Iraq's earlier invasion of Kuwait) was the control of oil.

With its rise as an economic, political, and military force, China too is poised to exert critical influence on the fortunes of resource-based economies around the globe—and to create anxiety for the incumbent powers as well. If

China were to become involved in the domestic politics of countries in which it holds large equity stakes in natural resources, it would not be the first major power to have done so.

China's rise occurs against the backdrop of attempts by the West—broadly encompassing Western nongovernmental organizations (NGOs), Western governments, and the multilateral institutions that Western governments dominate, such as the World Bank—to formulate new ways of better managing the resource curse. These initiatives—for example, the Kimberley Process Certification Scheme (KPCS) with regard to "conflict" or "blood" diamonds and the Extractive Industries Transparency Initiative (EITI)—can be regarded as a way to assuage troubled consciences, act as a precommitment mechanism to forestall more damaging forms of intervention, and promote more humane and rational uses of these resources. Whether they can be effective and, crucially, what role China will play with respect to these efforts remain open questions.

The commodity price boom or "supercycle" of recent years has raised the stakes and created an additional set of concerns for Western governments. The problem can be seen most clearly in the oil industry, where high oil prices in recent years, apart from representing a massive transfer of wealth from consumers to producers, have conferred enhanced financial and political power on producing states, which are generally underrepresented in the institutions of global governance where rules and procedures are formulated. The implication is that this enhanced power further weakens adherence to international norms, such as those governing human rights and participation in global environmental governance. Put simply, higher prices empower these regimes to pursue their aims.

Exporting states' aspirations are sometimes revisionist in nature: Believing that they have not received their just rewards under the status quo, they seek to weaken, circumvent, or otherwise undermine the liberal, rules-based international order that has prevailed since the end of World War II, in both its economic and political dimensions. China's emergence as a major importer and investor in extraction, and its willingness to accommodate revisionist exporters (Iran, Sudan, and, until recently, Myanmar), further exacerbates the diplomatic challenge, potentially undercutting international efforts in recent years to encourage greater transparency and improved management of natural resource wealth, as noted above, as well as Western diplomatic initiatives, including economic sanctions, targeted at resource exporters like Sudan. This issue is of particular salience for US policy toward Africa. By some estimates, China has surpassed the United States as the single largest provider of aid to the continent, and Chinese outward foreign direct investment is heavily targeted at the extractive sector. The resource boom may have catalyzed a "new scramble for Africa" (Carmody 2011). The last scramble for Africa ended badly, with European powers shooting it out in World War I. Although the war started in the Balkans, it was preceded by an intense naval arms race, motivated in large part by the desire to secure access to colonies (and commodities) around the world. The potential that this resource boom will occasion a geopolitical confrontation between the United States and China must be considered.

Internally, tightening commodity markets and higher prices facilitate repression, incentivize contestation of political control, and make it easier to finance insurgency. These conditions may also confer increased international political and economic clout on revisionist producers and investors. Many fear that the "Beijing Consensus"—a term applied to China's pursuit of marketization without democratization—is being exported around the globe, with illiberal regimes being propped up by the deep coffers of Chinese investors.

It is possible that these problems will be self-eradicating, as a decline in commodity prices from their current elevated levels would deprive revisionist countries like Russia, Iran, and Venezuela of revenues and thereby some power to influence events. Although real prices for oil and metals were flat or declining between 1980 and 2000, the past 13 years have seen rapid price increases and recurrent price spikes (see figure 1.1). But the general consensus appears that high prices reflect increased demand associated with the acceleration of growth in China, India, and other countries; relatively easy monetary conditions globally since 2001; anticompetitive action by OPEC; and possibly, in the case of oil, long-run constraints on supply (Carter, Rausser, and Smith 2011). Accelerated growth in China, India, and elsewhere may be secular in nature, easy money is a cyclical phenomenon, and the jury is still out on whether the global supply of oil is being exhausted (Simmons 2005, 2007). In short, although it is unlikely that commodity prices will remain at their current levels indefinitely, it would be a mistake to dismiss current prices as entirely the product of a speculative bubble. The *2013 World Energy Outlook* forecasts that global demand will rise by 33 percent by 2035 (IEA 2013).

These concerns have elicited a variety of policy responses to various facets of these issues. The West African civil wars of the 1990s generated two related policy initiatives: KPCS, to eradicate trade in conflict diamonds, and the Diamond Development Initiative (DDI), to address broader development concerns, particularly with respect to small-scale alluvial diamond mining. The role of diamonds in fueling violent political conflict has been attenuated, but this attenuation may be temporary; it is unclear how much of the decline in conflict stems from policy and how much reflects other factors and is subject to reversal. Immediate concern has shifted from civil war to the issue of militarized forced production in Zimbabwe.

EITI aims to strengthen governance, transparency, and accountability by encouraging companies to report payments and governments to report revenues in oil, gas, and mining. Recently, the United States has sought to construct a Kimberley-like certification process for certain minerals believed to have fueled mass violence in the Democratic Republic of the Congo and surrounding areas.

The other issue is the growing clout of revisionist producers. A possible response would be to deny them commodity export–derived revenues.

Unilaterally, consuming countries could reduce oil and gas consumption through conservation and development of alternatives. (One could argue that high prices represent implicitly "green" incentives, but conservation could have the same effect even if it resulted in a price reduction.) Although the United States has fruitlessly pursued "energy independence" since the Nixon administration, it now seems possible. An even more profound effect may be generated by the reemergence, through new discoveries and new technologies, of North America as a major source of hydrocarbon production.

North American energy independence would not signal an end to significant US involvement in and engagement with energy-exporting countries, however: Major trading partners in Europe and Asia will continue to be import dependent, and political instability in producing countries can propagate ever more quickly through the international system via global markets. Whatever its export position with respect to energy, the United States can scarcely afford to entirely retrench from an energy-focused foreign policy.

A number of multiauthor and edited volumes address aspects of the resource curse in considerable detail (for example, Humphreys, Sachs, and Stiglitz 2007; Lederman and Maloney 2007; Arezki, Gylfason, and Sy 2012; Arezki et al. 2012; Barma et al. 2012; Dobbs et al. 2013). This book differs from those works in two principal ways. It does not go into detail on the economics of contract and tax regimes for extractive industries; these issues are addressed adequately elsewhere. It does take seriously the critical and inadequately examined political economy of resource extraction in both its intra- and interstate dimensions.

The book is organized as follows. Chapter 2 briefly reviews the basic economics of the resource curse. It concludes that on purely economic grounds, there is reason to be concerned that the impacts are worse in poor countries than rich countries. Although a variety of policies and approaches can be implemented to mitigate harm, none is perfect; and for most countries, successful implementation depends critically on the capacity of the political system, which is weak in many poor resource-centric countries.

If there is a resource curse, it probably lies in the deeper political economy of institutions, rather than in economic management per se. These domestic political challenges are taken up in chapter 3, which makes the case that the resource curse operates primarily through political and institutional channels, with deleterious effects on democracy, bureaucratic and state capacity, and domestic political stability. In particular, it finds that the effects of natural resource wealth are conditional on preexisting institutions and price levels: When preexisting institutions are bad and prices high, the resource curse is more likely to emerge.

Chapters 4 and 5 move to the realm of interstate politics, examining first the ways that resource wealth shapes the foreign relations of resource exporters and then the rise of China as a major commodities importer. Oil exports in particular emerge as a driver of both more bellicose behaviors toward other countries and less participation in global governance institutions, which has implications for the adoption and observance of international norms. These effects are price sensitive: Higher oil prices embolden oil exporters to adopt more aggressive foreign policies.

China's rise as a commodity importer has drawn increased scrutiny of its foreign affairs, resulting in an emerging two-pronged conventional wisdom: (1) China's foreign policy stance is driven in large part by resource-seeking behavior and (2) China's resource-seeking behavior is "rogue," undermining democracy, human rights, and attempts to promote good governance in the developing world. This conventional wisdom has been great fodder for pundits but heretofore subjected to comparatively little rigorous scrutiny. Chapter 5 finds strong evidence that China's outward foreign direct investment is highly concentrated in extractives. It finds less evidence that China's official development assistance and arms transfers are as rogue as conventional wisdom suggests.

Chapter 6 examines multilateral good governance schemes. What is striking is that all of the initiatives reviewed are less the product of textbook economics than campaigns by Western NGOs. As a consequence, their success depends heavily on the efficacy of naming and shaming campaigns directed at producers and the willingness of Western governments to back these efforts up with legislation. The growing importance of non-Western consumers, who at least for the moment seem less sensitive to these concerns; non-Western producers, which may be less susceptible to shaming; and non-Western governments, which may be less supportive of these efforts may pose a profound long-term challenge to this approach.

Chapter 7 summarizes the core arguments and findings of the book and sketches out some policy responses, some aimed at alleviating the resource curse in new and emerging exporters via domestic policy decisions, others aimed at broader, multilateral accords for promoting good resource governance. Given the diversity of economies and commodities covered, no single policy choice, or even bundle of choices, provides a panacea. However, chapter 7 discusses how governments in countries grappling with newfound resource wealth can structure ownership in ways that are more likely to harness that wealth for improved developmental outcomes. In particular, it highlights the potential for partnerships between Western and non-Western entities to combine the flush capital reserves of non-Western investors with the good governance awareness of Western firms and the NGOs that follow them.

For the United States and other Western countries, it is important that this process produce a race to the top rather than the bottom: Just as the resource curse is contingent on institutional quality, so is its avoidance. Well-functioning institutions enormously improve the odds of successful implementation of the technocratic solutions sketched out in the chapter. Poor governance in resource-centric states is associated with state failure and attendant transborder spillovers, as well as a heightened likelihood of interstate conflict. The emphasis on enhanced transparency in the resource sector, going beyond the norms applied in other sectors or business activities, is no simple matter of wide-eyed altruism. Ultimately, good governance in the resource sector can help avoid the resource curse and the "public bads" that often follow it.

2

Natural Resources and Economic Performance

One can think of natural resources as a windfall, like a gift that should make you wealthier. An 18-year-old who gets a trust fund should be wealthier at age 40 than her twin who did not get the trust fund, unless the trust fund has some nefarious effects. But as revealed by a glance at table 2.1, countries whose wealth is heavily derived from the exploitation of natural resources generally are not rich—indeed they tend to be poorer and less democratic than countries whose wealth is based on the accumulation of human and physical capital. These relationships broadly hold for the entire sample for which data are available (figures 2.1 and 2.2).

What is driving this seemingly paradoxical relationship between the exploitation of natural resources and development? Understanding the precise channels through which resource dependency might affect outcomes is necessary for designing policies to address the issue. Is it an issue of abundance, the availability of resource-derived rents, or the centrality of resources in the economy? What is the direction of causality in this crude correlation? Are countries poor and undemocratic because they are dependent on the exploitation of natural resources—or are countries rich because they have developed the institutions and practices that have enabled them to move from extraction to the production of high-value-added services and manufactures? Is the dependence of poor countries on resources a manifestation of underlying institutional weaknesses that have prevented them from moving into more remunerative activities? In short, is the "resource curse" a cause or an effect?

This chapter surveys some of the channels through which the exploitation of natural resources may inhibit economic performance, examining in turn the possible roles of declining terms of trade, price volatility, resource pulls, and Dutch disease. It finds that there is cause for concern about all chan-

Table 2.1 Top and bottom countries by share of natural capital in country's total wealth, 2005

Country	Share of natural capital in total wealth (percent)	GDP per capita (2000 US dollars)	Polity IV score
	Top 10 percent		
Republic of the Congo	244	1,113	−4
Uzbekistan	144	684	−9
Burundi	123	128	6
Guyana	114	989	6
Angola	96	888	−2
Papua New Guinea	95	626	4
Liberia	95	187	5
Chad	93	308	−2
Central African Republic	87	227	−1
Bhutan	85	964	−6
Brunei Darussalam	79	18,312	n.a.
Azerbaijan	76	1,183	−7
Gabon	72	4,029	−4
Democratic Republic of the Congo	70	92	4
Saudi Arabia	66	9,440	−10

(continues on next page)

nels, at least with respect to the production of certain commodities and in certain settings. Even setting aside sustainability and optimal rate of extraction concerns, the exploitation of natural resources clearly poses particular problems for economic policy management. But the chapter concludes that whatever the nature of the resource curse, a complete understanding requires moving beyond economics, narrowly defined, and taking up the issues of political institutions (addressed in chapter 3).

Declining Terms of Trade

Although it may come as a shock to people who came of age during the long current bull market in commodities, for much of the last century, the real value of commodities was believed to be subject to long-term decline. In the 1950s, Argentinean economist Raúl Prebisch (1950) argued that commodities were subject to a long-term secular decline in their terms of trade relative to manufactures (see also Singer 1950). A variety of theoretical conditions could generate this empirical regularity. One would be a low income elasticity of demand for primary commodities, as a result of intrinsically low elasticities (for example, Engel curves for staple foods) or an indirect result of techno-

Table 2.1 Top and bottom countries by share of natural capital in country's total wealth, 2005 *(continued)*

Country	Share of natural capital in total wealth (percent)	GDP per capita (2000 US dollars)	Polity IV score
	Bottom 10 percent		
Macao, China	0	22,024	n.a.
Singapore	0	28,389	−2
Hong Kong, China	0	30,395	n.a.
St. Lucia	0	4,827	n.a.
Japan	0.4	39,295	10
Luxembourg	0.7	51,980	n.a.
Belgium	0.9	24,034	10
United Kingdom	0.9	28,261	10
Germany	1.0	23,564	10
South Korea	1.1	13,802	8
Seychelles	1.1	7,209	n.a.
Switzerland	1.3	35,860	10
Iceland	1.4	36,129	n.a.
Portugal	1.4	11,587	10
France	1.5	22,734	9

n.a. = Polity IV Project does not report these countries in its data

Note: Polity scores range from 10 (most democratic) to −10 (least democratic), based inter alia on the relative competitiveness of executive recruitment, constraints on the chief executive, and competitiveness of political participation.

Source: World Bank; Polity IV Project, www.systemicpeace.org/polity/polity4.htm (accessed on February 20, 2014).

logical change either generating alternatives (for example, artificial rubber) or conserving on the quantity of natural resources needed in industrial production. Another is lack of product differentiation, contributing to highly competitive markets and the dissipation of rents.[1] Such a secular deterioration in their terms of trade in the absence of significant productivity advances would create an ongoing balance of payments challenge for developing countries reliant on commodity exports, effectively forcing them to run uphill by exporting ever larger quantities of raw materials to finance industrial imports.[2]

---

1. In the case of nonrenewable resources, there is the Malthusian argument of exhaustion, which would imply that prices should rise in the long run. This view finds its greatest prominence with respect to "peak oil," but it has spawned a host of "peak" imitators, including water, potassium, and phosphate (Hendrix 2011).

2. If productivity increases are sufficiently large, countries could be better off even with declining terms of trade. Indeed, it is even possible that productivity improvements could be the cause

Figure 2.1   Relationship between per capita GDP and share of natural wealth in total wealth

log GDP per capita (constant 2000 US dollars)

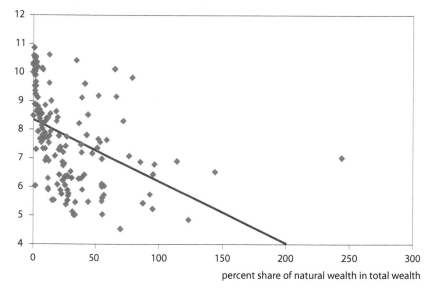

percent share of natural wealth in total wealth

Sources: World Bank, *Changing Wealth of Nations,* http://data.worldbank.org/data-catalog/wealth-of-nations (accessed on February 19, 2014); GDP per capita (constant 2000 US dollars): World Bank, *World Development Indicators.*

Whether what came to be known as the "Prebisch-Singer hypothesis" is correct is an empirical matter; unsurprisingly, there is a lack of consensus, turning in large part on highly technical statistical issues.[3] Perhaps the most exhaustive study, based on 400 years of price data, finds support for the Prebisch-Singer hypothesis for only a handful of the 25 commodities examined (aluminum, bananas, rice, sugar, and tea), meaning that their prices fell for all or some significant later fraction of the sample period (Harvey et al. 2012). For beef, coal, cocoa, coffee, copper, cotton, gold, hide, jute, lamb, lead, nickel, oil, pig iron, silver, tin, wheat, wool, and zinc, David Harvey et al. find

of declining prices (Tilton 2013). Chapter 7 examines the advisability of adopting policies to encourage diversification.

3. Studies finding confirmatory evidence for the Prebisch-Singer hypothesis include Spraos (1980), Sapsford (1985), Thirlwall and Bergevin (1985), Grilli and Yang (1988), and Powell (1991). Apart from nontrivial data issues (see Svedberg and Tilton 2006, 2011; Cuddington 2010; and Harvey et al. 2010), two statistical issues are at play: uncertainty regarding the true time series process generating the series and the possible presence of infrequent structural breaks in trend. Depending on how these two issues are handled, the same data set can generate apparently contradictory results regarding a secular deterioration in the relative price of commodities. See Cuddington, Ludema, and Jayasuriya (2007); Cuddington and Nülle (2013); and Harvey et al. (2013).

Figure 2.2 Relationship between democratization and share of natural wealth in total wealth

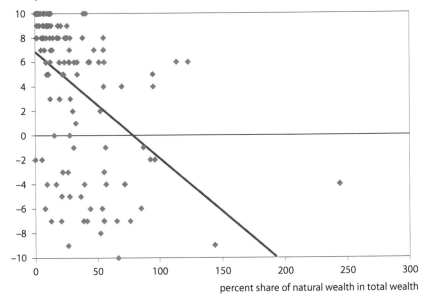

Polity IV democratization index score

percent share of natural wealth in total wealth

Sources: World Bank, *Changing Wealth of Nations*, http://data.worldbank.org/data-catalog/wealth-of-nations (accessed on February 19, 2014); Polity IV Project, www.systemicpeace.org/polity/polity4.htm (accessed on February 20, 2014).

no evidence of a price trend. Only in the single case of tobacco do they discover a positive price trend.[4]

Given the conceptual challenges of establishing a global price, the quality of the data, falling computational costs, and increasingly easy access to ever more sophisticated forms of time series analysis, it is not surprising that there is no consensus on these results. In particular, there is some evidence of "super-cycles" in the data and possible evidence of a positive upswing in the last decade or so (Cuddington and Jerrett 2008, Erten and Ocampo 2012, Harvey et al. 2013, and Yamada and Yoon 2013). Harvey et al. (2013) discover commodity price cycles of roughly 24 (cocoa) to 39 (copper) years. A period of 20 to 40 years is probably long enough to be relevant in terms of establishing a "new normal" and affecting economic and political behavior.

Developing countries typically do not export baskets of commodities: As Harvey et al. (2012) observe, three or fewer commodities account for virtually

---

4. The results reported in Harvey et al. (2010), which finds that nearly half the commodities had secularly declining prices, are erroneous because of an error in the way in which the various historical price series were converted to a common currency.

all exports for 40 least developed countries. And, regardless of the validity of the Prebisch-Singer hypothesis for commodities as a class, the hypothesis may well describe the experience of particular developing countries. In 2011, the five commodities that Harvey et al. identify as having experienced a secular deterioration in their terms of trade accounted for 45 percent of the exports of Guyana, 21 percent of the exports of Malawi, and 20 percent of the exports of Belize (table 2.2).[5] Fortuitously, Malawi also has the world's highest concentration of exports in tobacco (40 percent).[6]

The countries listed in table 2.2 are predominantly small and poor. As a rule, the exports of small countries tend to be concentrated in relatively few products, so the degree of specialization itself is not surprising. Presumably their low level of per capita income is linked to the fact that they specialize in commodities with secularly declining prices. As a group, they also have unusually conflictual political histories.

Commodity Price Volatility

If a few small developing countries defined the extent of the issue, it would amount to a significant, though relatively localized, problem. A related, though distinct, concern is that commodity prices may be highly volatile and the instability of export revenues may discourage saving and investment, complicating macroeconomic policy management, encouraging a boom-bust mentality, contributing to welfare-reducing instability in income and consumption, and ultimately slowing growth in income and consumption (UN 1952, Nurkse 1958). Developing countries do experience greater macroeconomic volatility than developed countries, and this volatility has a negative impact on economic performance. How much of this macroeconomic volatility can be attributed to commodity price volatility is an empirical issue.

The stylized facts, based on an examination of data on commodity prices going back as far as 1700, are that commodity prices are indeed more volatile than manufactures prices, there is little evidence of increased commodity price volatility over time, and periods during which global market integration is high are associated with less volatility than periods of wars or protectionism (Jacks, O'Rourke, and Williamson 2012). David Jacks, Kevin O'Rourke, and Jeffrey Williamson interpret their first finding—that commodity prices have

---

5. For the purposes of this calculation, exports of bauxite rather than aluminum were used. Researchers include aluminum in the commodity basket because good price data exist going back to the late 1800s, when an electrolytic reduction process was discovered that essentially turned aluminum from a precious into a mass-produced industrial metal. The process is very energy intensive, however, and today the local production of aluminum is very much a function of local energy prices rather than the location of bauxite ores. This characteristic explains the recent concentration of aluminum smelting in the Gulf countries. For our purposes, the location of the mining of the primary input, not the smelting, is more relevant.

6. Other countries with substantial concentrations in tobacco include Aruba (32 percent) and Zimbabwe (20 percent).

Table 2.2   Countries most specialized in exports with secularly declining prices, 2011

Rank	Country	Total goods exports in commodity basket (percent)[a]
1	Guyana	45.4
2	Malawi	21.1
3	Belize	19.5
4	Sri Lanka	14.8
5	St. Vincent and the Grenadines	14.1
6	Mauritius	13.7
7	Jamaica	12.9
8	Rwanda	12.7
9	Guatemala	12.2
10	Ecuador	10.5

Note: Countries have been ranked out of 148 countries by 2011 export data.

a. Basket of commodities with secularly declining prices includes bananas (including plantains, fresh or dried), tea, rice, sugar and confectionary, bauxite, and concentrates of aluminum.

Source: UN Comtrade Database.

always been more volatile than prices of manufactures, extending deep into the 18th century, before the Industrial Revolution—as contrary to the hypothesis that asymmetries in product differentiation or the degree of oligopoly contribute to the "rent dissipation" explanation for the secular decline in the terms of trade.

But in terms of economic performance, not all volatility is alike. Ultimately, one is concerned about the volatility of income and consumption, not prices per se. From this perspective, the implications differ, at least in a closed-economy model (figure 2.3). In the case of demand shocks, the impact on quantity magnifies the price impact on revenues. In the case of supply-side shocks, the price and quantity effects move in opposite directions, stabilizing revenue. Agricultural products may be more susceptible to weather-related supply shocks, whereas nonfood commodities may be more prone to business cycle–related demand shocks. Empirically, commodity price volatility appears to be predominantly a result of the less worrisome supply-side shocks.[7]

This argument has to be relaxed in an open-economy setting. In this situation, it is not enough for the shocks to emanate from the supply side: They must be common across producers. This may not be an issue if, for example,

7. See Murray (1978), Behrman (1984), and Lutz (1994). It is also the case that export instability may result from either domestic or foreign shocks, although the latter appear to predominate (Wong 1986).

Figure 2.3   Revenue effects of demand and supply shocks

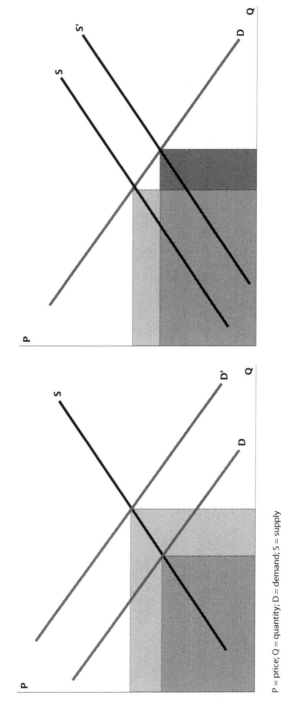

P = price; Q = quantity; D = demand; S = supply

Source: Authors' illustration.

16

common weather conditions affect agricultural producers, such as contiguous cocoa producers in Côte d'Ivoire, Ghana, and Togo. The opening of a new copper mine in Mongolia may be bad news for producers in Chile or Zambia, however.

The arguments of the United Nations' research group and Ragnar Nurkse (1958) regarding commodity price volatility launched a body of empirical literature that generated a mélange of apparently contradictory conclusions regarding the impact of price volatility on saving, investment, and growth among commodity exporters.

For a number of reasons, fiscal policy in commodity-exporting countries appears to have a procyclical bias (Heinrich 2011).[8] There is a tendency for governments to increase low-quality public investments, which cost money in the short term and do not generate adequate offsetting revenue flows in the long term, contributing to long-run fiscal woes. There is also a tendency to expand the size of the public sector, in terms of both the number of public employees and their wages, as well as to increase subsidies to food and other products. Once made, such commitments are difficult to reverse when export prices weaken.

External capital flows also tend to be procyclical. This response can be endogenous to the expansionary fiscal policy noted above. Also, if resource revenues contribute to a real appreciation in the exchange rate, the real resource costs of debt service can appear (temporarily) low, encouraging borrowing. There is therefore a tendency for fiscal policy to be procyclical. That said, in some countries there is evidence of learning and improved management. Chile, for example, makes better use of its copper revenues than it did a generation ago, and some Gulf energy producers made better use of their revenues during the recent boom than they did in the 1970s, allocating resources to improving human capital through education expenditures (see chapter 7).

What about private saving? The expected impact of either price or revenue volatility is not unambiguous. From a permanent income hypothesis perspective, if the saving response were asymmetric, with high saving in boom times not fully offset by dissaving in busts—as a result of uncertainty about the duration of the bust, for example—one might expect volatility to actually increase aggregate saving. Indeed, some studies make precisely this claim (Knudsen and Parnes 1975, Nugent and Yotopoulos 1976). But instability also creates "capital risk" (uncertainty regarding the value of and return on capital investment), which discourages saving. Christián Morán (1983) obtained results consistent with this interpretation.

The literature has generated conflicting results as to whether private investment is negatively or positively correlated with export instability. Peter Kenen and Constantine Voivodas (1972) find a negative correlation; Jeffrey Nugent and Pan Yotopoulos (1976) and David Dawe (1996) find a positive

---

8. See Caceres and Medina (2012) for an analysis of oil price volatility for the fiscal policies of oil exporters.

correlation. Both Alasdair MacBean (1966) and Kenen and Voivodas (1972) find that export instability is positively correlated with investment growth, which they associate with higher rates of investment.

Philip Brock (1991) develops a stochastic optimal control model based on the maximizing behavior of a risk-averse representative agent. It provides a useful framework for sorting through the evidence. He shows that the MacBean and Kenen and Voivodas results are consistent with a growth path in which instability reduces long-run accumulation by raising the risk premium. This interpretation appears to be borne out in results obtained by Sule Özler and James Harrigan (1988), who find that export uncertainty is negatively correlated with capital stock growth rates.

Ultimately, what matters is income and consumption growth. Although studies reach a variety of conclusions, the preponderance of evidence would appear to support the notion that export uncertainty is negatively correlated with income growth (van der Ploeg and Poelhekke 2008).[9] Matthias Lutz (1994) observes that although export instability may be negatively associated with growth, its influence on performance is weakest for the lowest-income countries and primary products exporters, noting that "there must be other important factors contributing to growth in these countries"; export instability is not the preponderant influence. Indeed, the direction of causality is ambiguous. Are these countries poor because the prices of their exports are unstable, or do they specialize in commodities because their weak business-enabling environments frustrate the emergence of more complex forms of production? To reiterate a point made earlier with respect to possible secular deterioration in the terms of trade, the conclusion that the volatility of commodity prices as a class may not be growing may be little recompense to a policymaker in a poor country whose exports are highly unstable.

Resource Pulls and Crowding Out

It is unsurprising that whatever their ultimate empirical validity, these arguments regarding the long-term trends in and volatility of commodity prices were used to justify the adoption of import-substituting industrialization policies in many developing countries, as well as the establishment of commodity cartels bent on stabilizing—and raising—commodity prices. The Organization of Petroleum Exporting Countries (OPEC) is the best known and most successful of these initiatives, but many others were tried—and largely failed— in commodities as diverse as coffee, copper, and tin, to name but three.

To be sure, some of the most successful economies of the last half-

---

9. See also the exchanges between Glezakos (1973, 1984) and Savvides (1984); Lam (1980), Tan (1983), and Glezakos (1983); and Özler and Harrigan (1988) and Lutz (1994). Dawe (1996) finds that instability is positively correlated with investment but negatively correlated with growth, which he asserts could be caused by uncertainty about future prices reducing the rate of return on investment and/or investment booms undertaken in the context of closed capital markets.

century—Japan, South Korea, and Taiwan, for example—have not been abundantly endowed in natural resources, but the cross-country statistical evidence on the relationship between abundance and growth is ambiguous (see Leamer et al. 1999, Rodríguez and Sachs 1999, Lederman and Maloney 2007). Figures 2.4 and 2.5 project labor, physical capital, human capital, and arable land endowments onto a two-dimensional diagram. (For reasons of data availability and tractability, arable land is used as a proxy in this illustration for natural resources more broadly. It is not the only resource; its use in this application is purely illustrative.) The average world endowment is represented by the intersection in the center of the triangle of the three rays emanating from its vertices. As one gets closer to the corner, the relative abundance of that factor increases. So, for example, in figure 2.4, Japan is very land scarce (i.e., it is far from the land vertex) and has a higher capital-labor ratio than South Korea, which, in turn, has a higher ratio than Taiwan.

It does appear that land- or resource-scarce countries developed manufacturing activities at an earlier stage in their development, specialized more intensively in those activities, or grew faster than land- or natural resource-abundant countries, however (Leamer 1987; see also Kuralbayeva and Stefanski 2013). In this distinctive "land- or resource-scarce" trajectory of development, natural resource–based activities do not crowd out the development of manufacturing to the extent that might occur in more resource-abundant economies. And distinct from some other development trajectories possible with greater resource abundance, real wages rise monotonically with the accumulation of capital: The interests of capitalists and workers are more closely aligned than in some other potential settings. Industrial promotion policies may be less politically contentious than in countries with greater resource abundance, thanks to the relative weakness of a rural landowner class.[10] Industrial policy may be "leaning with the wind" and relatively popular, if not Pareto-improving. Rates of return on education may be particularly high, encouraging the accumulation of human capital, facilitating the transition to industrial activities of greater complexity.[11] As a result, these economies experience relatively smooth industrial upgrading and rising welfare (Grossman and Helpman 1991). In contrast, development in more resource-abundant economies may be intrinsically more conflictual, regardless of the specifics of the political system. Of course, internal conflict may also contribute to the development of certain types of political institutions, as discussed in greater detail in the next chapter.

---

10. Kiminori Matsuyama (1992) distinguishes between open and closed economies. In an open economy, where prices are determined parametrically in the world market, high output and productivity in the agricultural sector may squeeze out the manufacturing sector, in some circumstances reducing welfare.

11. Thorvaldur Gylfason (2001) finds that the share of natural capital in national wealth is negatively associated with public expenditure on education relative to national income, expected years of schooling for girls, and gross secondary school enrollment rates.

Figure 2.4　Endowment triangle for labor, human capital, and land (1968 data)

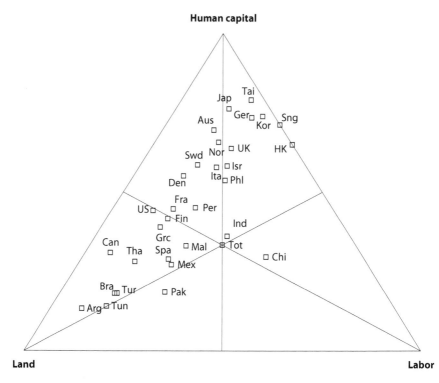

Arg = Argentina, Aus = Austria, Bra = Brazil, Can = Canada, Chi = China, Den = Denmark, Fin = Finland, Fra = France, Ger = Germany, Grc = Greece, HK = Hong Kong, Ind = India, Isr = Israel, Ita = Italy, Jap = Japan, Kor = Korea, Mal = Malaysia, Mex = Mexico, Nor = Norway, Pak = Pakistan, Per = Peru, Phl = Philippines, Sng = Singapore, Spa = Spain, Swd = Sweden, Tai = Taiwan, Tha = Thailand, Tun = Tunisia, Tur = Turkey, UK = United Kingdom, US = United States, Tot = Total

Source: Noland (1997).

Dutch Disease

A variant on the resource pull argument for the paradoxical result that the existence of valuable commodities may detract from economic performance is the "Dutch disease" phenomenon.[12] Named for the discovery of natural gas in the North Sea off the coast of the Netherlands in the 1950s, Dutch disease refers to the tendency of the real exchange rate to appreciate following the discovery of a valuable commodity or during commodity price booms, rendering traditional industries internationally uncompetitive. Especially if there are path

---

12. See Magud and Sosa (2010) for a survey of the literature. Gregory (1976), Corden and Neary (1982), and Neary and van Wijnbergen (1986) are early expositions. Jeffrey Sachs (2007) disputes the notion that Dutch disease is necessarily a problem to be avoided.

Figure 2.5 Endowment triangle for labor, physical capital, and land (1968 data)

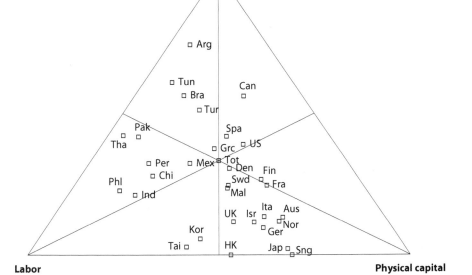

Arg = Argentina, Aus = Austria, Bra = Brazil, Can = Canada, Chi = China, Den = Denmark, Fin = Finland, Fra = France, Ger = Germany, Grc = Greece, HK = Hong Kong, Ind = India, Isr = Israel, Ita = Italy, Jap = Japan, Kor = Korea, Mal = Malaysia, Mex = Mexico, Nor = Norway, Pak = Pakistan, Per = Peru, Phl = Philippines, Sng = Singapore, Spa = Spain, Swd = Sweden, Tai = Taiwan, Tha = Thailand, Tun = Tunisia, Tur = Turkey, UK = United Kingdom, US = United States, Tot = Total

Source: Noland (1997).

dependencies, irreversibilities, or hysteresis effects (meaning that conditions will not return to their original state), such temporary booms can deindustrialize the economy, perhaps permanently. Policies to dampen the exchange rate effects would therefore be justified.[13]

In a meta-analysis of 60 papers, Nicolás Magud and Sebastián Sosa (2010) find evidence that Dutch disease shocks are indeed associated with real exchange rate appreciation and a shift in the composition of output away from tradables, but not with a reduction in growth. If the effects are reversible and do not affect growth, why worry?

If there are asymmetries in adjustment or hysteresis effects, Dutch disease could be a problem in the long run. Analyzing panel data, Rabah Arezki and Kareem Ismail (2013) find that there are indeed asymmetries in adjustment:

---

13. Pietro Peretto (2012) develops a model that generates similar effects in a closed-economy context.

Governments' current spending (as distinct from capital investment) increases during booms but is downwardly sticky during busts, as is the real exchange rate, which could generate hysteresis. Reda Cherif (2013) links such effects to the composition of output, illustrating this possibility in a two-country model with a differentiated-products–producing manufacturing sector subject to scale economies or learning by doing. A commodity boom (or indeed any transfer that generated a real exchange rate appreciation) could permanently retard the development of manufacturing in the poorer/lower-productivity/less developed country by shifting resources out of the tradables sector subject to the externality. Empirical analysis of cross-country data supports the notion that the interaction of resource dependence and an initial technology gap widens that gap over time, suggesting that the phenomenon is more problematic for less developed countries.

Possibly as, or more, important in terms of long-run economic performance is the fact that the procyclicality of booms facilitates engagement in ineffective industrial promotion policies to promote nonfavored activities, including downstream resource-based industry. Historically, such policies have included the expansion of high-cost domestic manufacturing via overly protective infant industry policies and the promotion of domestic food self-sufficiency, even in some Middle Eastern countries endowed with highly challenging climates from the standpoint of food production (Hendrix 2011). Programs to grow wheat in Qatar and Saudi Arabia are examples.

Richard Auty (1993) identifies four critical challenges in economies prone to Dutch disease:

- insufficiency of saving during booms,
- establishment of unsustainable patterns of saving and investment during booms,
- neglect of lagging manufacturing and/or agricultural sectors during booms, and
- tardy adjustment to the postboom downturn.[14]

The last point may present particular challenges in all but the lowest-income countries. Although at very low levels of development, it may be possible for agriculture to reabsorb some labor unemployed in the downswing, even in still relatively poor countries, such as Ghana, people are unlikely to move back to the farm. The result may be a surge in urban unemployment and underemployment.

The Dutch disease phenomenon has encouraged a variety of policies to dampen exchange rate swings and smooth procyclicality, as discussed in

---

14. He concludes by observing, "A striking feature of the policy response of governments in mineral economies is the persistent tendency towards over-optimism concerning future minerals prices" (page 21).

chapter 7. Yet although Dutch disease complicates exchange rate management and fiscal policy and may encourage misguided sectoral promotion interventions, it is unlikely to represent the whole explanation for the underperformance of commodity exporters; recent research suggests that it is probably not the primary channel through which natural resource abundance could negatively affect economic performance (Sala-i-Martin and Subramanian 2003, van der Ploeg 2006).

Assessing the Resource Curse

Reliance on the production of primary products may negatively affect economic performance through a variety of channels, including deterioration in the terms of trade, revenue instability, crowding out other activities with greater long-run potential, and Dutch disease. But the evidence on none of these factors is overwhelming. Taken together, are these factors a significant drag on growth or development?

Scatterplots display economic growth against the share of natural wealth in total national wealth (figure 2.6) and the ore and metal share of total exports (figure 2.7). (Natural capital is defined as the present discounted value of subsoil minerals, timber, cropland, and pasture land. The use of this broad definition in this illustration is driven by data availability.) Although there appears to be a modest negative relationship between growth and either of these measures of resource dependence, it is not dramatic. The question is whether this modest relationship is strengthened or disappears when other factors that might affect growth are taken into account.

Jeffrey Sachs and Andrew Warner (1997) examine the performance of a cross-section of countries for the period 1970–90. They find little if any correlation between resource intensity (measured as the share of primary product commodity exports in GDP) and either physical or human capital accumulation. They find a U-shaped relationship between resource intensity and the Sachs-Warner measure of openness. They argue that low resource intensity and extremely high resource intensity countries are open, but countries with high levels of resource intensity are tempted to pursue interventionist policies to promote the manufacturing sector, per Auty.

But resource intensity is negatively correlated with a variety of indicators of institutional quality. Sachs and Warner conclude that once the standard growth-theoretic explanators are taken into account, resource intensity has a large direct negative impact on growth and that the indirect effects through these other channels are relatively minor in comparison. In contrast, Halvor Mehlum, Karl Moene, and Ragnar Torvik (2006), anticipating the argument in chapter 3, maintain that institutions are the story: When they focus on lootable resources, they find a stronger direct negative impact of resources on growth and, notably, a strong negative interaction between resource abundance and the quality of institutions. They conclude that it is resource endowments in the presence of weak institutions that give rise to the result,

Figure 2.6 Relationship between per capita GDP growth (constant 2000 US dollars), 1990–2010, and share of natural wealth in total wealth

percent change in GDP per capita in 1990 and 2010

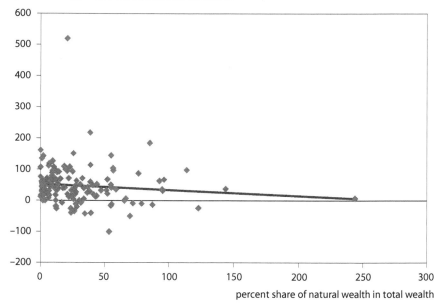

percent share of natural wealth in total wealth

Sources: World Bank, *Changing Wealth of Nations*, http://data.worldbank.org/data-catalog/wealth-of-nations (accessed on February 19, 2014); GDP per capita (constant 2000 US dollars): World Bank, *World Development Indicators*.

in contrast to the sort of Dutch disease interpretation proffered by Sachs and Warner.[15]

Francisco Rodríguez and Jeffrey Sachs (1999) provide a theoretical justification for this observed negative correlation between resources and growth. They argue that if a resource-based economy cannot invest its windfalls in international capital markets (for whatever reason—political restrictions, home bias, low rates of return abroad), it will experience temporary domestic investment and consumption booms. As originally noted by Brock (1991), convergence back to the steady-state growth path following such booms will be from above and generate the result that the country will simultaneously have a relatively high level of contemporary income and relatively slow growth.

---

15. Ann Boschini, Jan Pettersson, and Jesper Roine (2012) extend the analysis of Mehlum, Moene, and Torvik (2006) by examining the robustness of the results for different types of resources, measures of institutional quality, and time periods. They find that the resource curse, as well as its reversal with sufficiently strong institutions, is driven by the ores and metals component of primary product exports.

Figure 2.7   Relationship between per capita GDP growth (constant 2000 US dollars), 1990–2010, and share of ores and metals in total merchandise exports, 2010

percent change in GDP per capita in 1990 and 2010

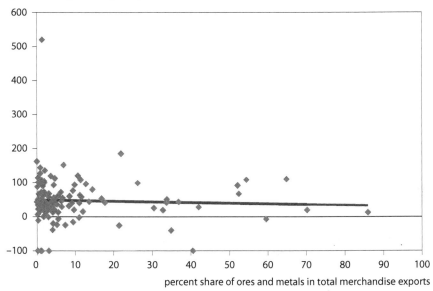

percent share of ores and metals in total merchandise exports

Sources: Ores and metal exports: World Bank, *World Development Indicators*, http://data.worldbank.org/indicator/ TX.VAL.MMTL.ZS.UN (accessed on February 19, 2014); GDP per capita (constant 2000 US dollars): World Bank, *World Development Indicators*.

This finding suggests that transitory acceleration or deceleration of growth may not be identical to a long-run rise or fall in welfare. John Boyce and Herbert Emery (2011) make this point explicitly, examining the conditions for a possible resource curse, setting aside market or institutional failures, in the context of well-functioning markets. They analyze data on US states for the period 1970–2001. Their results (similar to those shown in figure 2.7) confirm the negative correlation between economic growth and the mining share of employment. In the familiar cross-country growth model set-up, they confirm that US states exhibit convergence conditional on initial income levels. Their results also indicate that the rate of technological change in the manufacturing sector has exceeded that in the resource sector. But their results, like those of Rodríguez and Sachs, indicate that although resource-abundant states exhibit slower growth, they also have higher incomes—by a significant degree. On this basis, they conclude that if there is a resource curse, its origins lie in market, institutional, or policy failures, not intrinsic interactions between the resource and nonresource parts of the economy.[16]

---

16. Michael Alexeev and Robert Conrad (2009, 2011) reach similar conclusions based on their

In what is probably the closest thing to a definitive paper in the cross-country growth literature, Xavier Sala-i-Martin, Gernot Doppelhofer, and Ronald Miller (2004) find that the share of GDP originating in mining is strongly and robustly positively correlated with growth. With respect to the purely economic channels of effect, Daniel Lederman and William Maloney (2007), editors of a World Bank volume on natural resources and economic performance, conclude "put bluntly, *there is no resource curse*" [emphasis in the original, page 3]. Similarly, Otaviano Canuto and Matheus Cavallari (2012) find that the stock of natural capital, either in total or broken down by subsoil and other components, contributes positively to growth; the share of natural capital has no impact. They interpret this finding as indicating that natural capital is just another form of capital, providing no support for any sort of natural resource curse.

Conclusion

Economies in which natural resource production plays a central role face a variety of challenges that can impair economic performance. These challenges appear to be particularly acute for the poorest countries. A variety of policy tools is available to address these challenges, but none is perfect (as discussed in chapter 7). Achieving the desired effects depends critically on the quality of implementation, which in turn hinges on the quality of governance.

In this regard, as important as the cross-country statistical evidence is, the general tendencies appear to be marked by exceptions and counter-examples: Apart from high-income countries like Australia, Canada, and Norway, diamond producer Botswana, one of the most resource-centric economies on the planet, has also been one of its best performing; it maintains a quite open and liberal political regime as well (see Harvey and Lewis 1990; Acemoglu, Johnson, and Robinson 2001; Iimi 2006; and Noland and Spector 2006). Nigeria stands as a cautionary counterexample (see Bevan, Collier, and Gunning 1999; Sala-i-Martin and Subramanian 2003; and Human Rights Watch 2005). Analyses by Sala-i-Martin, Doppelhofer, and Miller (2004) and Lederman and Maloney (2007) examine the impact of resources on growth only through a direct economic channel. As intimated by Mehlum, Moene, and Torvik (2006), the primary channel through which resource endowments affect economic performance may be through the impact on institutions and political development. As Henning Bohn and Robert Deacon (2000) observe, insecurity of property rights may have a disparate impact on the rate of exploitation of natural resources—encouraging rapid cutting of forests, for example, but discouraging production in sectors such as oil, which require large sunk investments, which are vulnerable to exploitation. It is to these deeper institutional and political issues that we now turn.

---

work on transition economies, using the break-up of the Soviet Union as a kind of natural experiment.

3

Natural Resources and Domestic Politics

Chapter 2 assessed purely economic explanations for the resource curse and generally found them lacking. This chapter focuses on the effects of natural resource wealth for political institutions and political violence.

High-value mined commodities have negative effects on political democracy, bureaucratic and state capacity, and political stability—all of which exert direct or indirect effects on economic growth. However, the negative effects for bureaucratic capacity and political stability—the factors with the clearest implications for economic growth—are contingent largely on the quality of preexisting institutions and, in the case of conflict, certain attributes of the resources themselves.

Resource Curse and Political Democracy

Democracy has two principal effects on economic growth. First, modern democratic institutions impose checks on the executive that help overcome a basic problem of credible commitment—namely, that any government that is sufficiently powerful to enforce its territorial claim to sovereignty and provide domestic order is also powerful enough to deprive its citizens of their liberty and property (Madison 1799). For a society to make productive investments in human and physical capital, it needs assurances that these investments will not be expropriated and that contracts will be enforced by independent, nonpartisan courts, even when it is not in the short-term interest of the government to do so; in short, law must rule (North and Weingast 1989, McGuire and Olson 1996, Haggard and Tiede 2011). Independent courts have demonstrable positive effects for growth, although these effects are conditional on the courts having de facto independence—long tenures, budgetary autonomy—rather than just de jure independence (Feld and Voigt 2003). As there is no third party to enforce this government-society bargain, it must be self-enforcing. Society faces large costs of coordinating to punish the government from reneging on its assurances; democracy partially solves this problem by creating coordinating mechanisms, such as legislative assemblies, that reduce the cost to society of policing transgressions by the government (Root 1989, Weingast 1997). Although checks such as independent courts can arise in the absence of democratic institutions, elections and representative assemblies make these institutions self-enforcing and thereby have positive indirect effects on growth (Leblang 1996).

Second, democracy exerts large indirect effects on growth by incentivizing governments to invest in human capital accumulation. Building on the classic Solow (1956) growth model, in which growth rates are determined by the savings rate, population growth, and capital depreciation, endogenous growth models point to the importance of human capital accumulation, specifically education and health outcomes, in promoting growth (Barro 1991, 2001, 2012; Mankiw, Romer, and Weil 1992). More educated, healthier workers are associated with higher levels of development, rates of growth, and total factor productivity (Bloom, Canning, and Sevilla 2004, Weil 2007). David Lake and Matthew Baum develop a simple model of public goods provision in which the level of public services is a function of the rate of taxation of the economy and the rents that accrue to the government. Because democracy reduces the costs of deposing governments, for any given rate of taxation, the proportion of revenue invested in public services should be higher. In a series of papers, they demonstrate that democracies perform better in the provision of education and health care, particularly for women (Lake and Baum 2001, Baum and Lake 2003). They then link improvements in female life expectancy and secondary school enrollment to higher economic growth rates, although the effects of democracy are limited to poorer countries (GDP per capita less than $2,500). Although some more recent studies question the robustness of the direct link between democracy and better human capital (Ross 2006, Nelson 2007), democracy is still an important part of the development story. If natural resource dependence inhibits democracy, then natural resource dependence places a brake—albeit an indirect one—on development.

Despite recent debate, there is considerable evidence that at least since the late 1970s, point-source resource wealth—particularly oil—has inhibited democracy, although disentangling the specific influence of oil is confounded by the fact that in cross-country data the presence of oil is collinear with other influences that may inhibit democracy (Ross 2001, Noland 2008a, Gurses 2009, Tsui 2011, Andersen and Ross 2014).[1] The structural break in the oil-democ-

---

1. Stephen Haber and Victor Menaldo (2011) strongly dissent from the conventional wisdom regarding oil and democracy. Their estimates of the causal impact of oil income per capita on

racy relationship, which occurred during the early 1980s, reflects an important shift in both the volume of point-source resource wealth and the way it is managed. Before the 1970s, oil rents were relatively small and accrued primarily to the private sector, especially in the developing world. Between 1932 and 1972, world oil prices (in constant 2011 dollars) were low and declining (figure 3.1). In constant prices, oil actually fell 23 percent from its five-year average price from 1932–36 to 1968–72. Over this earlier period, oil traded on average at less than a third of its price in the post-1972 world. Moreover, exploitation in developing countries—the countries most associated with the oil curse—was generally conducted by large, Western multinationals. The "Seven Sisters"—the Anglo-Persian Oil Company (now BP); Gulf Oil, Standard Oil of California, and Texaco (now Chevron); Royal Dutch Shell; and Standard Oil of New Jersey and Standard Oil Company of New York (now ExxonMobil)—controlled 75 to 85 percent of the world's oil reserves (Sampson 1991).

Both of these realities—low prices and predominantly Western ownership—began changing in 1973. The oil embargo in response to the United States' rearmament of Israel during the Yom Kippur War more than doubled prices, and the Iranian Revolution of 1979 sent prices even higher. The structure of oil ownership began to change as well. As prices rose, nationalizations became more frequent: Between 1970 and 1980, governments in developing countries asserted direct control over their oil reserves; governments that did not invariably renegotiated contracts with multinationals on more favorable terms (Ross 2012, Andersen and Ross 2014). By 2010, only four of the world's 20 largest oil companies (BP, ExxonMobil, Lukoil, and Royal Dutch Shell) were fully private corporations. Their total reserves amounted to just 6.4 percent of reserves held by the top 20; 92.3 percent were held by national oil companies.[2] This transformation in ownership has meant that the unprecedented high prices of the past 40 years have been captured as resource rents by governments.

If oil hinders democracy, the outstanding questions are how much and why? Quantifying the effect of energy resources on democracy first requires that one quantify democracy. A common way of doing so is with the Polity scale (Marshall, Jaggers, and Gurr 2011), which measures the competitiveness of executive recruitment, checks on executive authority, and the degree of political competition allowed in a state on a scale that ranges from –10 (unconstrained hereditary monarchies, like Qatar) to +10 (consolidated democracies, like the United States and Japan). The focus on procedure, rather than on outcomes or degree of participation, has led to some criticism, but the Polity

---

democracy employ fixed effects, leveraging within-country variation in order to assess a causal relationship. Over a 202-year period (1800–2002), they find no evidence of a resource curse and some evidence of a resource blessing. Jørgen Juel Andersen and Michael Ross (2014) note that the positive relationship they find is confined to the pre-1970s era. In the more contemporary period, oil is negatively related to democracy.

2. Based on author's calculations from the Oil & Gas Journal Top 200/100, 2011.

Figure 3.1   Historic price of oil, 1861–2012

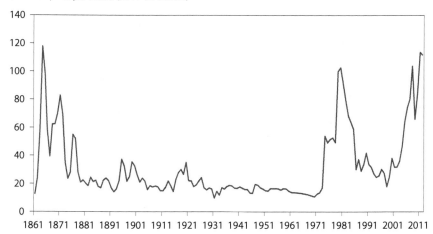

crude oil price per barrel (2011 US dollars)

Source: BP (2013).

scale is the most widely used comparative indicator of democracy. It is used by Kevin Tsui (2011) and Jørgen Juel Andersen and Michael Ross (2014), who represent the most recent attempts to measure the impact of oil on democracy.

Andersen and Ross show a modest effect of total oil income per capita on democracy, especially since 1980: Increasing total oil income per capita by 1 standard deviation—roughly equivalent to the difference between Denmark and Gabon in 2009—is associated with a small (2.2 percent) diminution of democracy.[3,4] However, these findings are based on fixed-effects models that leverage changes only within rather across countries.

Tsui's cross-sectional, comparative analysis suggests much larger effects. He looks at the effects of oil discoveries, rather than actual exploitation and resource rents, on changes in democracy between 1960 and 1990. His study yields two important findings. First, oil discoveries suppress democracy relative to the upward trend in democracy over that period for non-oil-producing countries. Second, the negative effect is larger in countries that were nondemocratic before the discovery of oil: The discovery of 100 billion barrels of oil (equivalent to the endowments of Iran or Iraq) in a nondemocratic country suppresses democracy by about 15 percentage points relative to nonproducers (Tsui 2011, 104).

---

3. Like many concepts in the social sciences, democracy can be measured a variety of different ways, with various operationalizations reflecting different theoretical constructions of the concept (Munck and Verkuilen 2002, Coppedge et al. 2011).

4. If 1984 is used as the structural break point, the effect is a 10 percent diminution of democracy.

There may be price effects as well. Thomas Friedman's First Law of Petropolitics holds that "the higher the average global crude oil price rises, the more free speech, free press, free and fair elections, an independent judiciary, the rule of law, and independent political parties are eroded."[5] Careful econometric work seems to bear out this proposition. Kristopher Ramsay (2011) leverages natural disasters as a source of random variation in oil prices to demonstrate that oil price shocks are negatively (and causally) correlated with democracy.

What are the causal mechanisms? A negative relationship between democracy and natural resource wealth may be the result of two different processes: Natural resource wealth may insulate nondemocratic states from democratizing pressures, but it also may undermine preexisting democratic institutions. The body of evidence developed over the past decade points to the former rather than the latter: Natural resource wealth helps autocratic regimes resist pressures to democratize (Smith 2004, Ulfelder 2007, Bueno de Mesquita and Smith 2010, Al-Ubaydli 2012). Indeed, the focus on oil wealth and authoritarianism may obscure a more general phenomenon: Oil wealth insulates existing regimes from regime transition, irrespective of regime type (Morrison 2009).

Linking authoritarianism to oil production, Michael Ross (2001) views the question from the perspective of the first causal process: If democracy has been on the rise globally since the mid-1970s, why have oil states been insulated from these pressures? He identifies three mechanisms. First, since the 1970s, massive resource windfalls have given oil states large resources to invest in avoiding the social and economic pressures that would otherwise challenge autocratic rule. In oil states, "no taxation without representation" may be recast as "no taxation, no representation." Governments that are reliant on their citizens for revenue have general incentives to defer to those citizens' preferences over policy and over process. Because enforcing compliance with taxation via the barrel of a gun is prohibitively costly, governments invest resources in establishing norms of quasi-voluntary compliance by providing desired policy outputs in the form of public goods and investing in a coercive apparatus to deter those individuals that do not comply voluntarily (Levi 1988, 1997; Ross 2004c). The existence of a plentiful, valuable natural resource base (particularly oil) exerts downward pressure on tax levels, as governments are able to finance themselves through the monopolization of these industries, obviating the need for high levels of taxation. Because these resources generate substantial revenue, oil states tend not to tax their populations much. As a result, their populations do not have this source of leverage with which to bargain for a greater say in governing; the "fiscal contract" linking government behavior to citizens' policy preferences does not develop.

Oil wealth also endows the government with resources to support patronage networks and thus "buy off" potential dissidents. However,

---

5. Thomas Friedman, "The First Law of Petropolitics," *Foreign Policy*, May 1, 2006, www.foreign-policy.com/articles/2006/04/25/the_first_law_of_petropolitics.

direct evidence for this patronage effect is limited—either because the actual effects are weak or because it is difficult to observe patronage networks and payments. Patronage is like obscenity—difficult to define but recognizable on sight. Studying the divvying up of oil rents requires delving into the arcana of government budgets in pursuit of evidence that many governments—especially those that make extensive use of patronage networks—actively try to obscure.

More generally, nontax revenue endows autocratic rulers with resources to invest in providing valued social services (Morrison 2009). By providing social services, resource-rich regimes can address some of the basic needs of the population without involving them in the policymaking process. These public services range from broad consumer subsidies for food and fuel (many oil-exporting countries subsidize fuel to the tune of 70 percent or more) to education, health care, and one-time direct transfers. After Arab Spring protests broke out in Tunisia and Algeria in January 2011, the Kuwaiti government announced that all Kuwaiti citizens would receive grants of 1,000 Kuwaiti dinars (about $3,500 in current dollars) and free food staples for 13 months. These policies, though ostensibly enacted to commemorate Kuwait's 50th anniversary of independence and the 20th anniversary of the expulsion of Iraqi forces, also addressed one of the key issues motivating Arab Spring protests in the region.

Despite investments in broad social services and systems of patronage, oil-rich regimes still may face domestic pressures for democracy. If carrots are not enough, sticks—repressive capacity—can be employed. As of 2010, major oil-exporting countries accounted for 4 of the top 10 military spenders in percentage of GDP terms, including the top three: Saudi Arabia, Oman, and the United Arab Emirates. Curbing domestic dissent is not the only reason why oil producers build strong militaries. Many, particularly in the Middle East and Africa, are located in some of the most conflict-prone regions in the world. Oil-exporting states engage in militarized interstate disputes—ranging from threats to actual uses of force—50 percent more often than non-oil-exporting countries (Colgan 2010; see discussion in chapter 4). Large militaries also help address surplus labor problems, providing both low- and high-skill job opportunities for men. However, oil-producing countries are significantly more repressive than nonproducers, even controlling for the external threat environment and a host of other factors (DeMeritt and Young 2013).

Figure 3.2 shows the average share of mineral wealth as a proportion of total wealth by quartile for respect for human rights.[6] Mineral wealth accounts for nearly twice the proportion of national wealth (i.e., it is statistically signifi-

---

6. The measure of respect for human rights is the Physical Integrity Rights Index, "an additive index constructed from the Torture, Extrajudicial Killing, Political Imprisonment, and Disappearance indicators" (Cingranelli and Richards 2010b, 3). The measure ranges from 0 to 8 on the criteria of absence of torture, summary execution, disappearance, or imprisonment for political beliefs, with 0 = no respect for these rights and 8 = full respect for these rights.

Figure 3.2   Relationship between mineral wealth as a share of national wealth and respect for human rights, 2005

mean mineral wealth as share of national wealth, 2005

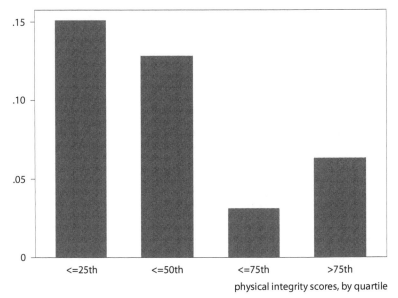

physical integrity scores, by quartile

Source: Human rights indicator is the CIRI Physical Integrity Rights Index (Cingranelli and Richards 2010a, 2010b). Mineral wealth data are from World Bank (2006).

cant) in countries below the median in respect for human rights versus countries above the median.

The differing outcomes associated with the Arab Spring protests demonstrate the regime-stabilizing effects of resource rents. Resource-poor countries, such as Egypt, Morocco, and Tunisia, experienced regime change (Egypt and Tunisia) or responded with virtually immediate pledges of economic and political reforms (Morocco). In contrast, resource-rich regimes proved much more difficult to oust from power. Only one resource-rich regime, Libya, fell as a result of the Arab Spring, and Libyan forces would likely have crushed the Benghazi-based opposition in the absence of NATO-led multilateral intervention. Resource wealth thus provides regimes with ample carrots (patronage, social spending) and sticks (repressive capacity) with which to resist pressures to democratize.

The third mechanism, the modernization effect, holds that resource export-led development does not promote the types of sociocultural changes that attend industrial development and therefore fails to produce the necessary social conditions for democracy to flourish. Building on initial insights from Lipset (1955) and Deutsch (1961), a large body of literature in sociology and political science indicates that stable democratic transitions are most likely where industrial development has taken root. Industrialization entails the attendant processes of urbanization, education, and occupational specialization leading to the development of a large middle class; these processes yield large, articulate middle classes that can pressure the government for a greater say in the policymaking process (Rueschemeyer, Stephens, and Stephens 1992; Inglehart 1997). Because resource-led development employs comparatively small, often imported labor forces, these conditions are less likely to obtain in resource-dependent countries. Ross (2001) finds evidence that the occupational specialization link is most compelling between oil, industrialization, and democracy. Countries with a larger proportion of male and female employment in industry are significantly more democratic.

Resource Curse and State Capacity

Another indirect channel through which natural resource dependence affects economic growth is the effect on state capacity. State capacity is a multifaceted concept, but at its most fundamental level, it is the ability of the state to provide market-sustaining goods (domestic order, property rights, and market regulation) and mobilize societal resources toward political ends (i.e., generate revenue). This definition of state capacity is separate from the notion of state autonomy: whether the state can act on its own or is beholden to the citizenry. If regime type is about who controls the state and whether government policy embodies the preferences of the citizenry, state capacity is about whether the state can implement these policies effectively.

The relationship between state capacity and economic development is less straightforward, contingent largely on the degree of state autonomy and specific government policies. Highly autonomous, capable states have been responsible for both growth miracles and tragedies: The divergent growth trajectories of North and South Korea—both strong states ruled by iron-fisted autocrats (until relatively recently, in the case of South Korea)—show that state capacity is not an unalloyed guarantor of growth. When, however, capable states are made beholden to society through checks on executive power and democratic institutions, state capacity, in particular fiscal capacity and property rights enforcement, is growth enhancing (Besley and Persson 2009).

In contrast, weak state capacity is almost always associated with poor development outcomes. At the extreme lower bound, failed states—states that have lost physical control of their territory and the ability to provide public services—are almost always poor states. Population-weighted GDP per capita among the top 10 countries on the Fund for Peace's Failed States Index is $1,497, with 4 of the poorest countries (Afghanistan, Haiti, Somalia, and South Sudan) missing data on this basic economic indicator. Among the top ten, population-weighted infant mortality, an excellent indirect indicator of the health of the poor, is 76.8 per 1,000 live births. In contrast, infant mortality in the bottom 10 (i.e., most functional) states stands at 3.9.

Most point-source resource-rich regimes have no problem generating revenue. Concentration of production and labor around mines and wells—including offshore platforms—constitutes a natural tax handle, or bottleneck, in the production of a good, which makes evasion inherently difficult. When revenues can easily be extracted from a few sources that are also easily controlled, they are more subject to direct capture by the state through a variety of mechanisms, including marketing boards, control of line ministries, and direct procurement (Isham et al. 2005). Figure 3.3 demonstrates this dynamic, plotting total government revenue as a percentage of GDP against natural resource rents as a percentage of GDP for countries where resource rents made up at least 5 percent of GDP in 2011. Each additional percentage point of natural resource rents is associated with a 0.34 percentage point increase in total government revenue.

The ease with which these resources generate government revenue leads to a "paradox of plenty": Resource-rich states tend to have weaker state capacity than their income levels would predict, because rulers have less need to develop capacity to access the resources of society in order to generate revenue (Chaudhry 1989, Karl 1997). The literature on the rentier state is an outgrowth of the fiscal sociology literature linking development of the modern state to large-scale mobilization for war. It notes that revenue demands generated by the increasing costs of warfare in the 17th and 18th centuries shaped the demand for political institutions capable of extracting the resources necessary to compete (Tilly 1975, Downing 1992). In these accounts, professional, Weberian bureaucracies developed as a response to both external threats and the difficulty of taxing increasingly mobile and thus concealable forms of wealth. Absent this pressure, resource-rich states fail to develop professional bureaucracies, and their staffs become dominated by patronage appointees rather than the best and brightest. Moreover, massive resource rents create their own political economy, wherein vested domestic interests, themselves a creation of state patronage, resist attempts at reform and constrain policy choices (Shafer 1994). These joint processes lead to pernicious policy outcomes and "grabber-friendly" economic and political institutions (Robinson, Torvik, and Verdier 2006), in which rent-seeking is more profitable than productive investment. Point-source resource–exporting economies thus perform worse across several key indicators of state capacity (Isham et al. 2005).

Figures 3.4 and 3.5 illustrate the relationship between natural resource rents per capita and two key measures of state capacity.[7] The first is government effectiveness, which captures "perceptions of the quality of public services, the quality of the civil service and the degree of its independence from political pressures, the quality of policy formulation and implementation, and the credibility of the government's commitment to such policies." The second is control of corruption, which captures "perceptions of the extent to which public power is exercised for private gain, including both petty and

---

7. Natural resource rents are "the sum of oil rents, natural gas rents, coal rents (hard and soft), mineral rents, and forest rents" (World Bank 2011a, 79).

**Figure 3.3   Relationship between natural resource rents and
government revenue as share of GDP, 2011**

total revenue as percent of GDP, 2011

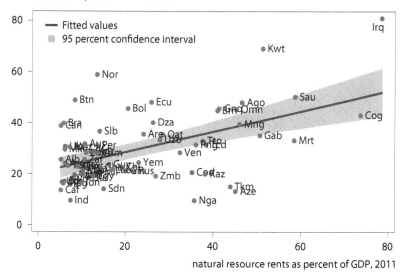

natural resource rents as percent of GDP, 2011

Note: $\beta = 0.34$, $p = 0.001$. See key to country abbreviations on page 50.

Sources: CIA World Factbook (for government revenue as share of GDP); World Bank, *World Development Indicators* (for natural resource rents as share of GDP).

grand forms of corruption, as well as 'capture' of the state by elites and private
interests" (Kaufmann, Kraay, and Mastruzzi 2010, 4). Both scatterplots are
weighted according to the size of the economy. In both, a clear downward
trend is evident: As natural resource rents become relatively more abundant,
governments are perceived as less effective and more corrupt. Brunei and Qatar
are well above the trend lines, indicating that some very resource-rich countries
with high-quality state institutions exist outside the West. However, these tiny
petrostates amount to 0.04 percent of global population and 0.3 percent of
global GDP.[8] Their experiences are atypical.

Chapter 2, however, indicates that economic evidence for the resource
curse is decidedly mixed. If natural resources have such pernicious effects on
state capacity, regulatory quality, and corruption, why is there no clear evidence
of an economic resource curse?

Natural resources are neither discovered nor exploited in an institutional
vacuum. Preexisting institutions are the key moderating factor. If these institutions are strong and the size of the mineral sector does not dwarf the rest of
the economy, resource wealth provides additional capital for productive invest-

---

8. Authors' calculations, based on Penn World Tables 8.0 (Feenstra, Inklaar, and Timmer 2013).

Figure 3.4 Relationship between natural resource rents and government effectiveness, 2011

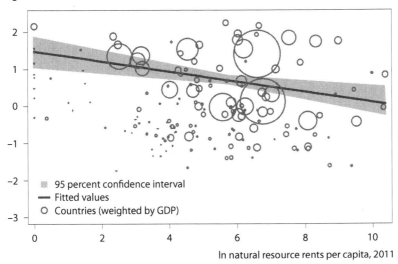

government effectiveness, 2011

■ 95 percent confidence interval
— Fitted values
○ Countries (weighted by GDP)

In natural resource rents per capita, 2011

Note: $\beta = -0.07$, $p < 0.05$.

Sources: World Bank, *Worldwide Governance Indicators* (for government effectiveness); World Bank, *World Development Indicators* (for natural resource rents).

ment. Even if Dutch disease dynamics come into play, these resources can be invested in ways that promote intergenerational equity and the accumulation of long-term wealth. Under these circumstances, resource income is growth promoting, and the "curse" becomes more of a blessing (Brunnschweiler and Bulte 2008, Alexeev and Conrad 2009). This condition seems to be the equilibrium path of Norway, the United Kingdom, the Netherlands, and the United States. If preexisting institutions are weak and the mineral sector is much larger than the rest of the economy (as in Angola, Nigeria, and Saudi Arabia), the resource curse dynamic emerges. Large resource windfalls in the context of autocratic, grabber-friendly institutions tend to increase perceptions of corruption (Bhattacharyya and Hodler 2010).

What does this pattern portend for new producers? The news is decidedly mixed. On the one hand, natural resource wealth is not destiny. Success stories may be rare, but they exist. Trinidad and Tobago, a tropical, plantation-based economy, has been a consolidated parliamentary democracy since independence in the 1960s. Its GDP per capita has grown 64 percent since 2000, thanks largely to windfall resource profits. Although mineral wealth makes up more than a third of total national wealth (a larger share than in Nigeria or Venezuela), Trinidad and Tobago appears to have dodged the political resource curse. Botswana's evasion of the resource curse is among the most celebrated

Figure 3.5 Relationship between natural resource rents and control of corruption, 2011

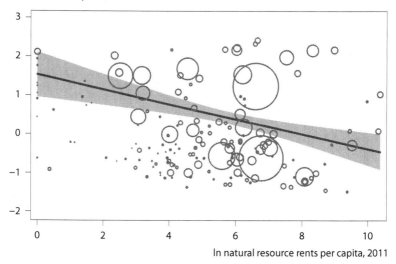

control of corruption, 2011

In natural resource rents per capita, 2011

▨ 95 percent confidence interval   ▬ Fitted values   ○ Countries (weighted by GDP)

Note: β = –0.09, p < 0.01.

Sources: World Bank, Worldwide Governance Indicators (for control of corruption); World Bank, World Development Indicators (for natural resource rents).

and oft-discussed positive cases in development economics (Sachs and Warner 2001; Acemoglu, Johnson, and Robinson 2002; Robinson, Torvik, and Verdier 2006). These examples show that natural resource wealth—and predominance in the economy—need not lead to economic stagnation. Strengthening institutions before resources come online may mitigate some aspects of the resource curse.

Despite this cause for optimism, preexisting institutions have deep determinants extending back centuries, even millennia, according to some (Engerman and Sokoloff 1997; Acemoglu, Johnson, and Robinson 2001; Easterly and Levine 2003; Rodrik, Subramanian, and Trebbi 2004; Hibbs and Olsson 2004). Institutions have distributive consequences, creating winners and losers and endowing winners with both incentives and capabilities to perpetuate the status quo (Acemoglu and Robinson 2006). Thus, the hope that good institutions can be developed before resources begin flowing runs up against a wealth of evidence that institutions are hard to change, especially in the short run.

Moreover, oil and other mineral resources are more likely to be discovered in states with weaker institutions, as weaker states tend to invest more effort in exploration, because it is difficult for them to attract foreign investment that is not collateralized by in-country fixed assets. States with weak institutions and property rights face significant problems of credible commitment, but the rents generated by energy extraction and the natural tax handles that follow from the technology of production make these investments particularly attractive to foreign partners. Victor Menaldo (2013) shows that weaker states—states with lower government revenues—are more likely to undertake energy exploration and discover larger amounts of oil, either through state-owned enterprises or in partnerships with private actors. Countries with the institutions most likely to lead to the resource curse are thus most likely to go looking for it in the first place.

Adding to this problem is the fact that the resource curse does not begin when the oil starts flowing. Components of it—such as corruption, perceptions of corruption and political conflict—start soon after oil discoveries are announced. São Tomé and Príncipe announced significant oil discoveries in 1997 and 1999. Pedro Vicente (2010) used surveys conducted there and in Cape Verde, a similar West African country sharing the same colonial past and recent economic and political trajectories, to show that perceptions of corruption related to vote buying, the allocation of scholarships, and customs duties increased significantly after the discoveries were announced. Oil played a large role in the public discourse surrounding a short-lived 2003 military coup, with the ousted president, Fradique de Menezes, and the coup leader, Major Fernando "Cobó" Pereira, stating publicly—albeit for different reasons—that the coup was in part about oil and the wealth that would follow from it. As of 2013, not a single barrel of oil had flowed from these discoveries.

The resource curse precedes actual exploitation in part because actors anticipate the rents that will flow from these new resources, raising the expected value of being in office (box 3.1). Oil exploration itself is big business for government officials, who can reap large financial rewards—both licit and illicit—from exploration licensing fees. The early stages of oil exploration tend to be handled by relatively minor players—wildcatters, as they were known in the United States in the 19th century—who face less public scrutiny and therefore have a comparatively free hand to engage in corrupt practices. The United States and the European Union recently passed laws requiring transnational mining firms to "publish what they pay" foreign governments (the subject of chapter 6), but these rules apply only to firms listed in the United States and the European Union.[9] As non-US and non-EU firms gain prominence and market share, the power of these laws may diminish.

---

9. As discussed in greater detail in chapter 6, the Securities and Exchange Commission (SEC) voted on August 22, 2012, to implement Section 1504 of the Dodd-Frank Act, which requires firms engaged in the development of oil, natural gas, or minerals to report their payments to the US or foreign governments. The same day, the SEC adopted a "conflict minerals" provision that requires firms to exercise due diligence on the minerals' sources and chains of custody for minerals originating in the Democratic Republic of the Congo or adjoining countries (Angola, Burundi, Central African Republic, Republic of the Congo, Rwanda, South Sudan, Tanzania, Uganda, and Zambia).

Box 3.1 The cautionary example of Ghana

In 2004, Kosmos, founded by two Texas wildcatters with a track record of discovering West African oil, and London-based Tullow acquired licenses to explore and develop offshore fields. In 2007, both firms struck oil in the Mahogany and Jubilee fields (and subsequently the Owo field); two years later Kosmos decided to sell out to a major company more capable of developing the field. After an auction that attracted interest from major companies from a number of countries, Kosmos signed an agreement to sell its stake to ExxonMobil for $4 billion.

The state oil company, Ghana National Petroleum Company (GNPC), objected, claiming that it had not been kept apprised of the Kosmos-Exxon negotiations. It was subsequently revealed that Kosmos did in fact share some geological data with Exxon as part of its negotiations without GNPC's knowledge.

GNPC was unable to either raise capital to counterbid or bully down the price (mooting an ex post windfall profits tax to claw back some of the rents expected to go to Kosmos); it was widely reported that the company was encouraging the China National Offshore Oil Corporation (CNOOC) to make a counterbid. CNOOC had not participated in the original auction, and some observers doubted both its interest and the credibility of the threat. BP, Total, and Sinopec were also reportedly interested in buying GNPC's stake if they could wrestle it away from Kosmos.

Reportedly tipped off by another stakeholder in the Jubilee field, the government of Ghana then prepared to file criminal corruption charges against Kosmos partner EO, a company established by two allies of former Ghanaian president John Kufuor, a move Kosmos termed a pretext to force a sale of the firm's stake at a firesale price.[1] EO initiated the deal that brought Kosmos to Ghana. In return, Kosmos fronted EO its share of the exploration and development costs. Apparently, it was willing to go where others declined to tread. The deal that Kosmos subsequently got on the concession was marginally better than the deal offered to other stakeholders. EO moved from Ghana to the Caymans after the opposition victory in December 2008 presidential elections. The US Department of Justice launched an independent investigation of Kosmos and EO, but in July 2010 it ended its probe, finding no evidence of wrongdoing by either. The Ghanaians then acceded to EO's sale of its 1.75 percent stake in Jubilee to Tullow for $300 million.

In August 2010, Exxon walked away from Kosmos deal amid signs that the Ghanaian government was going to steer the deal to China. The following month China's Export-Import Bank loaned Ghana $10.4 billion for infrastructure contracts; the China Development Bank offered a $3 billion loan to support the construction by Sinopec of a gas pipeline in return for oil.[2] Kosmos decided on

(continues on next page)

---

1. William Wallis, Martin Arnold, and Brooke Masters, "Corruption Probe into Role of Texas Group and Partner in Major African Oil Discovery," *Financial Times*, January 8, 2010; William Wallis and Martin Arnold, "'Sweat Equity' Probe Tests Ghana on Oil Jackpot," *Financial Times*, January 8, 2010.

2. Leslie Norton, "China's Sure Bet," *Barron's*, November 8, 2010; William Wallis, "Gas: Turf Wars Stymie Potential Increase in Employment," *Financial Times*, December 14, 2011.

Box 3.1 The cautionary example of Ghana *(continued)*

a public offering of a minority stake in the firm to raise capital for development, and the Ghanaians initiated talks with Norway's Statoil about joining a consortium to access deepwater skills that GNPC and CNOOC lacked.[3]

In December, the Ghanaians threw in the towel, absolving Kosmos of any wrongdoing.[4] But the episode underscored both the high stakes nature of the game and its intense politicization. One analyst estimated that if the terms of the other stakeholders were applied to the Kosmos stake, the state stood to gain $3.8 billion, a one-time equivalent of more than 10 percent of GDP or roughly one-third of the state budget.[5] In the words of respected Ghanaian political scientist Emmanuel Gyimah-Boadi, "In Ghana the capture of the state is still the name of the game."[6]

The magnitude of resources devoted to securing control of the state exploded. The 2008 presidential primary of the National Patriotic Party (NPP), the center-right party of outgoing president John Kufuor, involved 17 candidates, who collectively spent an estimated $50 million to $80 million. The nominee observed that the outcome of the election could determine Ghanaian politics for a generation, as the winner would have access to oil revenues with which to build an impregnable system of patronage.

The Petroleum Revenue Management Act of 2011 establishes mechanisms for collecting and distributing oil revenue, including the percentages that should be applied to the annual budget, set aside for future generations, and invested for a rainy day. Despite its passage, however, in Gyimah-Boadi's words, the 2012 presidential campaign in Ghana was "a proxy battle for control of Ghana's oil and gas revenue."[7] The election, the first since Ghana became an oil producer, was the most expensive in the country's history by a large margin: as of November 27, 2012, campaign expenditures were $288.4 million, or $11.55 per Ghanaian. (By comparison, per capita campaign expenditures in the 2012 election in the United States, a country 15 times wealthier than Ghana in per capita terms, were $18.62.[8]) In part, the competition reflected different coalitions competing for control—with the National Democratic Congress favoring a more resource nationalist approach, with a strong role for the Ghana National Petroleum Corporation, and the New Patriotic Party favoring an approach that would renegotiate existing development loans from China and court new investment from Western oil companies; in part, it reflected personal protection.[9]

---

3. Martin Arnold, William Wallis, and Leslie Hook, "Ghana Move for Kosmos Oilfield Stake," *Financial Times*, October 23, 2010.

4. Martin Arnold and William Wallis, "Ghana and Kosmos Sign a Truce Agreement," *Financial Times*, December 22, 2010.

5. William Wallis, "Curse of Oil Follows Ghana's Former President," *Financial Times*, October 26, 2010.

6. Tom Burgis, "Driven by Fear of Falling out of Power," *Financial Times*, December 4, 2009.

7. Sylvia Pfeifer, Xan Rice, and Andrew England, "Energy: Trial by Oil?" *Financial Times*, January 10, 2013.

8. "Parties Blow GHC549 Million on Adverts and Gifts," *The Finder*, November 27, 2012.

9. "After a Unifying Funeral, a Divisive Election," *Africa Confidential* 53, no. 17: 6–7.

Resource Curse and Political Instability

A final indirect mechanism linking economic development and natural resource wealth operates through political instability. The economic consequences of intrastate armed conflict (i.e., civil war) are dire. Low levels of economic development and low rates of economic growth are clear consequences of conflict (Collier 1999; Murdoch and Sandler 2002; Collier et al. 2003; Fearon and Laitin 2003; Collier and Hoeffler 2004; Miguel, Satyanath, and Sergenti 2004; Cerra and Saxena 2008). Conflict destroys human and physical capital; crowds out productive investment, both within the conflict-afflicted country and in its neighbors; and disrupts trade. Cerra and Saxena estimate the immediate cost of a civil war at, on average, 6 percent of GDP—significantly more than previous estimates (2.2 percent, in Collier 1999). Moreover, despite hopes of a Phoenix effect, in which postconflict societies quickly return to robust growth, evidence of such an effect is scant. To the extent that a Phoenix effect has characterized postconflict African countries, the effect is almost entirely attributable to influxes of development aid: Endogenous growth recoveries are rare, if not quasi-mythical (Cerra and Saxena 2008). Without postconflict growth, societies can become caught in a conflict trap, in which low development fuels conflict and conflict further curtails development. Ninety percent of all civil wars that have broken out in the 21st century were in countries that had previously experienced a civil war (World Bank 2011b).

If the causal link between conflict and economic development is clear, the link between natural resources and conflict is more contingent and highly qualified. Generally speaking, conflict is more prevalent in countries where natural resources—especially mineral resources—make up a larger proportion of national wealth and exports. However, this basic correlation reflects the fact that conflict and natural resource dependence are both highly correlated with poverty. Although the role of natural resources—particularly mined commodities—in conflict has become fodder for Hollywood movies (*Blood Diamond* and *Syriana*), it is clear that not even the most likely candidates for spurring conflict, diamonds and oil, have uniform effects. Whether natural resource wealth leads to violence is largely a function of attributes of the resource itself; the technology of its extraction; and the preexisting political, economic, and social environment.

Before addressing resource attributes and contextual factors, it is important to delineate causal mechanisms. Causal stories linking mined commodities to civil conflict fall into four basic categories: grievance, greed, resource mobilization, and state weakness.

Grievance-based explanations typically note that mining, although highly lucrative for some, generally entails significant environmental costs. When these costs are concentrated in communities that do not reap a large proportion of the benefits, severe grievances may arise, particularly if the local community is distinct in ethnic or religious terms from the dominant elite. Grievances over environmental costs and unequal access to benefits have been at the heart of rebel discourse in the Niger Delta (the Movement for the Emancipation of the Niger Delta [MEND], oil); Papua New Guinea (the Bougainville Revolutionary Army [BRA], copper and gold); and Aceh (Gerakan Aceh Merdeka [GAM], oil), among others (Bob 2005). This mechanism is plausible, although some skeptical observers note that rebels, whatever their actual aims, are more likely to receive favorable Western press when they couch their motives in environmental terms. All insurgent groups have incentives to state their group aims in terms of grievance rather than greed, for both domestic and international audiences. Public statements or manifestos may be directed toward developing domestic support for the group, either as a recruiting tool or as a means of making the group more palatable to the general population over which they intend to rule. Public statements may be directed at developing support at the international level, as during the Cold War, when insurgent groups and governments faced strong resource-based incentives to frame their goals in terms of communist or liberal democratic political and economic ideologies.

Greed-based arguments focus on rebel potential to "do well out of war": War creates conditions under which extralegal profits can be made from the sale of "conflict" resources appropriated by rebels or connected business interests. Because the government does not capture these resources, they do not generate revenues that can then be invested in public goods; rather, they enrich participants. Anecdotal evidence suggests that it is not only rebels who stand to do well out of war: Government officials and foreign militaries can also take advantage of anarchic conditions to engage in profiteering. In 2001, the UN Panel of Experts on Illegal Exploitation in the Democratic Republic of the Congo reported significant involvement in illegal diamond and gold mining by Rwandan and Ugandan military officers during the Second Congo War (1998–2003) (UN 2001).

Political opportunity arguments note that whether rebels fight for seemingly virtuous or venal reasons, they must generate operating capital in order to feed, clothe, and arm their troops. Access to resource rents—from either direct natural resource extraction or extortion of legitimate producers—makes rebel groups more viable than they might otherwise be. The example of the Fuerzas Armadas Revolucionarias de Colombia (FARC) is instructive. It was created in 1966 as an ostensibly Maoist communist insurgency in the Colombian department of Tolima. Most of its early activities involved capturing military equipment and supplies. During the 1970s and 1980s, the FARC expanded its base of operations to include more resource-rich areas, such as the oil-rich Magdalena valley and the gold mines of Antioquia and engaged in sabotage and extortion in order to raise operating capital (Rabasa and Chalk 2001). Later, the FARC developed ties to the illegal drug trade, which had initially been considered counterrevolutionary and an illegitimate source of funding. The decision to protect and promote coca cultivation was in part a defensive, reactive policy designed to keep its rural bases of support from being undercut by right-wing paramilitaries operating in regions that pioneered the protection of the coca crop. In keeping with the emphasis on group viability, valuable natural resources may also contribute to conflict by making a post-conflict independent territory an economically viable state. This discourse underpinned separatist conflicts in Angola's Cabinda province and Aceh in Indonesia (Ross 2012).

The state weakness channel relates to the relationship between state capacity and natural resource exploitation. States with capable bureaucracies and administration may deter or repress violent mobilization via nonmilitarized means (Goodwin 2001, Hendrix 2010). As the quality of the bureaucracy increases, the reach of the state—its ability to monitor its population or determine the identities and whereabouts of potential rebels—does so as well. Where the state is able to see its population, it can control and discipline its citizens even without force (Scott 1998). States with more capable political institutions will be better providers of public goods and rule of law, and aggrieved populations have responsive institutional channels through which to prosecute their aims. If resource-dependent states have weaker bureaucracies than their level of economic development would predict, state weakness may explain this correlation.

Attributes of the Resource

Whether natural resources lead to conflict is determined in large part by the nature of the resource itself. Commodities with high value-to-weight ratios, such as gemstones, oil, cocaine, and opium, are ideal contestable or "lootable" goods (Fearon 2004). Commodities with low value-to-weight ratios, such as staple grains, iron ore, and sugar cane, are less attractive, because they require the export of massive quantities to be profitable in international markets and few rebel groups have the resources—or the desire to operate in broad daylight—required to export low-value commodities. In order to purchase a single AK-47 rifle (at a black market price of $400), an insurgent would have to move more than a ton of sugar at world market prices (at the February 2013 price of $0.19 a pound). Eight grams of cocaine have the same purchasing power.[10] Bulk agricultural commodities are not robustly linked to conflict (Ross 2004a, 2004b).

Even among high-value, mined commodities, not all resource deposits are equal with respect to their effects for conflict. Regarding hydrocarbons, the relevant distinction is onshore versus offshore production. Onshore oil production increases the probability of conflict onset by 50 percent. In contrast, offshore production is not associated with conflict onset (Lujala 2010). Moreover, conflicts tend to last longer when oil reserves or gemstones are located within the conflict zone. These findings are consistent with all the causal mechanisms except state weakness; from a state revenue perspective, the location of the resource should be immaterial.

The differential effects of onshore and offshore production reflect the

---

10. Assuming average €40 ($54.45) per gram, based on inflation-adjusted wholesale prices in Europe; per statistics from the UN Office on Drugs and Crime (2012).

differential opportunities onshore versus offshore production create for rent-seeking by violent actors. Although both offshore and onshore production are capital intense and therefore characterized by high barriers to entry, transporting onshore hydrocarbons to terminals for export generally requires large, aboveground networks of pipelines. This onshore infrastructure creates a network of targets—ranging from derricks and pumpjacks to pipelines and the workers that service them—only a few of which can truly be hardened against attack. Deep-pocketed oil companies make attractive targets for insurgents, who may have limited capacity to hold and defend such installations but significant capacity to extort. Regarding motive, however, one person's extortion is another's revolutionary taxation; these findings do not help parse the competing explanations of greed versus grievance versus opportunity.

In contrast, offshore platforms are comparatively easy to defend, as most insurgent groups lack naval capacity and thus have limited capacity to extract rents from offshore production.[11] Figure 3.6 maps reported terror attacks against oil infrastructure from 1990 to 2011. Although many of the attacks occurred in coastal areas around export terminals, none of the reported attacks occurred offshore.[12] Using proprietary data, Norwegian researchers report very few attacks against offshore oil platforms, and attacks against submerged offshore pipelines are virtually unheard of (Kjøk and Brynjar 2001, Tørhaug 2006). In contrast, attacks on oil infrastructure are relatively common at inland installations in Colombia, Iraq, and Pakistan and are more numerous when international oil prices are high (Dube and Vargas 2013).

Regarding diamonds, the relevant distinction is primary versus secondary deposits. Natural diamonds occur under various geological conditions. These differences have profound implications for the political economy of their extraction. Primary, "deep-shaft," or kimberlite diamonds generally occur in rock formations or "pipes" in subsoil deposits, although part of the deposit may reach the surface. Although such deposits may be a rich source of diamonds, mining them is expensive, requiring significant investments in capital and technology. Secondary diamonds (including alluvial diamonds, found primarily in riverbeds) are primary deposits that have been weathered. Alluvial stones make up less than 10 percent of the volume of rough stones but more than a quarter of their value, because alluvial deposits yield higher shares of gem-quality stones (the better stones survive the tumble through the

11. Martin Murphy's (2007) study of maritime insurgency identified four groups that engaged in maritime attacks with some regularity: the Liberation Tigers of Tamil Eelam (Sri Lanka), Gerakan Aceh Merdeka (Indonesia), Abu Sayyaf Group (the Philippines), and al Qaeda (the USS Cole and the MV Limberg attacks in Yemen).

12. In 2008, the Movement for the Emancipation of the Niger Delta (MEND) claimed credit for an attack on Royal Dutch Shell's Bonga platform and a floating production, storage, and offloading vessel that serviced it. The attack, which occurred 120 kilometers off the coast of Nigeria, was later reported to have been the result of a dispute between Royal Dutch Shell and a private security firm contracted to guard the platform. See James C. K. Daly, "Nigeria's Navy Struggles with Attacks on Offshore Oil Facilities," *Terrorism Monitor* 6, July 10, 2008.

Figure 3.6   Heat map of attacks on oil and natural gas infrastructure, 1990–2011

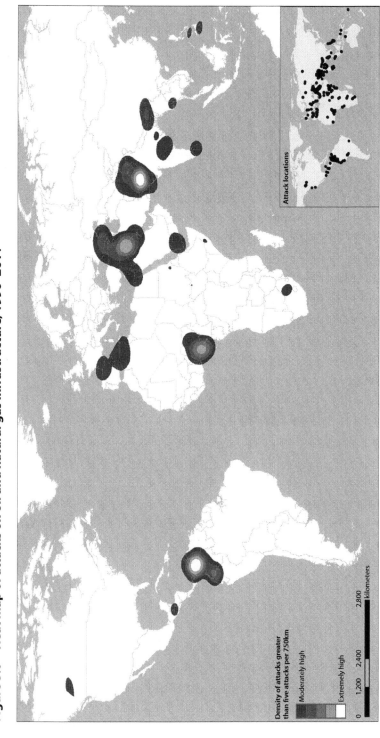

Density of attacks greater
than five attacks per 750km

Moderately high

Extremely high

0   1,200   2,400   2,800

kilometers

Attack locations

Note: Lighter colors within hotspots indicate a greater frequency of attacks.

Source: Global Terrorism Database, 2012.

riverbeds, erosion destroys flawed stones). These deposits are easily extracted with simpler methods, sometimes limited to a shovel and a sieve. This form of alluvial mining is often referred to as "artisanal" mining, a phrase that conveys an unduly benign or quaint air to what is often a grimly exploitative segment of the industry.

In geological terms, offshore marine deposits are a subset of alluvial deposits. From a political economy perspective, they more closely resemble "primary" kimberlite deposits, in that their recovery requires significant corporate investment and advanced technology. Primary and marine deposits are generally expensive to mine. These segments of the industry are therefore dominated by large multinational companies, such as De Beers or Rio Tinto, which account for about three-quarters of world output.

This distinction between capital-intense, corporate mining and artisanal mining is of great significance. Diamonds are easily tradable because of their high value-to-weight ratio. Because they are a natural resource whose locations of production are determined geologically and fixed, it is possible to gain phys-ical control over their locations and capture their economic value. In the case of corporate mining, this capturing is usually done by the state, which accrues benefits for society as a whole through taxes, royalties, and other payments. In the case of artisanal alluvial mining, which can be done by unskilled labor using simple implements, barriers to entry are low, transshipment costs are negligible, and potential returns are high, making them an ideal "contestable" or "lootable" resource.

In the case of diamonds, statistical analysis indicates that the existence of primary deposits actually contributes to stability, an argument consistent with the political experiences of the major southern African producers (Lujala, Gleditsch, and Gilmore 2005). (At least in the modern era: The Boer Wars were fought in part over control of the massive deep-shaft diamond deposits in present-day South Africa.) The argument that diamonds might be a drag on development would appear more plausible in the case of artisanally produced secondary deposits; a number of countries where these diamonds are found, such as Sierra Leone and Angola, have indeed experienced political instability and civil war. However, other African states with artisanal mining, such as Ghana and Tanzania, have not experienced comparable instability, and the statistical evidence in support of the proposition that secondary diamonds contribute to civil wars outbreak is weak at best (Lujala, Gleditsch, and Gilmore 2005). However, when precious gemstones—including secondary diamonds—are located in conflict zones, they more than double the average duration of a conflict (Lujala 2010).

Social, Political, and Economic Contexts

Certain types of natural resource wealth are clear contributors to conflict. But neither natural resource exploitation nor conflict occurs in a vacuum.

Whether resources are implicated in conflict is also a function of the social, political, and economic context. Many seemingly resource-related conflicts have occurred in societies that would be among the most likely candidates for conflict outbreak even absent the role of contestable resources: Countries like Colombia, Nigeria, and Indonesia are at elevated risk of experiencing conflict because of their histories of violence, comparatively low levels of economic development, and horizontal inequalities.

As implied by the conflict trap, conflict begets conflict, because of both the impoverishing effects of conflict and the legacies of violence and intercommunal mistrust that conflict leaves in its wake. This dynamic may be more acute in postconflict societies with mineral resources. Because of their reliance on fixed natural capital, extractive industries are a default sector in conflict zones; given the rents extractive industries generate, investment in this sector is harder to scare off. As a result, many postconflict societies are left more dependent on their natural capital than before conflict occurred (Brunnschweiler and Bulte 2009). Moreover, civil conflict is overwhelmingly a phenomenon of poor countries, and it is more likely to occur in countries experiencing slow economic growth (Blattman and Miguel 2010).

Ethnic, religious, and economic diversity are not, in and of themselves, strong predictors of conflict. Tanzania, one of the world's most ethnically diverse countries, has been largely peaceful since independence, and economic inequality in the United States is on par with Latin America yet has not led to widespread political violence. However, when ethnicity becomes a basis for exclusionary patterns of rule, as in South Africa under apartheid, conflict is more likely and more deadly (Heger and Salehyan 2007).

A similar story holds for economic inequality. More unequal societies experience more civil conflict, although the type of inequality is significant. Vertical inequality—inequality across individuals and households—is not robustly linked to conflict (Cramer 2003, Hegre and Sambanis 2006). Horizontal inequality—inequality across groups (where region, ethnicity, class, religion, or other political divisions define groups)—is associated with conflict (Østby 2008; Østby, Nordås, and Rød 2009; Cederman, Weidmann, and Gleditsch 2011). Such conflicts are often enabled by the fact that resource deposits are concentrated in distinct regions and not spread evenly throughout a country. Conflict is particularly likely to occur if deposit zones coincide with areas populated by people with distinct historical, ethnic, or religious identities.

Conclusion

Chapter 2 surveyed purely economic explanations for the resource curse and found them lacking. This chapter focuses on indirect mechanisms by which natural resource wealth affects economic development: democracy and the provision of public goods, state capacity, and violent conflict. It finds that the effects of natural resource wealth are largely contingent on preexisting institu-

Table 3.1   Growth in proven petroleum reserves, 2000–11

Country	Net growth (billion barrels per day)	Share of global net growth (percent)	Cumulative share (percent)
Venezuela	219.7	52.1	52.1
Iran	51.6	12.3	64.4
Iraq	30.6	7.3	71.6
Kazakhstan	24.6	5.8	77.5
Russia	19.7	4.7	82.2
Libya	11.1	2.6	84.8
Nigeria	8.2	1.9	86.7
Qatar	7.8	1.9	88.6
Angola	7.5	1.8	90.4
Brazil	6.6	1.6	92.0
Rest of world	33.8	8.0	100.0

Source: BP (2012).

tions and price levels: When preexisting institutions are weak and prices high, the resource curse is more likely to emerge.

What does this finding portend for new producers—and producers with significantly expanded production capacity and proven reserves—in the coming decades? Globally, the ratio of proven conventional petroleum reserves relative to current consumption has increased since 2000. However, virtually all of the gains have been made in Africa, the Middle East, and South America—regions where both preexisting institutions and histories of violence suggest a difficult future. As table 3.1 indicates, 10 countries have accounted for 90 percent of the growth in proven reserves since 2000, with one, Venezuela, contributing more than 50 percent.[13] Of the remaining nine, all but two (Kazakhstan and Russia) are in one of these three regions. North America, Europe, and Asia have seen minimal growth if not reserve depletion, until the recent North American shale oil boom. Several traditional Middle Eastern suppliers (Saudi Arabia, the United Arab Emirates, and Kuwait) have had comparatively modest increases.

Natural resource wealth can have pernicious effects on democracy, bureaucratic and state capacity, and political violence in the domestic arena.

---

13. During the 2000s, Venezuela surpassed Saudi Arabia as the country with the largest proven reserves of petroleum. Most of the additions came from exploration of the Orinoco belt region in eastern Venezuela. This region has large deposits of heavy crude, similar to the previously estimated petroleum resources in the Orinoco oil belt (Schenk et al. 2009). The estimated volume of heavy crude resources ranges from 380 billion to 652 billion barrels of oil, a quarter of total world reserves as of 2011.

Dependence on natural resources provides regimes with the resources to resist democratizing; access to comparatively free and easy revenue leaves resource-rich countries with weaker bureaucracies and state capacity than their level of economic development would otherwise suggest. Natural resource wealth can contribute both to the motives for and the opportunity to engage in armed rebellion. Indirectly, all three factors contribute to worse development outcomes. Although success stories exist, they are the exceptional cases.

What about international affairs? The commodities boom of the 2000s raises questions about the foreign relations of natural resource exporters, reminding many observers of the commodities boom of the 1970s and the strong hand it dealt oil-producing countries in international affairs. Chapter 4 addresses the foreign relations of major resource exporters.

Key to country abbreviations in figures 3.3 and 4.1

Ago = Angola, Alb = Albania, Are = United Arab Emirates, Arg = Argentina, Arm = Armenia, Aus = Australia, Aut = Austria, Aze = Azerbaijan, Bdi = Burundi, Bel = Belgium, Ben = Benin, Bfa = Burkina Faso, Bgd = Bangladesh, Bgr = Bulgaria, Bhr = Bahrain, Bhs = Bahamas, Bih = Bosnia and Herzegovina, Blr = Belarus, Blz = Belize, Bol = Bolivia, Bra = Brazil, Brb = Barbados, Bwa = Botswana, Caf = Central African Republic, Can = Canada, Che = Switzerland, Chl = Chile, Chn = China, Civ = Ivory Coast, Cmr = Cameroon, Cod = Democratic Republic of the Congo, Cog = Republic of the Congo, Col = Colombia, Cpv = Cape Verde, Cri = Costa Rica, Cyp = Cyprus, Dnk = Denmark, Dom = Dominican Republic, Dza = Algeria, Ecu = Ecuador, Egy = Egypt, Esp = Spain, Est = Estonia, Eth = Ethiopia, Fin = Finland, Fji = Fiji, Fra = France, Gab = Gabon, Gbr = United Kingdom, Geo = Georgia, Gha = Ghana, Gin = Guinea, Gnb = Guinea-Bissau, Grc = Greece, Gtm = Guatemala, Guy = Guyana, Cze = Czech Republic, Deu = Germany, Mon = Montenegro, Hnd = Honduras, Hrv = Croatia, Hti = Haiti, Hun = Hungary, Idn = Indonesia, Ind = India, Irl = Ireland, Irn = Iran, Isl = Iceland, Isr = Israel, Ita = Italy, Jor = Jordan, Jpn = Japan, Kaz = Kazakhstan, Ken = Kenya, Kgz = Kyrgyzstan, Khm = Cambodia, Kor = South Korea, Kwt = Kuwait, Lka = Sri Lanka, Lso = Lesotho, Ltu = Lithuania, Lux = Luxembourg, Lva = Latvia, Mar = Morocco, Mda = Moldova, Mdg = Madagascar, Mdv = Maldives, Mex = Mexico, Mkd = Macedonia, Mli = Mali, Mlt = Malta, Mng = Mongolia, Moz = Mozambique, Mrt = Maurita-nia, Mus = Mauritius, Mwi = Malawi, Mys = Malaysia, Nam = Namibia, Ner = Niger, Nga = Nigeria, Nic = Nicaragua, Nld = Netherlands, Nor = Norway, Npl = Nepal, Nzl = New Zealand, Omn = Oman, Pak = Pakistan, Pan = Panama, Per = Peru, Phl = Philippines, Png = Papua New Guinea, Pol = Poland, Prt = Portugal, Pry = Paraguay, Rou = Romania, Rus = Russia, Rwa = Rwanda, Sdn = Sudan, Sen = Senegal, Sgp = Singapore, Sle = Sierra Leone, Slv = El Salvador, Svk = Slovakia, Svn = Slovenia, Swe = Sweden, Swz = Swaziland, Syr = Syria, Tcd = Chad, Tgo = Togo, Tha = Thai-land, Tto = Trinidad and Tobago, Tun = Tunisia, Tur = Turkey, Tza = Tanzania, Uga = Uganda, Ukr = Ukraine, Ury = Uruguay, Usa = United States, Ven = Venezuela, RB, Vnm = Vietnam, Vut = Vanuatu, Yem = Yemen, Yug = Serbia, Zaf = South Africa, Zmb = Zambia, Zwe = Zimbabwe

4

Natural Resources and International Affairs

The fall of 2008 was a banner time for observers who argue that oil exporter status, and high oil prices, encourage oil exporters to adopt more provocative foreign policies. Russia's invasion of neighboring Georgia—ostensibly in response to Georgian aggression against the breakaway region of South Ossetia—occurred in August of that year, just one month after crude oil prices hit their highest point since 1980. A month later, Bolivia's Evo Morales and Venezuela's Hugo Chávez—both part of the left-leaning pink tide—expelled their US ambassadors as punishment for the United States' purportedly fomenting unrest (violent riots in Bolivia, a coup attempt in Venezuela). Venezuela threatened to cut oil exports to the United States—after earlier expropriating the ExxonMobil's Cerro Negro project. Earlier in the year, Venezuela's Petróleos de Venezuela, SA (PDVSA) suspended oil shipments to ExxonMobil in response to ExxonMobil's legal challenge of Venezuela's nationalization of the Cerro Negro project in the Orinoco belt. War raged between Israel and Hamas in the Gaza Strip. With Iranian backing, Hamas was able to launch rocket attacks on Bersheeba and Gedera. Khaled Mashaal, the chairman of the Damascus-based Hamas Political Bureau, would later say that Iran had played a "big role," providing money and moral support.[1]

Does resource wealth embolden aggressive behavior by exporting states, or are these prominent examples misleading with respect to broader trends? This chapter examines the systematic effects of natural resource dependence on exporting states' foreign affairs in two key arenas: participation in inter-

---

1. "Hamas Leader: Iran Played 'Big Role' in Helping the Gaza Fight," Associated Press, February 2, 2009.

national institutions and conflict behavior. In doing so, it moves from well-trodden terrain into less well marked territory.

Research on the systematic effects of natural resource wealth on interstate behavior is still in its infancy, but some preliminary conclusions can be made. Mineral exporters, energy exporters in particular, are characterized by what Michael Ross and Erik Voeten (2011) call "unbalanced globalization"—a high degree of economic integration but comparatively poor integration in the international organizations in which global governance takes place. Unbalanced globalization has practical effects for both adherence to international norms, such as those governing human rights, and participation in global environmental governance. The empirical record regarding conflict is more nuanced than the standard "resource wars" hypothesis: Oil-exporting states behave more aggressively than nonexporting states, but this belligerence rarely intensifies into actual armed conflict. This dynamic is amplified by high prices. Generally, oil endows exporting countries with a freer hand with which to pursue their aims.

Exports of high-value mined commodities promote economic integration, in terms of both trade and finance. Figure 4.1 plots the natural log of mineral rents per capita—a measure of the relative "ease" of exploiting resources and their predominance in the economy—against the KOF Economic Globalization Index, which includes trade, foreign direct investment (FDI), and portfolio investment, as well as tariff restrictions and capital account controls (Dreher 2006; Dreher, Gaston, and Martens 2008).[2] Although the relationship is essentially flat for most values of mineral rents per capita, there is a strong, positive relationship between mineral rents and economic globalization above a relatively high threshold of about $450, roughly the equivalent of Mexico's average per capita mineral rents, from 2007 to 2009.

The mechanisms through which this process works are several. Because the location of minerals is geologically determined, countries have uneven endowments: Together, Saudi Arabia and Venezuela account for 34 percent of world crude oil reserves but less than 1 percent of population and 1.3 percent of world GDP; Morocco has 75 percent of world rock phosphate reserves but only 0.5 percent of the world's arable land (BP 2012, FAO 2012, USGS 2012a). Thus, export is the only way to equilibrate global supply with global demand, given that most of the world's economic output is dependent on fossil fuels and minerals as agricultural and industrial inputs. Most countries with large extractive sectors are major traders.

Mineral wealth also encourages capital inflows and outflows, particularly in low-income countries, which lack domestic capital to invest in developing extractive capacity and, once the resources start flowing, the absorptive

---

2. Mineral rents are defined as the difference between the value of production for a stock of minerals at world prices and their total cost of production. Minerals included in the calculation are tin, gold, lead, zinc, iron, copper, nickel, silver, bauxite, phosphate, and crude oil. Estimates are described in World Bank (2011b).

Figure 4.1   Relationship between natural resource rents and economic globalization

KOF Economic Globalization Index, 2009

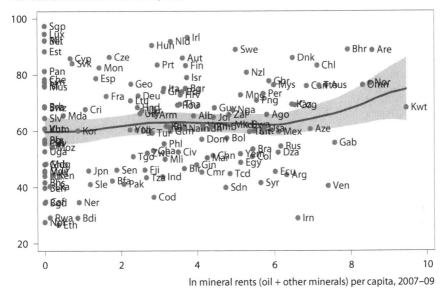

In mineral rents (oil + other minerals) per capita, 2007–09

— Fitted values, polynomial regression   ▧ 95 percent confidence interval

Note: The positive effect of resource rents on globalization does not appear in earnest until a relatively high threshold, equivalent to US$450 per capita. See key to country abbreviations on page 50.

Sources: Dreher (2006); Dreher, Gaston, and Martens (2008); World Bank (2013).

capacity with which to deal with the resulting resource rents. Net FDI inflows in Uganda averaged $252 million (in constant 2005 US dollars) between 2000 and 2005; late in 2005, Tullow Oil PLC and Energy Africa announced significant oil discoveries in the Albertine basin, followed by additional discoveries in 2006. By 2010, net FDI inflows in Uganda had tripled to more than $735 million.[3] Ghana's oil-fueled investment takeoff has been even more dramatic: Net FDI inflows in 2010 ($2.27 billion) were 19 times their average level between 2000 and 2005. Although FDI in resource-dependent economies faces greater threats of expropriation (Jensen and Johnston 2011), the massive rents that accrue to the extractive sector ensure that, in most circumstances, investment capital will be forthcoming.

Once resources begin to flow, countries become even more integrated, thanks to increased demand for imports—as a function of rising incomes—and a move toward capital outflows. Public and private capital outflows may be desirable, at least from the perspective of the resource-exporting country, for

---

3. UNCTADStat Database, 2013, http://unctadstat.unctad.org.

three reasons. First, they can help prevent real appreciation of the exchange rate (Dutch disease). Second, they can check inflationary pressures in the domestic economy. Third, capital outflows—particularly under the auspices of sovereign wealth funds—can provide additional income for developing countries, putting otherwise underutilized foreign exchange reserves to good—or at least potentially productive—use.

Very rarely, however, do policy discussions surrounding natural resource exporters focus on economic integration; rather, there is considerably more concern for the way resource wealth shapes their participation in global governance institutions, efforts to address global climate change, and propensity for armed conflict. In these discussions, Iran, Russia, and Venezuela have received the most scrutiny. Iran's pursuit of nuclear weapons, which flouts international law, is widely believed to be emboldened by its massive oil reserves and concerns stemming from the potential energy market effects of a preemptive strike against its nuclear facilities (Posen et al. 2010, Downs and Maloney 2011).[4] Russia's decisive 2008 invasion of neighboring Georgia was attributed to both the temporary emboldening effect of then near-record oil prices and Russia's longer-term interest in exerting influence over oil transport through the Caucasus.[5] Venezuela's Hugo Chávez used subsidized oil and resource-backed foreign aid to extend Venezuelan influence over other "pink tide" countries in Latin America. Once-secret documents implicate his regime in supporting the Fuerzas Armadas Revolucionarias de Colombia (FARC) against a more right-leaning and pro-US Colombian government (IISS 2011).

In each of these cases, mineral wealth is seen as empowering illiberal leaders to ignore international norms and complicate attempts by Western powers to impose consequences for "bad" behavior by curtailing market access for so-called rogue states. Commodities are, by definition, undifferentiated products. Just as the taste of wheat varies not according to whether it was harvested by "a Russian serf, a French peasant, or an English capitalist" (Marx 1859), the original sourcing of mined commodities, once refined for export and sale, is often impossible (or nearly impossible) to distinguish and of little interest to most end consumers. Moreover, intentional mislabeling of the source is common.[6]

Under these circumstances, attempts to freeze producers out of markets in order to punish bad behavior are difficult to implement in the absence of truly global collective action. The sanctions imposed by the UN Security Council against Iraq between 1990 and 2003 were effective at crippling the

---

4. George Friedman, chief intelligence officer of Stratfor, a private US intelligence firm based in Austin, Texas, opined that an Israeli strike on Iranian nuclear facilities could drive spot oil prices to $300 ("What Happens If Israel Attacks Iran," *Barron's*, February 11, 2012).

5. "Conflict Narrows Oil Options for West," *New York Times*, August 13, 2008; "Russian Offensive Imperils U.S. Aims on Iran, Energy," *Bloomberg News*, August 12, 2008; "Trigger Happy and Oil Mad," *Sydney Morning Herald*, August 16, 2008.

6. For a notable exception—diamonds—see chapter 6.

Iraqi economy because they were enacted and enforced by an essentially global coalition.[7] Unilateral sanctions on particular producing states, even if pursued in concert by major Western powers and Japan, are less likely to damage embargoed countries because of structural changes in the import market—particularly, the rise of non-Western countries as significant import destinations. Given that demand is growing significantly faster in non-Western economies than in the West, disciplining resource-rich states will only become more difficult as the number of key consumers in international markets expands. Moreover, short-run demand for most mined commodities—especially oil—is relatively price inelastic, meaning embargoes entail significant costs for imposing states as well. In contrast, mineral exporters can embargo their own production and shipment in order to impose costs on importers, as in the 1973 Arab oil embargo.

The remainder of this chapter addresses the role of natural resource exporters in global governance institutions and the effects of natural resource dependence for conflict behavior, with a particular focus on oil. It shows that oil exporters tend to be less integrated into international institutions, less supportive of global efforts to address climate change, and more inclined to adopt more confrontational foreign policies than nonexporting states. The chapter closes by addressing the question of whether the "illiberal exporters" singled out above—Iran, Russia, and Venezuela—are emblematic of a more general relationship between oil exports and global citizenship.

Institutional Integration

The proliferation of international institutions is one of the defining characteristics of the post–World War II international order. Political globalization has deepened even faster than economic globalization since the end of the Cold War.

States join international institutions for three reasons: to resolve basic coordination and bargaining problems, particularly problems involving trade, environmental issues, and collective security (Axelrod and Keohane 1985); to increase bargaining influence over third parties, especially in the realm of collective punishment (Martin 1992, 1993); and to enhance the cred-

---

7. New US and EU sanctions on Iran imposed in 2012 were a source of concern among trading partners like China, South Korea, and Turkey (Verleger 2012), but they did not lead to significant short-term disruption of global crude oil markets. They did lead to a significant short-term decline in Iranian oil exports: Shipments were down 40 percent and revenues down 27 percent (authors' calculations, based on USEIA 2013). Although sanctions targeted at the oil sector were significant, banking restrictions may have been more influential. In contrast to commodity markets, the United States and the European Union still have dominant positions in global banking, thus making collective action in this arena both more likely (given the smaller number of players and concordant preferences among them) and more effective. As of November 2013, US and EU sanctions—and the ability to lift said sanctions—appear to have provided the necessary leverage to produce a joint plan of action on Iran's nuclear program, the first such breakthrough in 30 years.

ibility of domestic policies, particularly those that affect international investors (Mansfield and Pevehouse 2008, Kerner and Lawrence 2014). Whatever the motive for joining these organizations, membership in international organizations and political globalization—hosting embassies, participating in UN Security Council missions, engaging in international treaties—have powerful implications for reducing international conflict behavior (Russett, Oneal, and Davis 1998; Shannon 2009; Choi 2010) and increasing respect for human rights (Hafner-Burton 2009; de Soysa and Vadlamannati 2011; Dreher, Gassebner, and Siemers 2012). Despite being characterized by the same type of horse-trading and power politics as other deliberative forums, international institutions can be important shapers and transmitters of international norms (Risse and Sikkink 1999, Checkel 2005). Active global citizenship is a stabilizing, peace-promoting force in international affairs.

For a variety of reasons, oil exporters may not "need" to join international institutions in the same ways as nonexporting countries. To the extent that international institutions—be they large, omnibus institutions like the United Nations or the European Union or bilateral agreements—constrain or at least change state behavior, they represent a loss of sovereign authority. That loss of authority is palatable only if it is offset by efficiency gains or facilitates outcomes that would be significantly more difficult to achieve in the absence of such institutions. For most states, the main impetus for integration is stabilizing trade and investment relationships—making sure their goods gain access to markets and investment capital is forthcoming—and bringing influence to bear on third parties, particularly in matters of collective security. Since the structural increase in prices after the 1970s, oil exporters have had little trouble finding markets for their main products. Because of Dutch disease dynamics, their agricultural and manufacturing sectors—the sectors where foreign competition is fiercest—seek protection, rather than integration, and this impulse is stronger the more oil exports predominate (Ross and Voeten 2011). Regarding investment capital, high prices and increasing global demand virtually ensure that investment capital will be forthcoming: Barclays Capital estimates that the energy industry will spend $644 billion on oil and natural gas exploration in 2013, not counting North America, where the shale revolution continues.[8]

Moreover, investment capital is usually forthcoming, despite the fact that investment in the resource sector is risky because of the threat of expropriation. The example of Venezuela under Hugo Chávez is telling. Between 2002 and 2006, 15 companies were nationalized. Beginning in 2007, the Chávez administration began a much broader program of nationalization, including foreign real estate holdings and oil exploration and production facilities. Over the next five years, 1,147 firms were nationalized, including oil facilities

---

8. "Global Markets to Drive 2013 Oil and Gas Spending—Barclays," Reuters, December 4, 2012.

belonging to ExxonMobil and ConocoPhillips.[9] Despite this wave of expropriations, and fiery anti-Western, anticapitalist rhetoric, Venezuela still saw annual FDI inflows of more than $1 billion a year (in constant 2005 dollars) between 2007 and 2011.[10]

Very little systematic work empirically assesses the relationship between natural resource exports and political globalization. To date, the only broadly cross-national analysis is that of Ross and Voeten (2011), who estimate the impact of oil revenue—operationalized as oil exports per capita—on four measures of political globalization:

- the KOF Index, which includes the number of embassies hosted, membership in international organizations, and participation in UN Security Council missions and international treaties;

- participation in standard-setting international organizations, which set benchmarks for behavior in human rights, the environment, or international business;

- economic international organizations, such as preferential trade agreements, currency unions, and development banks; and

- political international organizations, which have broad mandates to develop and coordinate policy across a range of issue areas (examples include the Organization of American States, the African Union, and the League of Arab States).

The findings of Ross and Voeten (2011) indicate that high levels of oil exports suppress political globalization and are associated with fewer memberships in standards-based and political international organizations. But oil exporters, in keeping with their economically globalized status, are no less prone to joining economic international organizations, including bilateral investment treaties. Bilateral investment treaties (BITs) establish terms for private investment by foreign nationals and companies. They are distinguished by provisions for channeling disputes through international arbitration rather than the host state's legal system. BITs are particularly relevant for investment in extractive industries, because the underlying assets are immobile, eliminating the possibility of using capital flight as a mechanism to keep host governments honest, and because the corrosive effect of mineral dependence on legal and bureaucratic institutions means that host-state legal institutions may not inspire investor confidence (Kerner and Lawrence 2014). Yet even when oil-exporting countries establish BITs, they are systematically less likely to delegate dispute resolution authority to a third party, such as the World Bank's International Centre for the Settlement

---

9. "Expropriations Stir Controversy in Venezuela," *Al-Jazeera*, October 6, 2012.

10. Following the expulsion of the US ambassador and threats to embargo exports to the United States in 2008, 2009 saw FDI repatriations of more than $2.7 billion. If this year is excluded, Venezuelan FDI inflows over 2007–11 averaged $1.64 billion.

of Investment Disputes, preserving for themselves more latitude (Ross and Voeten 2011).

Ross and Voeten call this situation "unbalanced globalization." Oil exporters are systematically more economically globalized than nonexporters but less politically globalized and integrated into international governance regimes. This circumstance has several important implications.

First, oil-exporting countries have more latitude in setting policy and face fewer formal, institutionally specified consequences for bad behavior. Although not all oil-exporting states flout international norms, they are systematically less likely to have precommitted themselves to not doing so. The relative paucity of institutional checks on their actions may help contextualize the heterodox behavior of some oil-exporting states.

Second, their lagging political integration complicates efforts to address issues that require global collective action, particularly regarding the environment. This dynamic is clearly at play in negotiations over how to address climate change, where oil-exporting countries' material interests are at stake. Carbon emissions reductions will be a necessary component of any climate change mitigation protocol; although emissions cuts will impose some costs on all economies, they will be greater for energy-intensive economies, particularly those with significant hydrocarbon reserves (Buys et al. 2009). Any global protocol on emissions reduction would have some negative economic effects for countries that produce hydrocarbons, but the proportional welfare effects would be particularly large for countries that export energy. Saudi Arabia and other members of the Organization of Petroleum Exporting Countries (OPEC) have long pushed for compensation, under the guise of aid for economic diversification, for reductions in carbon dioxide emissions that would lead to a decrease in fossil fuel prices and a devaluation of OPEC members' significant hydrocarbon reserves.[11] Following the partial successes of the REDD (Reducing Emissions from Deforestation and Degradation) scheme, which essentially pays rainforest countries to preserve forested areas, Ecuador has sought international funding not to develop the Ishpingo-Tambococha-Tiputini oil field, which is located in a national forest. This initiative ultimately proved unsuccessful, with the Ecuadorian government raising only $13 million for its UN-administered trust fund, well short of the $3.6 billion target.[12] Absent some sort of pecuniary offset, developing countries will find it almost impossible to leave valuable resources in the ground, and will likely push back against schemes to limit emissions.

---

11. "OPEC States Want to Be Paid if Pollution Curbs Cut Oil Sales," *New York Times*, September 16, 2000; "Saudis Seek Payments for Any Drop in Oil Revenues," *New York Times*, October 13, 2009.

12. "With $116 Million Pledged, Ecuador Moves Forward with Plan to Protect Rainforest," *Science Insider*, January 13, 2012; Rhett Butler, "As Rain Forests Disappear, A Market Solution Emerges," *Yale Environment 360*, http://e360.yale.edu/feature/as_rain_forests_disappear_a_market_solution_emerges/2097 (accessed on February 8, 2013); Jonathan Watts, "Ecuador Approves Yasuni National Park Oil Drilling in Amazon Rainforest," *Guardian*, August 16, 2013.

Material interests put oil producers at odds with many schemes for mitigating climate change, but their political isolation does not help, and it extends beyond issue areas where carbon emissions are of primary concern. Thomas Bernauer et al. (2010) find that membership in international organizations increased the probability that countries ratified multilateral environmental treaties such as the Montreal and Helsinki Protocols, which govern chlorofluorocarbon and sulfur emissions, respectively. Moreover, they find that economic integration—measured as trade intensity—decreased the probability of ratification. Thus, the unbalanced globalization of oil exporters decreases their propensity to participate in global environmental governance institutions via both mechanisms.

Third, because oil-exporting states participate in fewer international institutions, they are less likely to adhere to international norms regarding the use of force, both at home and abroad. Membership in international institutions can have powerful effects for state behavior even when the institutions in question have nothing to do with the specific issue at hand. Brian Greenhill (2010) finds that membership in institutions that do not focus on human rights has a positive effect on a state's respect for human rights.

Fourth, fewer institutional linkages mean that oil-exporting states have fewer forums in which tensions with other states can be moderated via socialization and routinized interaction, which may help explain why oil-exporting countries are also outliers with respect to conflict behavior, the subject of the next section.

Conflict Behavior

Both general trends and more careful econometric analysis indicate that oil exporters have more aggressive foreign policies and engage in interstate disputes more frequently. Moreover, higher prices further embolden exporters, increasing the frequency of dispute occurrence.

Jeff Colgan (2010) finds that "petrostates"—states in which revenues from net oil exports constitute at least 10 percent of GDP—have engaged in militarized disputes 50 percent more frequently than nonpetrostates in the post–World War II era.[13] Natural resource exporters—particularly oil exporters—engage in militarized disputes more often than nonresource exporters, though these disputes rarely escalate into full-blown wars. Indra de Soysa, Erik Gartzke and Tove Grete Lie (2011) note that oil is a highly contestable resource (see chapter 3). Because of its contestability, oil should make a state a more appealing target

---

13. "Militarized interstate disputes are united historical cases of conflict in which the threat, display or use of military force short of war by one member state is explicitly directed towards the government, official representatives, official forces, property, or territory of another state. Disputes are composed of incidents that range in intensity from threats to use force to actual combat short of war" (Jones, Bremer, and Singer 1996, 163). They are a commonly used measure of conflictual behavior between states that does escalate to actual warfare.

for conquest. Fighting over oil may ultimately be less attractive, however, than either purchasing it or cultivating close ties with governments in producing countries. As the United States learned firsthand in Iraq, it is easy to underestimate the costs associated with occupying and directly governing foreign territory (Wimberley 2007). Stability in oil-producing countries is often based on complex, dense networks of patronage that are much easier to destroy than to rebuild. The presence of oil veritably ensures that insurgents will have little trouble arming and equipping themselves, either through extortion—or "revolutionary taxation," depending on one's point of view—or direct third-party support.

The rents generated from oil export help finance large, technologically sophisticated militaries in exporting countries (Hendrix 2010). Table 4.1 shows the top 10 countries in military expenditures per capita from 2000 to 2011. Six are major oil exporters. Moreover, because oil is a strategic resource, major powers invest significant resources in securing global supply lines and have incentives to prevent large-scale conflict in oil-producing countries that might result in global price spikes. The US Fifth and Sixth Fleets have the smallest areas of responsibility of the Navy's numbered fleets, covering the Arabian Gulf and the Indian Ocean and the Mediterranean Sea, respectively, but they are among its most important assets for ensuring a steady supply of oil from and through the region. Given that all the members of the UN Security Council except Russia are major oil importers, maintaining stability in oil-producing states and deterring oil-seeking territorial aggression approaches an international norm. The 1991 Gulf War, in which a US-led coalition responded to Iraq's invasion of neighboring Kuwait, was waged under the auspices of a UN Security Council binding resolution. According to de Soysa, Gartzke, and Lie (2011), as a result of both domestic spending on defense in energy-exporting countries and their strategic significance for major powers, oil producers are less likely to experience wars and less likely to be perceived as rivals by major powers than nonexporting countries, even when their policy preferences, as expressed in voting patterns in the United Nations and military alliances, are opposed to those of the major power.[14]

Although energy exporters are, in the main, less likely to be involved in wars, they can still be irritants and instigators. de Soysa, Gartzke, and Lie (2011) argue that the implicit security guarantees perceived by energy exporters induce a form of moral hazard: Because they are essentially indemnified against large battlefield and territorial losses, they may be more casual

---

14. "Actors categorize other actors in their environments. Some are friends, others are enemies. Threatening enemies who are also adjudged to be competitors in some sense, as opposed to irritants or simply problems, are branded as rivals. This categorization is very much a social-psychological process. Actors interpret the intentions of others based on earlier behavior and forecasts about the future behavior of these other actors. The interpretation of these intentions leads to expectations about the likelihood of conflicts escalating to physical attacks.... Both sides expect hostile behavior from the other side and proceed to deal with the adversary with that expectation in mind" (Thompson 2001, 561–62).

Table 4.1 Top 10 countries in military spending per capita, 2000–11

Country	US dollars
United Arab Emirates	2,725
Israel	2,138
Kuwait	1,952
Qatar	1,883
United States	1,854
Oman	1,681
Singapore	1,671
Saudi Arabia	1,429
Norway	1,299
France	951

Source: SIPRI (2013).

about the use of force—or threats of force—in their dealings with other countries, especially countries that are not energy exporters and are thus not similarly insured themselves. They find that oil exporters tend to initiate more low-level disputes (militarized interstate disputes [MIDs]) with nonoil exporters, although the effect is small. These low-level disputes rarely escalate to actual war, but given the importance of oil for the world economy, they make headlines, contributing to the perception that resource-backed violence is a persistent feature of international affairs, even if actual oil wars are rare.

This moral hazard may embolden some leaders more than others. Colgan (2010, 2011, 2013) attributes the increased dispute propensity of oil producers to a confluence of two factors: resource rents and revolutionary leadership. Because state authorities can easily appropriate oil revenues, they provide rulers with greater resources with which to buy off opposition and spend on their militaries, reducing the domestic costs associated with more risky foreign policy behavior.

Although this logic establishes means, it does not establish motive. Leaders of many oil-rich states—Saudi Arabia, the United Arab Emirates, Nigeria, Gabon—are satisfied with their position in the status quo and lack revisionist ambitions: dissatisfaction born of a belief that they are not "receiving their due from the international order" (Kugler and Organski 1989). In contrast, revolutionary leaders—leaders who come to power by force and attempt to transform preexisting political and economic relationships, both domestically and abroad—often have revisionist ambitions and are less hesitant about using force to resolve international disputes. Revolutionary governments with oil wealth have both motive and means to initiate militarized disputes, a finding Colgan confirms with careful empirical analysis.[15]

Colgan also finds that the relationship between resources, revolutionary governments, and conflict does not hold for other extractives (bauxite, copper, iron, lead, nickel, phosphate, tin, zinc, gold, and silver). Oil is unique in its effect of emboldening revolutionary leaders. Whether this effect reflects its easy monopolization by state actors, the comparatively massive rents it generates, or its strategic significance cannot be determined conclusively, but the discussion of state revenue and state capacity in chapter 3 suggests that one can rule out the first mechanism: most other mineral resource rents are easily appropriable.

What about price effects? Although primarily focused on domestic politics in exporting countries, Thomas Friedman's First Law of Petropolitics suggests that high oil prices embolden producers to adopt more confrontational foreign policies.[16] Higher prices make strategic relationships between powerful importers and exporting states more valuable. If oil exporter status effectively insures leaders from retaliation for saber-rattling behavior, higher prices should further embolden oil-exporting countries and correlate with more bellicose behavior. If oil revenue is particularly emboldening to revolutionary leaders, then the price effect should be amplified for revolutionary-led petrostates.

Econometric evidence provides support for a general link between higher prices and more aggressive foreign policies in oil states; there is less support connecting higher prices to aggressive behavior by revolutionary-led oil states (Hendrix 2014). An increase in world oil prices from $23 per barrel (the price in mid-2002) to $73 (the price in the second quarter of 2007) in constant 2005 dollars increases the frequency with which oil-exporting states experience militarized disputes by roughly one quarter; oil prices are uncorrelated with dispute propensity in nonexporting states (see figure 4.2). A similar increase in oil prices

---

15. Colgan's definition of a revolutionary leader has two components. The first involves the means by which the ruler comes in to office: "First, has the individual leader used armed force against his own state at any time prior to coming to office as an integral part of coming to national influence, and ultimately, state leadership? Second, were there mass demonstrations or uprisings, violent or nonviolent, that were instrumental in deciding the outcome of the transition?" (Colgan 2012, 444–45). The second refers to the types of policies the leader implemented while in office: "Did the leader usher in a major change to the constitution? Did the leader adopt communism or fascism as the official ideology of the state/ruling party? Did the leader overhaul rules governing property ownership?" For a complete list, see Colgan (2012).

16. Friedman (2006) cites Hugo Chávez as "telling British Prime Minister Tony Blair to 'go right to hell' and telling supporters that the US-sponsored Free Trade Area of the Americas 'can go to hell'" in early 2006. Had he waited until September, he would have had even better copy. On September 20, Chávez addressed the UN General Assembly, one day after President George W. Bush. Chávez began his speech with a pitch for Noam Chomsky's *Hegemony or Survival* and followed with some choice remarks about the US president: "Yesterday, the devil came here. Right here. Right here. And it smells of sulfur still today, this table that I am now standing in front of. Yesterday, ladies and gentlemen, from this rostrum, the president of the United States, the gentleman to whom I refer as the devil, came here, talking as if he owned the world" (CQ Transcripts Wire, 2006).

Figure 4.2 Oil prices and militarized interstate disputes, 1945–2001

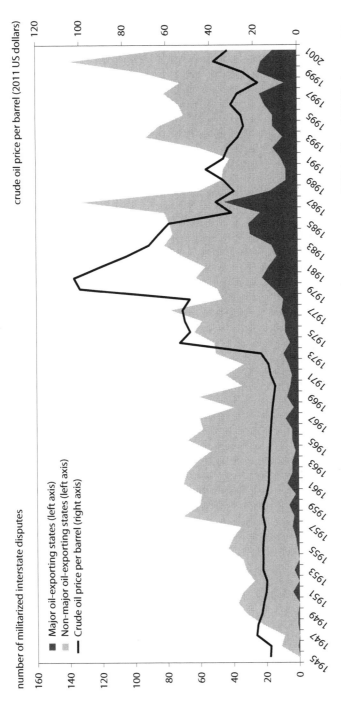

number of militarized interstate disputes

crude oil price per barrel (2011 US dollars)

- Major oil-exporting states (left axis)
- Non-major oil-exporting states (left axis)
- Crude oil price per barrel (right axis)

Note: Oil prices are strongly correlated with dispute behavior in oil states where net oil exports account for 10 percent or more of GDP (*r* = 0.5, *p* = 0.01). Oil prices are uncorrelated with dispute behavior in non-oil-exporting states (*r* = 0.07, *p* = 0.59).

Sources: Ghosn, Palmer, and Bremer (2004); Colgan (2010); BP (2012).

is associated with an increase in the frequency with which oil-exporting states clearly initiate these disputes; it has no effect on nonexporting states.

Evidence for price effects for revolutionary petrostates is less robust: Although there is some evidence that the relationship between prices and exporting state behavior is driven by revolutionary-led cases, this evidence does not hold up under the most rigorous specifications. Data availability limits the analysis to the period 1945–2001 and thus does not include the most recent commodities boom; it does include the oil shocks of the 1970s, which were of significantly larger magnitude than the shocks of the past decade.

This discussion highlights the unbalanced globalization—the high level of economic but comparatively low level of political integration—and more bellicose foreign policies of energy-exporting countries. How well do these findings illuminate the behavior of the "illiberal" producers that have received heightened scrutiny in the past decade (Iran, Russia, and Venezuela)?

First, none of the three is as politically isolated as its major exporter status might suggest: All three are above the median on the KOF Political Globalization Index. Figure 4.3 ranks OPEC members and non-OPEC members with significant energy exports according to their score on the KOF Political Globalization Index. Perhaps because of its former superpower status, Russia is extremely highly integrated, trailing only Norway and Nigeria. Iran and Venezuela, considered pariah states by many, are significantly more politically integrated than many other OPEC members and energy exporters, including Saudi Arabia and Bahrain, the home port of the US Fifth Fleet.

Second, only one of these countries (Venezuela) was presided over by a "revolutionary" leader, at least according to Colgan's definition. Hugo Chávez emerged on the Venezuelan political scene by attempting to violently overthrow the government in 1992. Once in office, he abrogated the constitution, abolished presidential term limits, and oversaw the reorientation of the Venezuelan economy via a program of nationalization and increased social spending based on socialist principles. Large swaths of Venezuelan society supported this program. Chávez came to power in elections no more problematic than those that brought Mohammed Khatami and Mahmoud Ahmadinejad to power in Iran or Vladimir Putin and Dmitry Medvedev in Russia. All four rose to power via conventional means, having been elected by questionable (at best) but nevertheless institutionalized electoral processes. In office, all four oversaw a continuation, rather than a complete overhaul, of the policies of their predecessors.

In terms of conflict behavior, Iran and Russia appear to have come by their petro-aggressive reputations honestly. Iran's Ayatollah Khomeini is the single most bellicose leader of the 1,020 leaders analyzed by one of us (Hendrix 2014), with an expected MID count of 3.9 per year, not far ahead of Ayatollah Hashemi Rafsanjani (2.8, ranked sixth). Both Putin and Boris Yeltsin rank in the top 3 percent of all leaders for conflict propensity.[17] The modeling indicates that

---

17. US presidents Dwight Eisenhower, John F. Kennedy, Lyndon Johnson, Richard Nixon, George H. W. Bush, Ronald Reagan, Gerald Ford, Bill Clinton, and George W. Bush do as well.

Figure 4.3 KOF Index of Political Globalization scores for major energy exporters, 2009

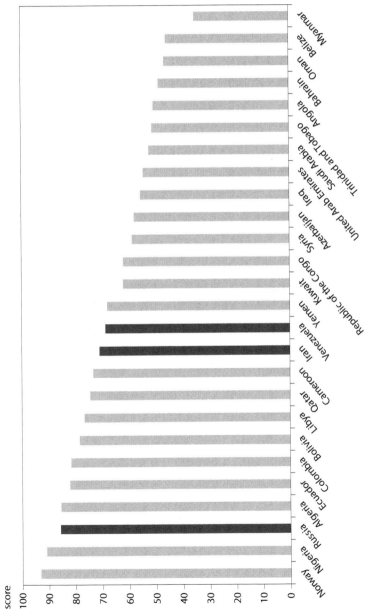

Note: The higher the score, the greater the globalization. Figure includes member states of the Organization of Petroleum Exporting Countries and all countries where energy exports accounted for more than 35 percent of merchandise exports in 2009.

Sources: Dreher, Gaston, and Martens (2008); World Bank (2013).

Russia is the single most conflict-prone country, followed closely by China and the United States, two major oil importers. Iran is the only nonmember of the UN Security Council—whose members are able to project military power at a global scale—to crack the top five.

Will the United States' reemergence as an energy exporter fundamentally alter this picture? Imports as a share of total US energy consumption hit their post-1973 peak in 2005 at 30 percent, but by 2035, the International Energy Agency forecasts that the US energy trade deficit will shrink to less than 4 percent, thanks to both expanding production and increasing energy efficiency (IEA 2012). One of the purported benefits of increasing efficiency and expanding US production capacity is that they will make the United States much less dependent on energy imports, thereby diminishing incentives to intervene in the domestic and external affairs of energy-exporting countries. An energy-independent United States would be freed of its implicit commitment to stabilize oil producers; realizing that they no longer have this implicit security guarantee, producers would adjust their behavior accordingly.

The hydrocarbon boom in North America may also lead to lower global prices. Many medium-term forecasts for crude prices have spot prices either up slightly or in some cases doubling from recent prices by 2020.[18] However, some industry experts believe these forecasts massively underestimate the potential impact of the ongoing shale revolution, which some believe may lead to a halving of prices.[19] If oil prices were to stabilize at 50 percent of their present real value, the logic goes, it would rob petrostates of the vast resources with which to prosecute their aims. Of course, it would expose the United States to the same price shocks, although the proportional effects on US terms of trade would be much smaller than for oil exporters for which oil exports account for large shares of total exports.

Despite these projections, the rise of the United States as an energy exporter is unlikely to markedly diminish the importance of foreign oil producers for US foreign policy, for at least two reasons. First, key US allies—and lynchpins of the global economy—in Europe and Asia will remain import dependent for the foreseeable future. North Atlantic Treaty Organization (NATO) members Germany, the Netherlands, France, and Italy are all among the top 10 oil importers, as are Japan and South Korea (and China, for that matter). To the extent that the health of the US economy is contingent on the health of some of its largest trading partners and military allies, supply shocks in global markets will continue to have clear economic implications

---

18. Benes et al. (2012) and OECD StatExtracts (accessed on January 11, 2013).

19. These experts include John Llewellyn, former head of international forecasting at the Organization for Economic Cooperation and Development (OECD); Francisco Blanch, head of the commodities research department at Bank of America; and Joseph Petrowski, CEO of Gulf Oil. See "Shale Gas Revolution 'Could Halve Oil Price,'" *The Times*, July 1, 2013; Benjamin Alter and Edward Fishman, "The Dark Side of Energy Independence," *New York Times*, April 27, 2013; and "Expect $50 Oil, but Not $2 Gas, Gulf Oil CEO Says," CNBC, July 15, 2013.

for an energy-independent United States, from which US security interests in these places necessarily follow.

Second, the security implications of the price effects that might accompany the United States' rise as an exporter are murky. On the one hand, lower prices should mean less bellicose behavior by producers in the international arena. On the other hand, lower prices would mean lower revenues for governments that have made large public expenditures a key pillar of domestic political stability. Consumer subsidies have long been part of the "authoritarian bargain" between the state and citizens in many authoritarian countries. Attempts to withdraw them have been met with upheaval, as during the bread *intifada* (uprising) after Egyptian President Anwar Sadat's decision in 1977 to roll back food subsidies. The resulting unrest killed 800 people, and the subsidies were quickly reinstated. The political logic of these subsidies is both straightforward and pernicious: They explicitly encouraged citizens across the region to evaluate government effectiveness based on its ability to maintain low consumer prices. When the government is flush, these large public expenditures are tenable. When revenues decline, governments find themselves in the uncomfortable position of having to roll back price supports, sparking unrest.[20] As current events suggest, it is unlikely that domestic unrest in oil-producing countries will lead to less attention from US policymakers.

Conclusion

This chapter discussed how energy exporter status affects state behavior, endowing these states with a freer hand, maintaining independence from international organizations, and pursuing more confrontational foreign policies. It established that high prices amplify these conflict effects. Thus, in addition to their direct economic effects, resource booms have demonstrable impacts for international security. Security concerns related to resource booms should consider not just what they allow exporters to get away with, however, but also what they may (or may not) compel major importers to do. The next chapter addresses the rise of China as a major mineral importer and investor in resource extraction and the extent to which its rise has shaped its foreign policy in the 21st century.

---

20. The resulting domestic instability in oil-exporting states would likely both push prices back up and result in significant price volatility, suggesting that the lowest projections for global oil prices would not be a stable equilibrium.

5

China as a Major Importer and Investor

The previous chapters addressed both the domestic and international economic and political effects of the natural resource curse in resource-producing and resource-exporting countries. But the implications of the resource curse may not be confined to countries in which the resources are located. The resource curse may affect large consumers as well, insofar as it shapes their foreign policies to a significant degree.

As of 2011, China and the United States together consumed 40 percent of the world's primary energy, 32 percent of its oil, and 26 percent of its natural gas (USEIA 2012).[1] The rise of China as an energy consumer has been meteoric. In 1973, China accounted for less than 5 percent of world energy consumption, and the United States accounted for 32 percent. By 2011, China had surpassed the United States as the single largest energy consumer (BP 2012). The true takeoff, however, has been a more recent occurrence. Between 2000 and 2011, China's energy consumption more than doubled, growing at an annual rate of 8.6 percent. Although China's economy will become more energy efficient as it develops, its expanding middle class and growing manufacturing sector ensure that conventional energy demands will continue to grow, likely at a rate three to four times that of the United States (USEIA 2011). As documented below, China's emergence as a major consumer (and investor) is not limited to oil but extends to a broad array of potentially contestable commodities, including industrial metals and diamonds and gold associated with luxury consumption.

Although both China and the United States have large conventional energy reserves in the form of coal, both are net oil and natural gas importers,

---

1. Primary energy comprises commercially traded fuels, including modern renewables (biomass, geothermal, hydropower, etc.) used to generate electricity (BP 2012).

dependent on international markets to satisfy domestic energy demand. As of 2011, domestic production accounted for 42 percent of total oil consumption in both countries. Over the medium term, China and the United States are headed in opposite directions in terms of their reliance on these markets. The shale gas revolution is radically altering the US outlook. The International Energy Agency forecasts that the United States will surpass Saudi Arabia to become the biggest oil producer by 2020 and that it will shift from net importer to net exporter by 2030, reversing nearly two decades of declining domestic production (IEA 2012). The upturn in US production is already evident. As figure 5.1 demonstrates, domestic production as a share of total consumption in the United States has increased significantly since 2005, when it stood at 33 percent. In contrast, China's rapid economic growth and relatively modest increases in domestic capacity have meant a monotonic decline in domestic production as a share of total consumption, down from 52 percent in 2005. China's domestic oil production is forecast to grow by only 4.4 percent between 2013 and 2035, not nearly enough to keep pace with increased demand (USEIA 2012). In the 21st century, China will assume the United States' mantle as the world's preeminent oil importer.

Since 2000, global oil markets have been characterized by the highest prices and price volatility since the 1970s (see figure 3.1). High prices and volatility are the result of both market fundamentals (increasing demand in developing countries has not been offset entirely by new production elsewhere or increases in refining capacity) and the rise of commodities as an asset class for institutional investors. Michael Klare (2002, 2004) argues that a resource scramble has supplanted (or will supplant, at some point in the near future) the capitalist-communist ideological struggle as the main source of conflict in the post–Cold War era, both within resource-exporting states (or states with export potential, in the case of new discoveries) and as part of a larger pattern of geopolitical competition between the world's two largest importers (the United States and China) over access to the oil reserves of the Middle East, North Africa, and Central Asia.

The United States' relative decline as an energy importer does not mean that energy security will cease to be a significant foreign policy issue. The idea that US energy independence will clear energy issues from the agenda is a nice campaign slogan but a specious claim, as major trading partners and allies in Europe and Japan will continue to be import reliant. Moreover, price shocks as a result of political instability in producing countries will still have the capacity to roil consumer markets. What happens in global markets will necessarily affect the US market and US interests abroad. Natural resource needs will continue to shape the foreign policies of both countries.

China's appetite for natural resources extends beyond oil and natural gas. China's economy accounts for 14.3 percent of world GDP in purchasing power parity but more than 60 percent of global iron trade and more than 30 percent

Figure 5.1   Domestic oil production in the United States and China as a share of domestic consumption, 1980–2011

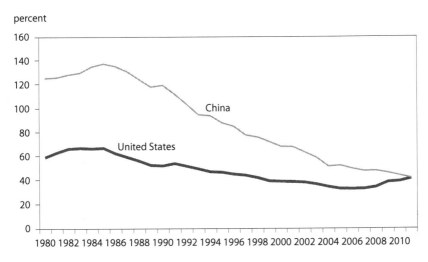

Source: BP (2012).

of global metals trade.[2] Growing consumption of natural resources, particularly energy and metals, is the handmaiden of industrialization and economic development. As the manufacturing sector grows, per capita demand for industrial inputs—especially base metals like aluminum, copper, lead, nickel, tin, and zinc—rises. Even among rapid industrializers, China's demand for energy and base metals is unprecedented. Demand intensity can be measured by commodity consumption per capita relative to GDP; China's rapid industrialization has been more energy and metals intensive than that of either Brazil or South Korea (Roache 2012).

As China has become a major resource importer, its economic growth and large current account surpluses have fueled greater scrutiny of its foreign affairs. Although China has been a major power throughout the post–World War II era, with a permanent seat on the UN Security Council, it was the least economically integrated of the permanent members until its rapid economic ascent in the early 1990s. In the early 1980s, China accounted for less than 1 percent of global trade flows (imports plus exports); by the early 2000s, it was second only to the United States, having surpassed the United Kingdom and France (see figure 5.2). Its rise as a trading power has been accompanied by persistent current account surpluses that reached 10 percent of GDP in 2007 (Cline 2012). Although these current account surpluses have dipped recently,

---

2. The United States is the world's number one exporter and importer of foodstuffs (FAOSTAT Database, accessed on January 12, 2013).

Figure 5.2   Share of total world trade accounted for by permanent UN Security Council members, 1950–2009

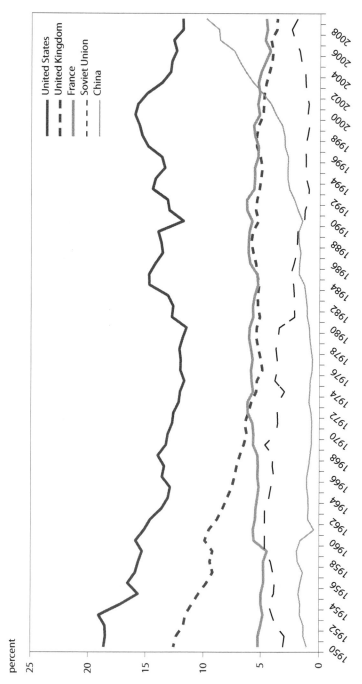

Source: Barbieri and Keshk (2012).

they are forecast to remain at 3 to 4 percent of GDP through 2017 (Cline 2012). At least since 2000, China has been flush with cash, enabling it to significantly expand its economic and security ties with the rest of the world, in terms of outward foreign direct investment (OFDI), development finance, and military assistance/sales.

From a market liberal perspective, this increased integration into the world economy could be heralded as good news. Trade and financial integration tend to pacify relations between states, raising the opportunity costs associated with conflict and creating vested domestic interests in both that prefer peace to war (Oneal, Russett, and Berbaum 2003; Gartzke 2007). The rise of global supply and production networks only enhances these tendencies (Brooks 2007).

However, not all observers are cheerful about China's rise as a major trader, source of FDI, and aid donor. Indeed, the prevailing conventional wisdom is highly skeptical, if not downright contemptuous. Moisés Naím (2007, 95) has called Chinese development assistance "rogue aid," claiming, "It is development assistance that is nondemocratic in origin and nontransparent in practice; its effect is typically to stifle real progress while hurting average citizens." Stefan Halper (2010a, 102) alleges that China's economic rise is "marginalizing the values that have informed Western progress for 300 years."

These concerns have arisen around the loose banner of the "Beijing Consensus," an alternative economic model to the prevailing market-oriented logic of the Washington Consensus. Rather than emphasizing open markets, private ownership, and retrenchment of the government's role in the economy, the Beijing Consensus—to the extent that it is a meaningful concept—means pursuing economic development along Chinese lines: gradual policy changes; experimentation and incremental reform and policy changes, as opposed to great leaps; state enterprises working within a predominantly market framework; and authoritarian rule (Williamson 2012).[3]

The term, which is also applied to China's foreign economic engagement, comes in several flavors. The most benign is that China simply does not account for democratic institutions and practices in its investment and aid allocation decisions: It is driven entirely by economic concerns, particularly securing natural resources; politics are largely irrelevant (Bräutigam 2008, 2009). Dambisa Moyo (2012, location 1496) casts this perspective in starkly resource-seeking terms: "Like a 19th-century colonial power, China has ranged the world over to secure the resources needed to meet its ambitions. Unlike many of those earlier colonial powers, though, its strategy has been less to

---

3. "In a lecture I delivered in Birmingham, I tend to take a somewhat cynical view about that. I argued first of all that there's not a lot of content in the concept of the Beijing Consensus beyond saying, 'This is what the Chinese do.' There's no list of propositions [comparable] to those [that] I suggest constituted the Washington Consensus. Instead it's what China does, and I've identified four things." John Williamson, "Beijing Consensus vs. Washington Consensus," Peterson Perspectives interview, November 2, 2010.

plunder the natural wealth of the countries it deals with than to strike long-range aid and trade agreements."

More strident definitions point to an illiberal, antidemocratic bent in China's investment and development assistance. Halper, in particular, argues that China prefers to invest in nondemocratic countries and that Chinese investment and development assistance are part of a strategy for developing a pro-China (and often anti-Taiwan) voting coalition in multilateral institutions like the United Nations and World Trade Organization. In this version, China's rise is qualitatively different from that of other developing countries, particularly South Korea, in the postwar period (Halper 2010c). Rather than integrating into the West-led economic and political order, it seeks to develop its own: "China will not join the club. It cannot be housebroken. It marches to its own drummer" (Halper 2010b).

Hyperbolic statements aside, the factors that shape China's foreign policy have not been subjected to rigorous empirical analysis. Are China's 21st century investment, aid, and security ties disproportionate to nondemocratic countries? If so, does this pattern reflect an affinity for authoritarian governments, or is China interested in natural resources, particularly mined commodities, which stifle democracy via the mechanisms discussed in chapter 3? The remainder of this chapter investigates these claims with respect to China's OFDI, official development financing, and arms transfers.

Outward Foreign Direct Investment

Most discussions of FDI involving China focus on its rise as an investment destination. In 1990, China attracted 1.7 percent of total FDI inflows; by 2011, it attracted more than 8 percent, second only to the United States.[4] Since 2000, China's OFDI has grown at an average annual rate of 50 percent, taking off particularly sharply after 2003 (see figure 5.3). Although China has moved into the ranks of the world's major sources of OFDI, the United States still accounts for nearly eight times as much OFDI, and Japan nearly twice as much. Chinese OFDI has attracted attention because of its role in China's broader policy of exporting capital in order to achieve domestic price stabilization and prevent real exchange rate appreciation and because of China's dependence on global markets to satisfy its resource needs. China's emergence as a major destination for and exporter of FDI has been facilitated by its aggressive pursuit of bilateral investment treaties (box 5.1).

Chinese OFDI is clearly targeted toward extractive industries. Previous Peterson Institute research found that 73.5 percent of Chinese OFDI in Latin America was targeted at metals, coal, oil, and natural gas (Moran, Kotschwar, and Muir 2012). Global and regional analyses point to the significance of host-country oil and mineral exports in attracting Chinese OFDI (Asiedu 2006; Kolstad and Wiig 2012; Ramasamy, Yeung, and Laforet 2012; Aleksynska and

---

4. UNCTADstat Database, 2012, http://unctadstat.unctad.org (accessed on December 10, 2012).

Figure 5.3 Chinese outward foreign direct investment flows, 1990–2012

millions of constant 2005 US dollars

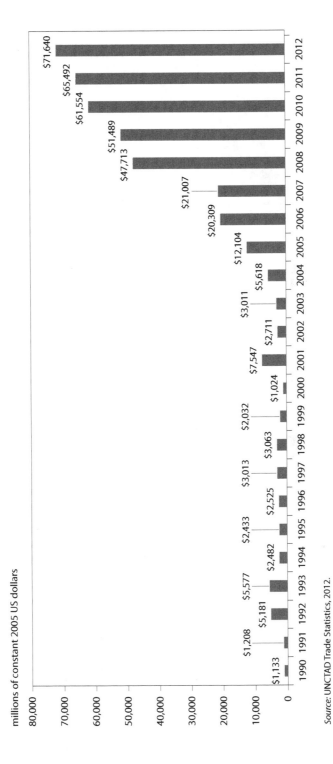

Source: UNCTAD Trade Statistics, 2012.

Box 5.1   Bilateral investment treaties

Bilateral investment treaties (BITs) establish terms for private investment by foreign nationals and companies. They are distinguished by provisions for channeling disputes through international arbitration rather than the host state's legal system. BITs are particularly relevant for investment in extractive industries because the underlying assets are immobile, eliminating the possibility of using capital flight as a mechanism to keep host governments honest.

The United States has negotiated and enacted BITs with 41 countries; BITs with another six have been signed but not entered into force. China has been much more active in securing BITs, with 128 signed and 101 in force. China's role as both a destination and source of foreign direct investment (FDI) partially explains the gap, as does the fact that US outbound and inbound FDI tends to flow between developed economies with strong domestic legal systems and investor protections.

Havrylchyk 2013). Ivar Kolstad and Arne Wiig demonstrate that Chinese OFDI targets countries that combine large natural resource endowments and weak rule of law. China lacks the same domestic constraints on engaging in corrupt practices abroad that many developed countries face (a subject addressed in chapter 6). A more permissive environment for corrupt practices back home gives Chinese firms a competitive advantage over more constrained developed-country firms in corrupt environments. State-owned enterprises (SOEs) may have a particular advantage. Bala Ramasamy, Matthew Yeung, and Sylvie Laforet (2012) find that OFDI by state-owned firms is more attracted to countries combining weak political institutions and large resource endowments, whereas OFDI by private firms is attracted to larger markets. However, the correlation between Chinese investment and high natural resource endowment yet institutionally weak countries does not imply nefarious intent or a preference for corrupt environments on the part of Chinese firms: If Western firms are constrained from investing in these countries by their home-country regulatory environment, more corrupt countries will be relatively undercapitalized, implying higher potential rates of return for unconstrained firms. Politically connected SOEs may also have an advantage in obtaining resolution of disputes via diplomatic intercession in weak institutional environments.[5]

Chinese investment in extractive industries may be driven by a much more prosaic concern: return on investment. Following two decades of stagnant, if not declining, real prices, commodities have boomed in the 21st century.

---

5. North Korea may present an extreme case. Survey evidence indicates that Chinese participants in cross-border trade regard North Korea as a very corrupt and challenging business environment. As a consequence, they undertake a variety of hedging strategies. In particular, fearing expropriation, they are reluctant to invest; much of the investment and provision of credit that occurs is done by Chinese SOEs, which have a greater expectation of calling upon political connections to resolve disputes (Haggard, Lee, and Noland 2012; Haggard and Noland 2012).

Although the metals index of the International Monetary Fund is down from its high in February 2011, metals were nevertheless trading at 250 percent of their 1990 prices in 2012.[6] Oil prices were up 450 percent. Profits in extractive industries reflect these increases. Margins may be larger in other industries, but the 2011 profits of the Big Five oil companies—BP, Chevron, ConocoPhillips, ExxonMobil, and Shell—were $137 billion, up 75 percent from 2010 (Weiss, Weidman, and Leber 2012).

That Chinese OFDI is heavily invested in energy and minerals is beyond argument. Whether this behavior reflects China's desire to corner the world's energy and mineral reserves and thus bodes ill for other economies is up for debate. As Theodore Moran, Barbara Kotschwar, and Julia Muir (2012) point out, the answer turns crucially on whether Chinese investment simply reallocates property rights within an essentially fixed stock of natural capital or expands those stocks by spurring new exploration and relieving upward pressure on prices by enhancing competition in the global supplier system.

How fixed is the stock of natural capital? All the relevant commodities are nonrenewable resources. Barring developments in asteroid mining, the resource stock is, in some sense, fixed. Although the world can ill afford to be sanguine about depleting nonrenewable resources, there are several reasons why the natural resource stock is less fixed than its nonrenewable status would seem to imply. All mined commodity reserve estimates are based on surveys, from which estimates of geologic resources (mineral concentrations that have been sampled and surveyed) and reserves (the subset of resources "from which a usable mineral or energy commodity can be economically and legally extracted at the time of determination," i.e., given present technology and market prices) are made (USBM/USGS 1980). Until the 2000s, real prices for many mined commodities had been stagnant or falling for at least a decade. Higher prices should spur more investment, the search for new concentrations of valuable minerals, and the conversion of known resources into reserves, resulting in higher reserve estimates for most commodities.

Table 5.1 reports changes in estimates of reserves of crude oil, natural gas, and several key minerals from 2000 to 2012. For all commodities except tin, the 2000s saw increases in reserve estimates, despite higher consumption. Clearly, prices are up more than reserve estimates, partly because of the often multiple-year lags between initial exploration and resource discovery and discovery and extraction. Mined commodity exploration and production—ultimately, supply—is simply slower to adjust to rapid price increases than other primary commodities. Grain producers responded to surging world food prices in 2007–08 with the largest two-year increase in area under cultivation (4.5 percent) in more than 40 years, leading to lower prices in 2009 and the

---

6. The index includes prices of copper, aluminum, iron ore, tin, nickel, zinc, lead, and uranium, and their relative trade values compared with the total world trade as reported in the UN Comtrade Database (IMF Primary Commodity Price Tables 2013, www.imf.org/external/np/res/commod/index.aspx).

Table 5.1   Spot prices and estimated global reserves of crude oil and key industrial metals, 2000–12

Metal	Estimated global reserves (metric tons)		Price change, 2000–12 (percent)	Estimated reserve growth, 2000–12 (percent)
	2000	**2012**		
Bauxite	25,000,000	29,000,000	23	16.0
Copper	340,000	690,000	199	103.0
Iron	74,000	80,000	815	8.0
Lead	64,000	85,000	155	33.0
Crude oil	171,600,000,000	225,400,000,000	360	31.4
Natural gas[a]	154.3	208.4	459	35.1
Nickel	46,000,000	80,000,000	98	74.0
Tin	7,700,000	4,800,000	247	−38.0
Uranium[b]	3,700,000	6,950,000	402	88.0
Zinc	190,000	250,000	28	32.0

a. Unit is trillion cubic feet.
b. The most recent reserve estimate is for 2011.

Sources: US Geological Survey (USGS 2000, 2012a, 2012b); OECD (2012b); BP (2012); IMF (2013).

largest global stockpiles since 2003 (Hendrix 2011). Moreover, more careful firm- and project-level analysis indicates Chinese OFDI is having a positive impact by diversifying the global supplier system. Moran's (2010) analysis of Chinese foreign investment in extractive industries concludes that the predominant form of investment involved equity stakes and/or long-term contracts with comparatively minor players. In Latin America, the majority of Chinese natural resource investments were aimed at "new frontier or even fringe" projects (Moran, Kotschwar, and Muir 2011, 50). Although Chinese OFDI is clearly targeted at extractives, the evidence does not support the simple neo-Malthusian notion that Chinese companies are controlling a larger share of a dwindling pie.

Development Assistance

Whatever its humanitarian aims, development aid is an important mechanism for governments to curry favor with or discipline other governments. Many studies confirm that aid is given for many reasons beyond—and in some cases, in place of—economic need: to maintain former colonial ties, build coalitions in the UN General Assembly, and garner support from newly elected members of the UN Security Council (Alesina and Dollar 2000; Kuziemko and Werker 2006; Dreher, Thiele, and Nunnenkamp 2008; Bueno de Mesquita and Smith 2009).

In the past, virtually all development assistance[7] flowed from wealthy to poorer countries, coordinated through the Organization for Economic Cooperation and Development's Development Assistance Committee (OECD-DAC).[8] Rapid development in the BRIC (Brazil, Russia, India, and China) economies and near-record oil prices have transformed several developing, middle-income, and high-income non-OECD countries into increasingly important aid donors. OECD estimates put annual non-DAC development commitments (promises of funded assistance projects) at 3.4 to 7.5 percent of DAC commitments, which ranged from $107 billion to $128 billion over the past five years.[9]

Official OECD data vastly underreport the extent of non-DAC development assistance, largely because of the murky reporting practices of many non-DAC donors. Data on DAC members' assistance—project descriptions, aid amounts, targeted countries and sectors, etc.—are available through the DAC Creditor Reporting System (CRS); official non-DAC development assistance does not adhere to a similar reporting standard. China, believed to be the largest nontraditional donor, has argued strongly that such a transparent standard should not apply to nontraditional donors. At the 2011 High Level Forum on Aid Effectiveness in Busan, South Korea, Chinese officials stated that the "principle of transparency should apply to north-south cooperation, but...it should not be seen as a standard for south-south cooperation."[10] China and many other nontraditional donors are signatories to the Paris Declaration on Aid Effectiveness, which stresses transparency and mutual accountability, but they have generally argued that their signatures govern their activities as aid recipients rather than donors (Grimm 2011).

Nevertheless, China periodically divulges data on its development assistance activities. A 2013 White Paper entitled "The Diversified Employment of China's Armed Forces," released by the same office, reports that since 2002, the People's Liberation Army has been involved in 36 humanitarian aid opera-

---

7. "Grants or loans to countries and territories on the DAC List of ODA Recipients (developing countries) and to multilateral agencies which are: (a) undertaken by the official sector; (b) with promotion of economic development and welfare as the main objective; (c) at concessional financial terms (if a loan, having a grant element of at least 25 percent). In addition to financial flows, technical co-operation is included in aid. Grants, loans and credits for military purposes are excluded. Transfer payments to private individuals (e.g., pensions, reparations or insurance payouts) are in general not counted" (OECD 2012a).

8. The OECD-DAC members are Australia, Austria, Belgium, Canada, the Czech Republic, Denmark, the European Union, Finland, France, Germany, Greece, Iceland, Ireland, Italy, Japan, Luxembourg, the Netherlands, New Zealand, Norway, Poland, Portugal, Slovakia, Slovenia, South Korea, Spain, Sweden, Switzerland, the United Kingdom, and the United States.

9. OECD StatExtracts, http://stats.oecd.org (accessed on January 11, 2013).

10. Mark Tran, "Transparency Could Be the Sticking Point for China at Busan," *Guardian's* Poverty Matters Blog, November 14, 2011, www.guardian.co.uk/global-development/poverty-matters/2011/nov/14/busan-aid-china-rejects-transparency.

tions, with disbursements amounting to roughly $200 million (Information Office of the State Council of China 2013). In addition, the Chinese military has provided in-kind assistance, in the form of military training, to almost 40 countries. A 2011 White Paper entitled "China's Foreign Aid," released by the Information Office of the State Council of China, provides some highly internally vetted data on where China's development assistance goes.[11] Instead of reporting project-level or country-level statistics, the report reveals regional and income-level aggregates. The data, which cover only China's aid activities in 2009, show that roughly half (45.7 percent) of aid went to Africa, with the next largest blocks flowing to Asia (32.8 percent) and Latin America (12.7 percent) (see figure 5.4).[12]

These three regions have the highest oil export potential (measured as the ratio of proven oil reserves to annual domestic consumption [BP 2012]). They are also home to most of the world's poor and food insecure, with China itself home to one in five of the world's undernourished (FAO 2012). Export potential and poverty are related: Countries can have high export potential by having small populations relative to their reserves, large populations with low per capita fossil fuel consumption rates, or truly massive reserves. Kuwait and Qatar fit the first profile; Saudi Arabia, Venezuela, and Iran fit the third. Virtually all sub-Saharan African oil producers fit the second: The top five oil producers in sub-Saharan Africa—Nigeria, Angola, Sudan, the Republic of the Congo, and Gabon—emit roughly 22 times fewer carbon dioxide emissions per capita than the United States. These data are hardly conclusive evidence of either proauthoritarian or resource-seeking tendencies in Chinese aid disbursement.

Africa is comparatively poor in investment capital and rich in natural capital, with large endowments of many key mineral commodities. African countries have 32 percent of world reserves of bauxite and aluminum, 58 percent of industrial-grade diamonds, and 76 percent of rock phosphate, a key, nonsubstitutable input for agriculture.[13] Although Africa accounts for only 8 percent of global proven oil reserves and 7 percent of natural gas reserves, exploration effort—and FDI more generally—lagged in the 1990s and early 2000s because of political instability and concerns about corruption and currency instability (Rogoff and Reinhart 2003, Asiedu 2006). Continentwide, new FDI projects have more than doubled since the early 2000s, and 2011 saw Africa achieve its highest proportion ever of global FDI projects, although that proportion was still smaller than the continental population and economic growth rates

---

11. Tellingly, the elaboration of the "White Paper on Chinese aid included interministerial communication but does not appear to have involved consultations with researchers" (Grimm 2011, 4).

12. Chinese development statistics do not recognize North Africa and the Middle East as a separate geographic region. North African countries are included in Africa; Western Asian countries are included in Asia.

13. Figures are authors' calculations, based on data from USGS (2012b).

Figure 5.4   Geographic distribution of China's foreign aid funds, 2009
(percent)

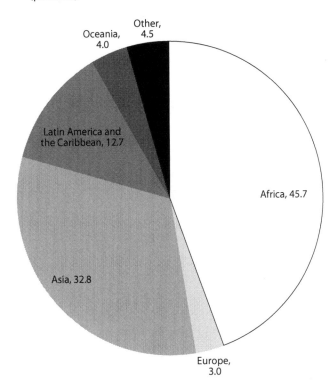

Source: Information Office of the State Council of China (2011).

would seem to justify (Ernst & Young 2012). Africa is both resource rich and capital scarce, making it an ideal target for Chinese development assistance and FDI. Moreover, the continent has widely varied governance structures, ranging from consolidated democracies (Ghana, South Africa) to soft autocracies (Sudan, Uganda); hybrid regimes (Tanzania); and hard authoritarian regimes (Eritrea and, until 2011, most of North Africa). If Chinese development assistance were particularly resource seeking or proauthoritarian, Africa would be the place these tendencies would be most manifest.

New data on Chinese development assistance and investment in Africa allow these propositions to be tested. AidData researchers at the College of William and Mary scrutinized media reporting on Chinese development assistance and FDI to develop systematic data on official Chinese financial flows to Africa from 2000 to 2011 (Strange et al. 2013a). These data indicate that China has become a, if not the, major player in development assistance in Africa. In the early 2000s, China was already providing nearly as much official development finance (ODF) as the United States.[14] Over the entire period, China committed $107.5 billion to the region, equivalent to 26.6 percent of all official OECD-DAC commitments ($404 billion)—and $17.5 billion more than the United States over the same period.

Table 5.2 shows the top 10 recipients of Chinese ODF in Africa for the period 2000–11, along with their average Polity score and the country's share of all oil, natural gas, and mineral capital on the continent as of 2005, the most recent year for which comparable data are available.[15] The Polity IV Project ratings range from 10 (most democratic) to –10 (least democratic), based on, inter alia, the relative competitiveness of the head of government's recruitment, constraints on him or her, and the competitiveness of political participation (Marshall, Jaggers, and Gurr 2011).

At first blush, the resource-seeking hypothesis seems to receive some support. The top 10 countries account for 50 percent of the region's natural capital and 41 percent of the region's population but receive 67 percent of Chinese aid. Because data for oil-rich Equatorial Guinea are not available, the proportion of natural capital belonging to the top 10 aid recipients is biased downward. Nigeria, the second largest aid recipient, is also the best endowed with natural capital, accounting for more than one-third of the continent's total. The proauthoritarian hypothesis does not receive much support: Countries on the list range from strongly democratic Ghana to highly authoritarian Libya, and the mean Polity score for the top 10 countries is not significantly different from the mean Polity score for non–top 10 countries.[16]

Moving beyond simple ranking orderings, regression analysis indicates that in the main, neither democracy nor natural resource wealth drives

---

14. Per the AidData coding scheme, ODF includes "official development assistance (ODA)-like," "other official flows (OOF)-like," and "vague official finance." It includes only project records that have not been cancelled, suspended, or sourced from suspicious reports. OOF come from governments but do not meet ODA criteria. They could be loans with a grant element of more than 25 percent, or they could be "official bilateral transactions, whatever their grant element, that are primarily export facilitating in purpose" (OECD 2010, quoted in Bräutigam 2011a, 757). This category includes "grants with a representational or commercial purpose (i.e., grants that do not have a primary objective of promoting economic development or welfare in the recipient country), loans from a Chinese government institution that do not have any apparent grant element (commercial loans based on Libor or Libor plus a margin) or a grant element that does not exceed 25 percent, and export credits from a Chinese government institution to a recipient institution" (Strange et al. 2013b, 36). OOF activities also include "short-term credits to Chinese exporters (export sellers' credits) to help them finance foreign sales, and...longer-term credits to foreign buyers to assist in the export of Chinese goods and services" (Bräutigam 2011b, 206). OOF also include lines of credit that the Chinese government provides to a Chinese enterprise (state-owned or not-state-owned) to do business overseas (Strange et al. 2013b, 36).

15. In addition to oil and natural gas, this measure includes 10 other mined commodities: bauxite, copper, lead, nickel, phosphate, tin, zinc, gold, silver, and iron ore (World Bank 2006).

16. Mean Polity score = –0.1 for top 10 aid recipients, = 1.8 for non–top 10 (two sample t-test t-statistic = 1.09, $p > 0.10$).

Table 5.2　Top 10 recipients of Chinese official development finance in Africa, 2000–11

Country	Official development finance (billions of dollars)	Average Polity score, 2000–10	Percent of Africa's oil, gas, and mineral capital, 2005
1. Ghana	13.8	7	0.01
2. Nigeria	11.1	4	35.05
3. Democratic Republic of the Congo	7.8	3	0.28
4. Mozambique	7.1	5	0.15
5. Zimbabwe	6.4	−3	0.02
6. Sudan	6.2	−5	3.54
7. Ethiopia	6.0	1	0.01
8. Mauritania	5.2	−4	0.26
9. Angola	4.7	−2	11.09
10. Equatorial Guinea	3.8	−5	n.a.
Total Africa	107.5	1	100.00

Sources: Strange et al. (2013a); Marshall, Jaggers, and Gurr (2011); World Bank (2006, 2011a).

Chinese aid allocations: Although countries with larger mineral stocks receive larger ODF commitments, the effects are both small and relatively poor predictors of aid allocation.[17]

We regress Chinese ODF on the two key variables of interest—the Polity score and various measures of a country's mineral wealth—and a sparse set of controls.[18] We split the sample into two periods, 2000–05 and 2006–11. The Polity score proxies democracy. Given Beijing's stated principle of nonintervention in domestic affairs, we expect democracy to exert no effect on aid targeting. In order to measure mineral wealth, we include stock measures of mineral capital. These measures—of oil reserves, natural gas reserves, and mineral reserves and oil, natural gas, and minerals combined—are taken from the World Bank's Measuring Capital for the 21st Century Project. They represent the present discounted value of economic profits over the life of the resource (World Bank 2006).[19] Virtually all studies of Chinese aid and OFDI use measures of current energy and/or mineral exports to proxy natural resource wealth. Stock measures are preferable to measures of current (or

---

17. See appendix A for regression tables.

18. Summed and log-transformed across the periods 2000–05 and 2006–11.

19. The value of the resource stock is calculated as $v_t = \pi_t q_t \left(1 + \frac{1}{r^*}\right)\left(1 - \frac{1}{(1+r^*)^T}\right)$, where π is the unit rent, q is the volume of production, r is the social discount rate, and T is the lifetime of the resource (World Bank 2006).

past) production, because they are more likely to affect long-term investment decisions.

The minerals category includes bauxite, copper, gold, iron ore, lead, nickel, phosphate, silver, tin, and zinc, which have been prominent in discussions of Chinese investment in Africa's resource sector (Halper 2010b, Bräutigam 2009, Moyo 2012). If the resource-seeking hypothesis were correct, we would expect ODF to be significantly and positively associated with the various measures of mineral wealth.

We also include controls for population and level of development (real GDP per capita). Population proxies both the need for aid—ceteris paribus, more aid should flow to countries with larger populations, because they need more resources to develop—and the potential size of the domestic market, as Chinese aid is also believed to be market seeking. Real GDP per capita proxies recipient need, with poorer countries expected to receive more development financing. We also include a control for whether the country extends diplomatic recognition to Taiwan, because previous studies highlight China's use of aid to further its One China policy of denying diplomatic recognition to Taiwan (Bräutigam 2009, Halper 2010b, Dreher and Fuchs 2013).

For the period 2000-05, the most striking finding is that only (non) recognition of Taiwan robustly predicts Chinese ODF. For the entire period, no ODF flowed from China to the three countries in the sample—Burkina Faso, the Gambia, and Swaziland—that recognize the government in Taipei. In keeping with our expectations, democracy does not affect aid targeting. In contrast with our expectations, neither population nor real GDP per capita predicts ODF. The resource-seeking hypothesis does not find support either: None of the coefficients on the resource variables is significant.

For the period 2006-11, we find some evidence that mineral wealth attracts Chinese ODF. For each near tripling (171.8 percent, to be exact) in the dollar value of a country's mineral resource endowment, Chinese ODF increases by about 8 percent. This effect holds for mineral resources in the aggregate (oil plus natural gas plus minerals) and for mineral stocks when each resource type is analyzed separately. Although the effect is statistically significant, it would be misleading to say that, in the main, mineral resource stocks are driving Chinese ODF allocations: The target country's mineral resource endowment explains only 1 percent of the variation in Chinese ODF allocations.

For the period 2006-11, the single strongest predictor of aid targeting remains (non)recognition of Taiwan. Neither democracy nor real GDP per capita affects aid targeting. Significantly more Chinese aid went to more populous countries, but neither democracy nor natural resource wealth significantly predicted ODF flows. As expected, democracy does not seem to affect Chinese aid targeting in Africa. Aid is somewhat disproportionately targeted at countries with larger mineral resources. However, mineral resources contribute only a small fraction to the explanatory power of the models: China's aid may be somewhat resource seeking, but it is not only, or even in the main, resource seeking. In the aggregate, population and (lack of) diplomatic relations with Taiwan seem to be the primary drivers of Chinese aid on the continent.

These relatively weak findings are at odds with conventional wisdom—that China's development assistance is primarily resource seeking. They are more consistent with the only other quantitative analysis of Chinese aid allocation. Axel Dreher and Andreas Fuchs (2013) use project aid, food aid, medical staff, and total aid money to developing countries to analyze Chinese aid allocation patterns. They find no relationship between oil production and aid projects or volumes of food aid. The only systematic evidence of oil increasing aid allocations in their analysis is for the period 1979-95, well before China's 21st century ascendancy. During that period, China provided more medical staff to oil-producing countries. For the period 1996-2006, Dreher and Fuchs find no systematic evidence of a pro-oil exporter bias in Chinese aid. Looking at slightly different measures of mineral resource wealth, we find some evidence that China accounts for mineral resource endowments in its aid allocation decisions, but the effect is relatively small.

Arms Transfers

Even more than development assistance, arms sales and military aid are tried and true mechanisms by which governments can develop new strategic partnerships and reward and punish existing partners. Because arms are crucial to a recipient government's ability to defend its interests—and often, the regime itself—they are a natural lever for influencing both the domestic and foreign policies of recipient governments. This section analyzes patterns in Chinese military transfers—sales, in-kind military aid, and aid that is tied to purchases—in order to assess whether Chinese military sales and assistance provide evidence of resource-seeking behavior.

China's rapid, outward-oriented growth has both facilitated and necessitated a large increase in its military spending. As China's global economic ties deepen, its national interests increasingly require the ability to project force on more than a regional scale, especially in the case of extractives, which entail massive investments in fixed assets abroad. Even if China were not so heavily invested in extractives, its dependence on natural resources sourced from abroad compels it to invest in significant military capacity in order to secure supply lines.

Since 2000, China's military spending has grown significantly more rapidly than GDP per capita (286 versus 178 percent). China's $143 billion in military spending in 2011 places it second only to the United States, with twice the spending of its closest rival, Russia (SIPRI 2013). In 2012, China commissioned its first aircraft carrier, the *Liaoning,* and details of its stealth fighter program—including photographs of a new prototype—were leaked to media outlets in March 2013.[20]

Like many other large industrial countries, China has pursued a policy of

---

20. The *Liaoning* is not an entirely new ship. Her stripped hulk was purchased in 1998, from Russia,

self-sufficiency in the production of arms, resulting in a large defense sector with an exportable surplus that has made China a top 10 exporter of military technology. Chinese arms transfers to the developing world have been criticized for both facilitating state repression and spurring armed conflict. In *China Safari: On the Trail of Beijing's Expansion in Africa*, Serge Michel and Michel Beuret report that "China appears increasingly willing to support repressive African regimes and rebellions alike, and to profit from the resulting chaos by selling weapons and improving its access to natural resources" (2009, 135). These arms transfers, along with FDI and development assistance, form what Halper calls "the Chinese exit option," a diplomatic place for countries to turn when under pressure from the incumbent Western powers.

An influential background report by Amnesty International (2006) criticizes Chinese arms transfers to, among others, Liberia and Sudan, in contravention of the then-active UN arms embargo, arguing that these transfers allowed state forces to increase repression in the midst of already protracted and intense civil wars. In 2012, the *Washington Post* ran a story with the headline "China's Arms Exports Flooding Sub-Saharan Africa" (August 25). It noted that "Chinese arms have surfaced in a string of U.N. investigations in war zones stretching from the Democratic Republic of the Congo to Ivory Coast, Somalia and Sudan" and that although Chinese arms are not the only ones implicated in these conflicts, "China has stood apart from other major arms exporters, including Russia, for its assertive challenge to U.N. authority, routinely refusing to cooperate with U.N. arms experts" during investigations.

The conventional wisdom, then, is four pronged:

- Chinese arms transfers have increased significantly, especially in Africa.
- Chinese arms are helping fuel conflict and human rights abuses.
- Arms flows are motivated by Chinese national interests, in particular the pursuit of natural resources.
- These flows are different from those from other major arms exporters.

How well does this conventional wisdom stand up to scrutiny? First, Chinese arms transfers should be placed in the broader context of global arms transfers. Figure 5.5 presents the share of global arms transfers for the nine largest exporters—the United States, the Soviet Union/Russia, Germany, France, the United Kingdom, China, the Netherlands, Italy, and Israel—for the period 1990–2011. Since the end of the Cold War, the United States, Germany, France, the United Kingdom, the Netherlands, and Italy (all core North Atlantic Treaty Organization members) have been responsible for, on average, 63.6 percent of global military transfers per year. China's share of global arms transfers averaged 3.1 percent. For much of the post–Cold War era, China's total military transfers were comparable to those of the Netherlands,

---

where she served as the *Varyag*. The ship was modified and refitted by the Dalian Shipbuilding Industry Company.

Figure 5.5   Share of global arms transfers by exporting country, 1990–2011

percent

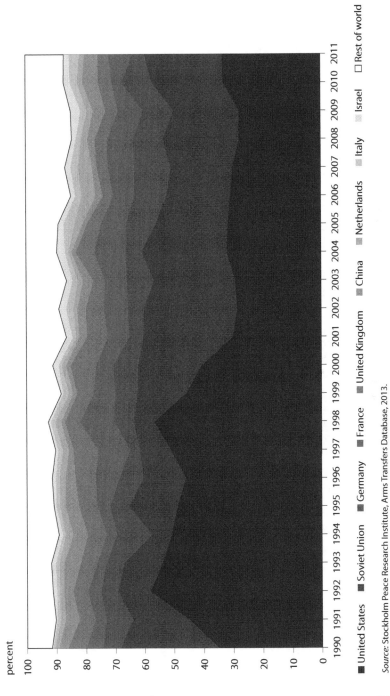

■ United States   ■ Soviet Union   ■ Germany   ■ France   ■ United Kingdom   ■ China   ■ Netherlands   ▨ Italy   ▨ Israel   □ Rest of world

Source: Stockholm Peace Research Institute, Arms Transfers Database, 2013.

an economy roughly 1/16th the size of China's. China is a major player, but it is far from dominant.

China's relatively minor position may mask its relevance for certain regions or types of regimes. If Halper is correct, China has carved out a niche as an arms provider for regimes that have fallen out of favor with the West; its transfers should disproportionately target countries with poor human rights records and illiberal political institutions. However, any correlations between arms transfers and authoritarian institutions, human rights violations, and violent conflict may be the result of the effect of natural resources on arms transfers through multiple channels. On the supply side, China may target arms transfers to countries with larger natural resource endowments as part of a policy to secure long-term access by currying favor with resource-rich governments. On the demand side, resource rents inhibit democratization and respect for human rights and, under certain circumstances, promote conflict, as chapter 4 shows. The stylized profile of a Chinese arms importer is thus very similar to the stylized profile of a resource curse country, characterized by nondemocratic institutions, poor human rights performance, and violent conflict.

We test the proposition that Chinese arms transfers are resource seeking, focusing on Africa. We regress each measure of arms transfers on three variables of interest—the Polity score, the Physical Integrity Rights Index, and various measures of a country's mineral wealth—and a sparse set of controls.[21] The Physical Integrity Rights Index proxies human rights conditions, measuring "the rights not to be tortured, summarily executed, disappeared, or imprisoned for political beliefs" (Cingranelli and Richards 2010a, 403). It ranges from 0 (no government respect for these rights) to 8 (full government respect for these rights). If China disproportionately targets its arms transfers to human rights abusers, we would expect the relationship between arms transfers and human rights conditions to be negative. Alternatively, if China's noninterference principle extends beyond political institutions and to human rights practices, we would expect no correlation. We include an additional control, conflict intensity, to proxy "need" for arms shipments. Conflict intensity refers to the scale of domestic armed conflict; higher values indicate more violence and should generate more government demand for military resources (Gleditsch et al. 2001).

---

21. The data are summed and log-transformed across the periods 2000-05 and 2006-11. For regression tables and expanded discussion, see appendix B. The units for arms transfers are trade in value (TIV) units, constructed by the Stockholm International Peace Research Institute (SIPRI). "These prices are based upon the average unit costs for core conventional weapons. Weapons for which the cost is unknown are compared with core weapons based upon size and performance characteristics (weight, speed, range, and payload); type of electronics, loading or unloading arrangements, engine, tracks or wheels, armament and materials; and finally the era in which the weapon was produced. SIPRI then calculates the volume of transfers to, from, and between all end-users using the TIV/price and the number of weapon systems or subsystems delivered in a given year. The quantitative data provide a common unit for measuring trends in the flow of arms to particular countries and regions over time—in effect it is a price index" (de Soysa and Midford 2012, 846, footnote 10).

In order to place Chinese arms transfers in context, we run these models using total arms inflows and US arms inflows as well. Much of the discourse surrounding Chinese arms transfers focuses on their purported "rogue" status, breaking with international norms governing arms shipments to countries in which they would be used to violate human rights.[22] As with the ODF estimates, we split the sample into two periods, 2000-05 and 2006-11.

Across both time periods, more populous countries, wealthier countries, and countries experiencing more intense armed conflict received a higher volume of total arms transfers. Neither democracy nor respect for human rights is correlated with Chinese arms transfers, seemingly confirming the noninterference hypothesis. Yet if China is practicing noninterference, it is hardly alone: Neither total arms inflows nor US arms transfers are correlated with either measure. These nonfindings, consistent across both time periods, belie the notion that Chinese arms transfers are systematically "different" or "rogue" with respect to democracy and human rights abuses, at least in Africa.

Evidence of a resource-seeking bias in Chinese arms transfers is slightly more convincing. Between 2000 and 2005, China transferred significantly more arms to countries with larger stocks of total oil, natural gas, and mineral resources. Disaggregating according to resource type, mineral resources appear to drive the main result; they are positively correlated with Chinese arms transfers. For the 2006-11 period, however, there is no evidence of Chinese arms transfers disproportionately favoring countries with large natural resource endowments. Context is important: During this period, countries with larger stocks of total oil, natural gas, and mineral resources received significantly more *total* arms transfers, with both oil stocks and mineral stocks predicting arms inflows when assessed independently. If anything, the evidence suggests a resource-seeking bias in US arms transfers, which are positively correlated with oil stocks and mineral resources.

The data have some limitations. They do not include small arms and light weapons—assault rifles, pistols, submachine guns, or light machine guns—which can change hands easily once exported and are responsible for the vast majority of deaths in contemporary armed conflicts. As with ODF, however, data on arms transfers indicate that China's military assistance/sales are not quite as rogue as believed.

Conclusion

As an import-dependent major power, China is hardly unique in shaping its foreign policy by natural resource-related concerns. Dependence on energy imports has exerted a profound influence on US foreign policy since World

---

22. The United States, Canada, the European countries, and Russia are all parties to the 1993 Organization for Security and Cooperation in Europe (OSCE) Principles Governing Conventional Arms and the Wassenaar Arrangement on Export Controls for Conventional Arms and Dual-Use Goods and Technologies. China is not.

War II. The Foreign Petroleum Policy of the United States, released in 1944, encouraged a shift from domestic production and export to conservation of Western Hemisphere petroleum and the supplying of demand domestically and in Europe via exports from the Middle East. Thirteen years later, President Dwight Eisenhower specifically cited the Middle East's oil deposits in committing the United States to a policy of military aid and assistance—including troops, if need be—to "secure and protect the territorial integrity and political independence" of Middle Eastern countries against Communist aggression.[23] From the Carter Doctrine to the Iraq wars, US foreign policy reflects the primacy of energy concerns.

This assessment of whether Chinese FDI, ODF, and arms transfers flow disproportionately to countries with large endowments of oil, natural gas, and mineral capital finds that in the main, the resource-seeking hypothesis holds for FDI and, to a lesser extent, ODF. However, arms transfers are not as robustly correlated with recipient-country resource wealth as conventional wisdom suggests.

---

23. Dwight D. Eisenhower, Special Address to Congress, January 5, 1957.

6

Good Governance Initiatives

Over the past decade, a number of international good governance initiatives have emerged to address the resource management challenges documented in chapters 2 and 3. They share common origins in human rights campaigns by Western nongovernmental organizations (NGOs) that eventually induced the extractive industries and Western governments to put into place procedures to heighten disclosure and improve transparency, with the long-term goal of improving development outcomes. Although much of the attention has centered on Africa, where abundant point-source resources and weak institutions have created a witch's brew, the issues are global, affecting Latin America and emerging resource exporters in Asia, such as Myanmar and Mongolia. The growing importance of consumers, investors, and producers, who are less sensitive to the concerns of Western NGOs and governments, threatens to undercut these initiatives.

This chapter examines three of these efforts: the Kimberley Process Certification Scheme (KPCS), or Kimberley Process for short, for diamonds and its progeny, the Diamond Development Initiative; the Extractive Industries Transparency Initiative (EITI) and its progenitor, the Publish What You Pay coalition; and the US attempt via the Conflict Minerals Trade Act provisions of the Dodd-Frank bill to unilaterally create a Kimberley-like certification process for trade in minerals in the Democratic Republic of the Congo and neighboring countries. These programs initially aimed at attenuating the impact of lootable resources on civil conflict, increasing the odds that resource revenues would be used in economically rational, prodevelopment ways and directly contribute to political stability and the improvement of human rights. Over time, the initiatives were expanded in an attempt to address longer-term development considerations beyond the immediate cessation of civil conflict.

The effectiveness of these initiatives has varied depending on the industry structure, the vulnerability of major extractive firms to shaming, the relative importance of participants sensitive to human rights concerns, geological and other considerations that affect the availability of alternative sources of supply, the technical ability to implement certification procedures, and the political interests of the dominant powers. It is not a coincidence that these initiatives have targeted primarily poor, weak states and not major resource producers such as Russia or the Gulf states, where challenges with respect to transparency and human rights can also be found. In the end, how one evaluates the success of these measures is a function of the criteria against which they are judged. With respect to the issues of internal political stability discussed in chapter 3, there is evidence that they have made positive contributions; with respect to the economic performance issues discussed in chapter 2, the evidence is more elusive.

Conflict Diamonds and the Kimberley Process Certification Scheme

Diamonds have long held a prominent place in popular imagination, but in the late 1990s, the romantic image the gems held began to tarnish due to a long-running conflict in Angola and civil wars in Sierra Leone and Liberia that involved "severe human rights abuses, massive internal population movements, and the destabilization of internationally recognized governments" (Cook 2003, 2).[1] Beyond the obvious humanitarian concerns, "conflict diamonds" have also been linked to the financial activities of al Qaeda and other terrorist groups (Farah 2004, Zarate 2005).[2]

In addition to their use as gemstones, diamonds have a wide range of industrial uses in cutting, grinding, and boring other hard materials. Today, most of the world's diamonds are synthetically produced, with natural diamonds making up only 20 to 25 percent of supply. Approximately half of the world's natural diamonds have only industrial use; only a small percentage ultimately is used in jewelry. Only a minority of stones are of gem quality, but they account for most of the industry's profits.

Natural diamonds occur under various geological conditions (as discussed in chapter 3). These differences have significant implications for the political economy of their extraction. Primary, "deep-shaft," or kimberlite diamonds generally occur in subsoil deposits, requiring significant investments in capital

---

1. This section draws extensively on Noland and Spector (2006).

2. The United Nations defines conflict diamonds as "diamonds that originate from areas controlled by forces or factions opposed to legitimate and internationally recognized governments...and used to fund military action in opposition to those governments, or in contravention of the decisions of the Security Council" (www.un.org/peace/africa/diamond.html).

and technology to mine.[3] Production is dominated by large multinational companies such as De Beers and Rio Tinto, which account for about three-quarters of world output.

Secondary diamonds (including alluvial diamonds, found primarily in riverbeds) have been weathered from primary deposits. Alluvial stones make up less than 10 percent of the volume of rough stones produced but more than a quarter of their value, because alluvial deposits yield a higher share of gem-quality stones. Artisanal production refers to the mining of alluvial diamonds using relatively simple techniques, sometimes involving nothing more than a shovel and a sieve. It is this segment of the industry that gave rise to the phenomenon of "blood" or "conflict" diamonds. Artisanal production can be divided further into two categories: licit mining and illicit mining, the latter of which typically involves unlicensed activities or cross-border smuggling.

Artisanal miners might engage in extralegal activities for a myriad reasons unrelated to conflict, including the expense of obtaining the required licenses, the desire to obtain better prices than offered by local oligopsonist middlemen, and the desire to evade export taxes, to name a few. Conflict diamonds are a subcategory of illicit diamonds. They are mined illegally for the purpose of supporting political rebellion and are thus politically determined. The critical factor is the existence of conflict, without which a blood diamond is just another illicitly traded gem—undesirable, to be sure, but not a contributor to mayhem.

When concerns about conflict diamonds began to coalesce, the United States accounted for nearly half of the final demand for gem-quality diamonds (Cook 2003), and relatively high-income European and American consumers accounted for the bulk of final demand for diamond jewelry. Insofar as this demand represented a "created" or nonessential need, the industry depended heavily on the norms and values of Western consumers for one of its most profitable segments. The industry's great fear was that adverse publicity could affect these consumers' perception of their product and attenuate demand—that, in short, diamonds could "go the way of fur."

The launch of the Fatal Transactions campaign by a coalition of NGOs in October 1999 demonstrated that these fears were not unfounded. Ironically, the noncompetitive structure of the industry, and the dominance of a single firm, De Beers, facilitated addressing this emerging threat (and associated ethical concerns of third-party NGOs). De Beers responded by announcing that it would stop buying Angolan diamonds, which had been the focal point of the initial campaign by the NGO Global Witness. It issued commercial guarantees that it would not buy or sell diamonds from conflict zones and suspended all outside buying of diamonds with the exception of a few partners with which it had long-standing formal agreements (Cook 2003; Taylor and Mokhawa 2003;

---

3. In geological terms, offshore marine deposits are a subset of alluvial deposits; from a political economy perspective, they more closely resemble "primary" kimberlite deposits, in that their recovery requires significant corporate investment and advanced technology.

Grant and Taylor 2004; Marciano, Porter, and Warhurst 2006).[4] The credibility of De Beers' claims was called into question, however, and the United Nations independently attempted to impose "smart sanctions" on conflict diamonds in Angola (1998), Sierra Leone (2000), and Liberia (2002).[5] Responding to the sanctions on Sierra Leone and Liberia, neighboring West African countries, such as Guinea and Côte d'Ivoire, tried to protect themselves from collateral damage by introducing national certification systems to distinguish licit from sanctioned diamonds, but the patchwork of inconsistent national systems proved inadequate.

The current international system to deal with the conflict diamonds issue, the KPCS, grew out of this milieu. In May 2000, three large southern African producing countries (South Africa, Botswana, and Namibia) initiated talks with three major importing countries (the United States, Belgium, and the United Kingdom). Together with representatives from industry (including De Beers) and NGOs (including Global Witness), they began talks on an international certification scheme. The initial meeting was held in Kimberley, the historic center of the South African diamond mining industry. Although the major southern African producers had no conflict diamond problems, the potential adverse externalities associated with the phenomenon were so profound that they took the lead in addressing the issue. The near-monopolistic nature of the industry facilitated the industry response led by De Beers, which by the late 1990s mined roughly half the world's stones and accounted for 80 percent of sales.[6] An agreement was concluded in November 2002, remarkably quickly by the standards of multilateral negotiations.

The KPCS, initiated on January 1, 2003, is a nonbinding international accord among signatory governments aimed at "eradicating trade in 'conflict diamonds' and thus addressing the negative consumer perceptions around all diamonds, which could damage diamond demand, by ensuring the legitimate pedigree of rough diamonds from their mined sources through to the cutting room to the customer" (Kaiser Associates 2005, 45). Contrary to common understanding, the Kimberley Process talks were not a UN negotiation, although General Assembly and Security Council resolutions endorsing the group's work conferred legitimacy (Wright 2004).

The system is based on two underlying principles: that participants will

---

4. One ex post analysis of these events concluded that the firms operating in Angola benefited from the status quo insofar as stock markets perceived the death of rebel leader Jonas Savimbi, the subsequent ceasefire, and resolution of the war as bad for firms operating in Angola. This finding was ascribed to perceptions that the lower transparency standards associated with the ongoing conflict permitted relatively profitable unofficial dealings. As a result, the conclusion of hostilities meant a strengthening of the government's bargaining leverage vis-à-vis incumbent producers and anticipation of improved access for rival producers in the postconflict period (Guidolin and La Ferrara 2005).

5. See www.diamondfacts.org for a timeline of these developments.

6. "Betting on De Beers," *Economist*, November 12, 2011.

not import or export diamonds without the necessary certification and that participants will not trade diamonds with nonsignatory countries.[7] The implication is that countries that did not join the system could not sell to signatories such as the United States or trade with diamond-processing countries such as Belgium, India, and Israel.[8] Kimberley Process participants produce virtually all rough diamonds worldwide.

Under the KPCS, all exports of rough diamonds have to be shipped in sealed containers, accompanied by a uniquely numbered Kimberley certificate issued by a duly authorized body within the exporting country stating that the diamonds are conflict-free. Imports may be processed only if a shipment arrives with a Kimberley certificate. The warranty system requires a declaration on the invoice accompanying every transaction of rough diamonds, polished diamonds, and diamond jewelry that the diamonds are "not involved in funding conflict and are in compliance with United Nations resolutions." These warranties and declarations are subject to audit and oversight by the relevant national authorities. The system relies on national laws and enforcement systems for its implementation. As such, it may require implementing legislation by national governments, and implementation is partly dependent on the institutional capacities of local authorities.[9]

Despite the expected growing pains in implementation, the system initially met with success. A study sponsored by Global Witness estimated that illicit diamonds as a share of total diamond sales may have been as high as 25 percent, and the share of conflict diamonds as high as 15 percent in the mid-1990s. After implementation of the KPCS, the conflict diamond share fell to less than 1 percent (Wexler 2006). Another study estimated blood diamonds at 0.2 percent of African rough diamonds (Herbst and Mills 2006). In effect, the KPCS drove the illicit industry above ground: With the end of its civil war in 2000, Sierra Leone registered a more than fivefold increase in official diamond exports, which rose from $26 million in 2001 to $142 million in 2005. In 2003, the first year of the system's implementation, the Democratic Republic of the Congo reported a 62 percent increase. As an unanticipated side effect, the UN peacekeeping operations in Liberia and the Democratic

---

7. *Participant* is the term used to describe states and/or regional economic integration organizations that have met the minimum requirements of the KPCS and are eligible to trade in rough diamonds under the auspices of the Kimberley Process. *Applicants* are states that have expressed their commitment to the Kimberley Process but have not yet met the minimum requirements of the KPCS. *Observers* are industry and civil society groups that play an active role in monitoring the effectiveness of the certification scheme and provide technical and administrative expertise to the secretariat, working groups, applicants, and participants. There are three main Kimberley Process observers: the World Diamond Council, representing industry, and Global Witness and Partnership Africa Canada, representing civil society.

8. The World Trade Organization issued a waiver permitting this restriction on trade.

9. US obligations under the KPCS are implemented via the Clean Diamond Trade Act (see Noland and Spector 2006 for details).

Republic of the Congo may have succeeded, at least partly, because the KPCS reduced the economic returns to trafficking conflict diamonds, depriving the fire of oxygen.

It was apparent from the outset that the system had its weaknesses. In lieu of an independent monitoring system, in October 2003 participants adopted a voluntary scheme of "review visits." There were concerns that member willingness to host such reviews was uneven and that the reviews were not as rigorous as they could have been (Smillie 2010). There were also problems with late or inadequate data submissions by national authorities.[10] Although participants are required to implement the Kimberley Process in their territories, sharing information and insight is an integral part of making the certification scheme work. Recognizing that more had to be done about fraudulent certificates, in 2012 participants agreed to a standardized system to share information among KPCS members and the World Customs Organization.[11] Another weakness is that the initial design of the system unintentionally created a giant loophole that has been impossible to close—namely, that illicit diamonds that bypass the early tracking stages of the process can in essence be laundered by willing companies in the cutting and polishing segment of the industry (Smillie 2010).

Problems with noncompliance, which had been problematic with respect to a number of countries, came to a head when rich alluvial diamond deposits were discovered in Zimbabwe, already under sanctions by the United States and the European Union because of the lawless rule of autocrat Robert Mugabe (Smillie 2010).[12] Russia and China vetoed the adoption of sanctions

---

10. See Noland and Spector (2006) for discussion of US problems implementing KPCS requirements.

11. The existing system relies on certification because it is the only technologically feasible tracking system at this time. In the long term, the paper trail system could be complemented with alternative approaches, such as geochemical identification or tagging through identifying marks. These approaches have yet to be perfected and are currently prohibitively expensive, but they could become viable in the future (Cook 2003).

12. The Central African Republic was suspended from the KPCS in March 2003. It was readmitted following rectification of its policies, despite the unease of some participants (Wright 2004). The Republic of the Congo, which admitted involvement in improperly "legitimizing" smuggled diamonds, was suspended in 2004; it is making an active effort to gain readmission. In 2005, the KPCS suspended Côte d'Ivoire as a participant eligible for trading but retained it as a member eligible for eventual reinstatement as a full participant. The same resolution was reached with Venezuela in 2008. Partnership Africa Canada claims that Venezuela officially produces no diamonds but that 150,000 carats are smuggled out each year to Brazil and Guyana, where they receive fake Kimberley certificates (Roxane Horton, "For Kimberley Process, Next Challenge Is Broadening the Mandate on Conflict Diamonds," *World Politics Review*, December 6, 2012). According to a Global Witness spokesperson, Lebanon's export of "significantly more gem-quality rough diamonds than it imports" has been "known for months," but the KPCS has allegedly been "sluggish" in its response. In Guinea, which experienced an "astonishing 500 percent increase" in diamond exports, "the government has acknowledged widespread corruption in the mining industry." The country was visited by a KPCS review team in August 2008, "but a year later the report [had] still not been completed," according to Global Witness ("Credibility of the Kimberley

by the UN Security Council.[13] The Zimbabwe case tested the KPCS in more ways than one. The Kimberley Process was envisioned as a means of solving two problems. First, conflict diamonds were funding often brutal insurgencies, and Western consumers were—absent ways to differentiate between conflict and conflict-free diamonds at point of purchase—complicit. Second, the diversion of resource rents to insurgent groups sapped sovereign governments of a vital source of revenue. The Zimbabwe case did not fit the mold. There was no insurgent group, and the resource rents were accruing to a sovereign government.

Thus despite extensive documentation of gross human rights abuses—including murder, rape, and the enslavement of children at military-controlled mines at Marange—in June 2010 Zimbabwe was judged to have met the minimum standards of KPCS participation (Partnership Africa Canada 2010, Global Witness 2010).[14] Zimbabwe is not a marginal producer. According to one estimate, production from the Marange mine could propel Zimbabwe to the world's largest producer by 2013.[15] In August 2010, Zimbabwe sold 900,000 carats of rough stones from Marange. That the auction coincided with the "blood diamonds" phase of the trial in the International Criminal Court of former Liberian strongman Charles Taylor for crimes against humanity refocused attention on the issue and called into question the utility of any certification process sufficiently lenient that Zimbabwe would qualify.

In response, Partnership Africa Canada and Global Witness, which had been among the original proponents of the KPCS, jointly called for the classification of conflict diamonds to be redefined, and Human Rights Watch called for suspension of Zimbabwe as a Kimberley Process participant, claiming that the abuses were continuing and that its continued participation would undermine the credibility of the whole Kimberley Process.[16] A proposal to expand the definition of conflict diamonds to encompass not only the activities of insurgent groups seeking to overthrow governments but also the use of "armed force between states or protracted armed violence between governmental authorities and organized armed groups or between

---

Process on the Line, Say NGOs," June 22, 2009, www.irinnews.org/Report.aspx?ReportId=84949; see also Centre for Natural Resource Governance 2013).

13. See Kleine-Ahlbrandt and Small (2008) for more on the relationship between China and Zimbabwe.

14. The involvement of a Chinese entity in paramilitary organizations in Marange is documented by Global Witness (2012b). See Centre for Natural Resource Governance (2013) for a comparison of the Botswana and Zimbabwe diamond policy regimes and suggestions as to how Zimbabwe's policy might be improved.

15. "Zimbabwe to Become World's Largest Diamond-Producing Country by 2013," Panapress, September 15, 2010.

16. Because of its emergence as a major diamond exporter, Canada, like De Beers, has a stake in maintaining the industry's reputation. It has been an avid participant in the KPCS and the associated Diamond Development Initiative.

such groups within a state," which was supported by Western governments, created a rift with African and Asian states. Under the KPCS procedure of requiring unanimity in decision making, Zimbabwe could veto the change. When the US chair was unable to secure the change in 2012, hopes for reform evaporated.

The Zimbabwean example underlines the political nature of the issue. Although the role of diamonds in fueling violent political conflict narrowly defined has been attenuated, the outbreak of new conflicts in countries with alluvial diamond deposits could reverse these gains, even if alluvial diamonds themselves are not associated with a higher probability of conflict outbreak. Moreover, demand for diamonds has soared in Asia, the Middle East, and Russia. In China, the share of brides receiving diamond engagement rings rose from about 1 percent in the early 1990s to 31 percent in 2010, similar to the United States in the 1940s.[17] Some have even spoken of "peak diamonds," as demand outstrips production and inventories are destocked.[18] Such developments foretell both a shift in leverage toward producers and an increase in the relative influence of consumers in countries whose governments have shown less enthusiasm for the KPCS—and other forms of consumer conditionality—than traditional Western powers.

Diamond Development Initiative

The origins of the KPCS lay in concerns over intrastate conflict in Angola and West Africa. Yet it became apparent that the KPCS alone would not address the deeper development issues afflicting diamond mining in Africa. Artisanal miners, of which there may be 1 million in Africa, produce perhaps 10 percent of gem diamonds (Smillie 2005). Many lead lives of almost Hobbesian grimness. In certain respects, the KPCS has acted like a mandate, with the unintended effect of increasing the costs to producers of exporting, which has fallen heavily on small diggers. As one pair of observers characterize the situation, "The problem with artisanal mining activities is that the activities are largely illegal (not licensed), and the diamonds produced therefore have to be sold to intermediaries outside of formal frameworks" (Herbst and Mills 2006). As a result of their illicit status, these diamonds then trade at a discount, depressing the earnings of the diggers.

Meeting this challenge will require an extensive mix of microeconomic and regulatory interventions, which will probably require the intervention of national governments, public and private donor organizations, and ultimately the major corporate mining houses. For legal and reputational reasons, the response of some large multinationals has been to abandon production in countries where governance is weak. But this understandable private response

---

17. Helen Thomas, "Diamond Industry Cuts and Reshapes," *Financial Times*, August 18, 2012.

18. William MacNamara, "Why Diamonds Might Not Be Forever," *Financial Times*, April 27, 2010.

does not constitute a fully adequate solution—it simply clears the field for less reputable operators, ultimately lowering the prices diggers receive.

Given the hellish existence of many artisanal diggers under the status quo, a more coherent and developmentally focused set of policies and practices could significantly improve their welfare and would also presumably be less prone to political conflict than the KPCS. As specifics vary from country to country, these programs will have to be devised and implemented on a country-specific basis—there is no one-size-fits-all solution to this nexus of problems. However, certain commonalities and opportunities for learning underlie the Diamond Development Initiative (DDI), launched in Accra, Ghana, in 2005 by the World Bank, Global Witness, Partnership Africa Canada, De Beers, and several governmental aid agencies.[19]

The ultimate goal of the interventions should be to regularize the artisanal sector in a way that generates increased earnings for the diggers. DDI has produced standards for an ethical diamond certification system. In 2012, it began running a pilot project in Sierra Leone with the support of the German aid agency. To work, a reformed system has to provide more income to the diggers than they earn under the status quo organization of the supply chain. The first step is educational—informing diggers of their rights as well as of opportunities afforded under various programs and initiatives. DDI is actively engaged in this educational work.

A reformed sector also has to embody a marketing system that permits the government to observe, regulate, and tax diamonds before they are exported, bringing them under the KPCS and generating revenue for the state. DDI has proposed a regulating and tracking system that would both protect diggers and strengthen state compliance with the KPCS. In 2012, the regulation and tracking system was introduced in the Democratic Republic of the Congo, with support from the Canadian aid agency. In its first year, the program registered more than 100,000 diggers.

At its root, the status quo in this area reflects capital market failure—the formal banking sector shies away from extending credit to diggers, who are instead financed by middlemen, who act not only as oligopsonist purchasers of rough stones but also as oligopolist suppliers of digging implements, food, and other household items (Even-Zohar 2005). Under such arrangements, the potential for exploitation and abuse is vast.

Addressing this situation will require reducing the costs of obtaining licenses and doing business more generally, resolving property rights uncertainty and undertaking proper cadasters, forming cooperatives or other forms of collective organization to make diggers more attractive borrowers to banks and other financial institutions, and encouraging the formal financial system to begin extending credit to these entities. De Beers has pioneered

---

19. In 2007, the organization was registered as a nonprofit in the United States. The original founding organizations gave way to a larger board and advisory group.

the introduction of "smart wallet" technology similar to an "e-wallet" or a "digital wallet," which are systems that store a user's payment information and credentials electronically. This information can then, for example, be accessed by means of a smart phone to do SMS-based banking, which is prevalent through much of Africa and facilitates remote access to the banking system. Implementation of such a program would erode the rents currently captured by middlemen; as such, it would face opposition from them and their political allies. Regularization would probably also mean consolidation of the sector. As a consequence, alternative opportunities will have to be fostered for redundant diggers (Diamond Development Initiative 2005).

Such schemes are subject to regulatory capture, in which incumbent producers use regulation to deter new entry.[20] It has been argued (e.g., Spar 2006) that initiatives such as the DDI will solidify De Beers' eroding position in the diamond market. Such concerns about regulatory capture by De Beers and other large multinationals are understandable. However, these apprehensions must be set against the fact that the competitive fringe includes some fairly unsavory characters. Bill Gates they are not.

Precisely because of its prominence, De Beers internalizes industry reputational considerations to a greater extent than other producers. As one first-hand witness of Sierra Leone's civil war trenchantly observed:

> The quick reestablishment of legitimate mining operations should be seen as a positive development and it would be a welcome investment if the country continued to stabilize enough for De Beers to play a role once again.... Some critics will balk that a partnership between De Beers and Sierra Leone will add yet more decimal points to the company's wealth, but it's a far cry better than the utter anarchy that dominated the 1990s. If De Beers' greed for diamonds leads Sierra Leone's leaders to be greedy for the good of the nation, then who loses, other than those who may be paying too much for their jewelry downstream? In terms of free market economics they are already paying too much. The only difference would be that they would be paying legally employed miners, not men who cut off arms with machetes. (Campbell 2002, 207–208)

Indeed, one of the industry's current challenges is that De Beers' eroding market dominance means that it is increasingly unwilling to internalize externalities for the whole industry.[21] Yet DDI has been relatively successful in attracting support from other mining companies, such as BHP Billiton and Rio Tinto; retailers, such as Tiffany and Co. through its foundation; and a number of African governments and Western aid agencies.

From the standpoint of local governments, it would be advantageous to increase the role of the formal financial system. Doing so would both serve their own regulatory and taxation aims and enhance their coordination with the multilateral Financial Action Task Force, an intergovernmental

---

20. The airline industry is the classic case.

21. Helen Thomas, "Diamond Industry Cuts and Reshapes," *Financial Times*, August 18, 2012.

body established in 1989 to combat money laundering, in order to prevent diamonds from being used for this purpose (Reuter and Truman 2004) and to facilitate compliance with anti–money laundering regulations. In this respect, their interests align with the foreign policy objectives of the major consumer countries, such as the United States. As such, it is appropriate that they have lent political and financial support to the DDI both directly and via the international financial institutions (see GAO 2006 for a description of US efforts in this regard).

In addition to these financial sector reforms, there is need at the local level for improved due diligence rules regarding the allocation of exploration licenses and strengthened disclosure laws with respect to local politicians (Even-Zohar 2005). Ghana appears to have made the greatest progress in addressing these issues. Smillie (2005, 5) describes its Precious Minerals Marketing Company (PMMC), which pays sellers by check, with funds placed on deposit by registered buyers, as "simple, open, and secure." Another analyst describes the Ghanaian diamond bourse as having "increased transparency significantly and contributed to reducing illicit dealings in the region" (Olsson 2006, 1148).[22]

Nevertheless, as this brief discussion suggests, progress via DDI is likely to be more akin to trench warfare than blitzkrieg. Conditions vary from location to location, and although there are general lessons to be drawn and best practices to be adopted, real progress is contingent on the ability of market participants, local governments, and outside funders to craft sustainable solutions under challenging conditions.

Extractive Industries Transparency Initiative

As in the case of the KPCS, industry response to reputational concerns played a key role in the emergence of the Extractive Industries Transparency Initiative (EITI). During the 1990s, problems in the Nigerian oil industry attracted increasing public attention. The 1995 hanging of internationally known playwright and activist Ken Saro-Wiwa, who publicly implicated Royal Dutch Shell in the events leading up to his execution, was a turning point. In 1999, Human Rights Watch published *The Price of Oil: Corporate Responsibility and Human Rights Violations in Nigeria's Oil Producing Communities*, which linked oil company activities to a variety of abuses in the Niger River Delta.

At the same time, while researching the role of conflict diamonds in the Angolan civil war, it became apparent to Global Witness that the Angolan government relied on oil revenues to finance the war. In 1999, it published the report *Crude Awakening: The Oil and Banking Industries in Angola's Conflict*. The emphasis on transparency in the report resonated with other groups, including the International Monetary Fund (IMF), which was promoting greater transparency in Angola's fiscal affairs (Gillies 2010). A coalition including Human

---

22. For details, see www.pmmcghana.com.

Rights Watch, the Catholic Agency for Overseas Development, the Open Society Institute, and the World Bank began to coalesce around a campaign to promote greater transparency and less corruption in the extractive sector (Aaronson 2011).

The Publish What You Pay (PWYP) coalition, formed in 2002, was initially an ad hoc group of London-based NGOs. As a tactical issue, they decided to focus pressure on payments paid by major Western oil companies, which were relatively vulnerable to shaming, and Western governments, among whom their campaign would have the greatest traction, rather than focusing on the practices or expenditure patterns of host governments (van Oranje and Parham 2009).

A turning point came in 2001, when BP decided to disclose payments to the state-owned oil company and government in Angola, one of the most notoriously corrupt countries in the world. Its announcement caused a backlash. Sonangol, the national oil firm, stated that such a disclosure would violate confidentiality agreements and threatened to revoke BP's license and the licenses of any other firms that followed suit. BP backed down.

The Angolan episode demonstrated the vulnerability of companies going it alone. PWYP drew the lesson that to solve the collective action problem, disclosure would have to be mandatory. It adopted an agenda focused on regulatory solutions such as stock exchange listing rules; accounting standards setting bodies, such as the International Accounting Standards Board; and lending requirements for multilateral banks, private sector banks, and national aid and export and investment finance agencies.

It was in this context that British Prime Minister Tony Blair formally launched the EITI in September 2002.[23] Politically, the British government was looking for low-cost strategies to address governance challenges in the developing world, specifically Africa; the transparency initiative fit the bill (Gillies 2010). Despite its somewhat indirect linkage to, and weak evidence on, transparency's impact on economic performance, EITI did resonate with an intellectual argument emerging principally from the World Bank: that institutions, governance, and specifically transparency were key to development (Kolstad and Wiig 2009). For these reasons, it was understandable that the issue was framed primarily around production in developing countries, concentrated in sub-Saharan Africa and Central Asia, rather than larger producers such as Russia or the Gulf states, where problems of governance and corruption would appear to be on a comparable scale. In this respect, the outcome fit a familiar pattern in which Western governments and institutions essentially establish

---

23. It is often claimed that Blair launched the initiative at the World Summit on Sustainable Development in Johannesburg, South Africa. EITI is mentioned in the written version of his speech. But for unknown reasons, when delivering the speech, Blair skipped that portion of the address and did not make the announcement of EITI until he returned to London (van Oranje and Parham 2009). In 2007, a secretariat was established in Oslo, and two trust funds were established within the World Bank to support implementation by developing countries.

the norms and set the rules for a less powerful group of countries, while the actions of more powerful states are subject to less scrutiny.

EITI consists of two components: disclosure, which is supposed to generate the information needed to reduce corruption, and the establishment of country-level multistakeholder bodies, which in principle absorb and propagate this information with the aim of enforcing accountability.

The aim of the first component is to build double-entry accounts, which can be checked for consistency. Governments must require extractive firms operating within their territory to disclose payments to governments to explore or extract energy or minerals. Governments must record revenues that they receive from extraction. A third party, an independent administrator, reconciles these figures. Western firms argued that voluntary acceptance by the host countries of the notion of disclosure was essential, as many of their operations were joint with state oil firms that required confidentiality as a matter of course. A current source of contention is whether those payments are aggregated or reported on a company-by-company basis, as required by the Dodd-Frank law in the United States.

The second component is the establishment of a formal multistakeholder group that evaluates the information provided by the firms, the government, and the third-party administrator. An outside body validates the reports in conjunction with the stakeholder group, in an effort to close a loop between the government and the governed.

As in the KPCS, there are two tiers of countries in EITI: candidate countries, which have signed up to implement the EITI protocol, and compliant countries, which have fully and successfully implemented EITI.[24] Norway is the only developed-country participant. The United States has indicated to the EITI Secretariat its intention to join but has not begun the process of implementation. None of the BRIC governments is an EITI stakeholder. Petrobras (Brazil) is an EITI supporter; other large non-Western oil companies, such as the China National Petroleum Company, Lukoil (Russia), and Petronas (Indonesia), are not.

Although EITI was originally oriented toward the oil sector, several signatories—Mongolia, Niger, Guinea, Mali, and, until recently, Ghana—produced other minerals and were not primarily oil producers. EITI is being expanded to include fisheries and forestry in some countries. Liberia, for example, includes rubber and forestry in its EITI protocol.

The effectiveness of EITI is in significant part a function of the degree of buy-in by host governments. The pact is voluntary. A government committed

---

24. As of February 2013, compliant countries included Azerbaijan, the Central African Republic, Ghana, Iraq, Kyrgyzstan, Liberia, Mali, Mauritania, Mongolia, Mozambique, Niger, Nigeria, Norway, Peru, Tanzania, Timor-Leste, Yemen, and Zambia. Candidate countries included Afghanistan, Albania, Burkina Faso, Cameroon, Chad, the Republic of the Congo, Côte d'Ivoire, the Democratic Republic of the Congo, Gabon, Guatemala, Guinea, Indonesia, Kazakhstan, São Tomé and Príncipe, Sierra Leone, the Solomon Islands, and Trinidad and Tobago.

to behaving corruptly may simply not participate. There is no mechanism for directly sanctioning noncompliance, although there may be reputational or signaling costs.[25]

EITI focuses on a single point in the production chain (the transfer of money from the firm to the government). It ignores critical upstream (contracting and procurement) and downstream (expenditure) activities. This set-up reflects the origins of the initiative and the tactical decisions made by the PWYP coalition. Even the African Development Bank, which might be expected to adopt more of a cheerleading stance, echoes this criticism (ADB 2009). There is no standard way of disseminating this information, even to the stakeholder body.

The stakeholder body is also potentially a point of weakness, depending on the preexisting strength of civil society and the attitude of the government toward EITI. EITI creates a platform for communication between the government, companies, and civil society, and it establishes a set of internationally accepted norms and procedures. Some governments—for example, Azerbaijan —have used EITI proactively to strengthen civil society (Gillies 2010).

In other countries, the press and the NGO sector remain weak, making effective civil society participation difficult. And in some countries, the government appoints the stakeholder representatives, allowing it to pack the body with cronies who may have little interest in rocking the boat.

Similarly, EITI may serve as a spur to national legislation to strengthen regulation of the extractive sector. For example, in Chad activities around EITI had an indirect beneficial effect, through the enactment of new legislation and the development of monitoring bodies, even if EITI compliance, narrowly defined, was weak (Gillies 2010).

One barrier to implementation has been a simple lack of accounting expertise. PWYP and Transparency International train budget activists, and the Revenue Watch Institute has developed educational materials for journalists and civil society groups. The World Bank has launched an EITI++ program, which assists host governments from the initial bid tendering stage through expenditure management. The ability of these initiatives to foster civil society, as distinct from providing technical assistance to functioning civil society groups, is unclear. Ultimately, EITI is only as effective as the mechanisms, including a free press, that allow citizens to exert accountability over their government. Some of the major emerging oil exporters in sub-Saharan Africa—Chad, Gabon, Cameroon, and Equatorial Guinea to name four—are corrupt autocracies where it would seem the seeds of EITI would be falling on rocky soil. The situation in other producers, such as Ghana, Kenya, and Sierra Leone, is more promising.

---

25. For example, Rex Tillerson, ExxonMobil CEO, subsequently argued that host-country adherence to EITI signals a commitment to strengthen the business-enabling environment and encouraged Equatorial Guinea to join (Aaronson 2011). The country began the implementation process but was delisted in 2010.

Market structure helps explain the variety of responses to EITI. In contrast to diamonds, where a single firm (De Beers) effectively constituted the industry, the initial reaction to the initiative varied among the major Western oil producers, reflecting their differentiated interests. The high-level involvement of the British government presumably influenced attitudes toward EITI within the London-based majors BP and Shell. Having been burned in Angola, BP was an early supporter of EITI. Shell became the first company to come out in favor of mandatory disclosure, although it later shifted positions and opposed the proposed EU Transparency Directive (Moran 2012).

Chevron and Total were initially more reluctant than BP and Shell. ExxonMobil was the least enthusiastic of the Western majors. It had enlisted World Bank support, arguably as a kind of Good Housekeeping seal of approval for reputational reasons, in the construction of a pipeline from oil fields in Chad to the Cameroonian port of Kribi (Pegg 2005, Gillies 2010).[26] But after becoming embroiled in allegations of complicity in corruption by officials in Equatorial Guinea during the 2004 Riggs Bank scandal in Washington, DC, it reversed course and initiated more proactive involvement with EITI (van Oranje and Parham 2009).

Responses from major Western oil firms also varied according to their identifiability in the consumer market. The majors, which sell gasoline to the public, were more vulnerable to shaming than smaller "nonbranded" firms, like Canada's Talisman, or non-Western, particularly Chinese, firms.[27] Even if this group of firms constitutes a relatively small share of the global market, their existence as an alternative to the EITI-compliant majors confers negotiating leverage on recalcitrant governments, a consideration cited by Western firms reluctant to push transparency for fear of loss of competitiveness (Gillies 2010, Haufler 2010).[28]

---

26. At $3.7 billion, the Chad-Cameroon pipeline project was a major initiative, at the time the largest private investment in sub-Saharan Africa. The project, started in 2000, was completed ahead of schedule, in 2003. With world oil prices high, it generated larger revenues more quickly than expected. Commitments by the government of Chad to complementary social investments lagged, however, with some revenues channeled to military expenditures, in contravention of the agreement. The agreement between the World Bank and Chad was quietly terminated in 2008 when Chad paid back the loan.

27. Talisman, for example, resisted pressure regarding its operations in the Sudan for years. When it finally caved and withdrew, it sold its interests to India's national oil company, which does not participate in EITI (Gillies 2010). Talisman later became an EITI stakeholder. See Shankleman (n.d.) for a discussion of Chinese producers' relative insulation from transparency concerns.

28. EITI compliant or not, the entry of Chinese firms into the market has permitted host governments to strike better terms with incumbent producers. For accounts of such episodes in Nigeria, see the following articles in the *Financial Times* by Tom Burgis: "Chinese Seek a Huge Stake in Nigerian Oil," September 29, 2009; "Nigeria Feels Pull from East and West," September 28, 2009; "Oil Groups Battle Plans for Nigerian Overhaul," October 12, 2009; and "Groups Dig Deep for Nigerian Leases," December 14, 2009.

Nevertheless, the non-Western firms are steadily becoming entangled in the regime. One prong is EITI itself: As more countries begin implementing EITI and validation standards tighten, more and more companies will be subject to host government pressure to participate, as is beginning in places like Gabon and Kazakhstan.

The other prong consists of laws and regulations in the United States, the European Union, and other jurisdictions. Foreign firms listing on US stock exchanges must observe US law, which embodies increasing rigor with respect to transparency and disclosure.[29] Disclosure legislation was introduced in Congress in 2008. The following year, Senators Benjamin Cardin (D-MD) and Richard Lugar (R-IN) proposed the Energy Security through Transparency Act (ESTTA), which essentially made company-by-country EITI reporting requirements compulsory in the United States. (Roughly half of EITI member countries publish only aggregate amounts; the others publish their results by company.)[30] The ESTTA was unable to pass Congress. When the Dodd-Frank bill came up for consideration, supporters were able to insert it as an amendment. It was enacted as Section 1504 of the Dodd-Frank bill, which was signed into law by President Obama on July 21, 2010. Companies are expected to begin reporting in 2015–16.

In the European Union, the European Commission proposed one set of rules in June 2012, but the European Parliament passed stricter regulations in September 2012. After consultations, in April 2013 the European Parliament overwhelmingly passed legislation that went farther than Dodd-Frank. It requires resource companies to publish total payments, taxes on profits or production, royalty dividends, bonuses, related fees, and payments for infrastructure improvements for any project generating more than €100,000 in revenues.[31] Together the US and EU regulations cover about 70 percent of value in global extractive industries. In 2013, Canadian Prime Minister Stephen Harper announced that Canada would pass similar legislation.

The American Petroleum Institute filed a lawsuit to block implementation of Section 1504 by the Securities and Exchange Commission (SEC). Chevron, ExxonMobil, and Shell publicly supported the lawsuit; BP did not comment publicly; and Statoil indicated that although it did not support the lawsuit, it shared the others' objections to the provision.[32] Peter Rees, the legal director of Shell, laid out the industry's objections—namely, that subjecting US and EU firms to these requirements would create an unlevel playing field with respect

---

29. The Hong Kong Stock Exchange adopted similar rules in 2012 (Moran 2012).

30. Moran (2013b); see Darby (2009) for the rationale for company-by-company disclosure.

31. Alex Baker and Verity Radcliffe, "EU Deal to Expose Resource Group Payments," *Financial Times*, April 9, 2013; Mark Tran, "EU's New Laws Will Oblige Extractive Industries to Disclose Payments," *Guardian*, June 12, 2013.

32. Ed Crooks, "Rift in Push for Oil Industry Transparency," *Financial Times*, October 28, 2012.

to their non-Western competitors and that the disclosure requirement could conflict with confidentiality agreements required by some host governments, including Angola, Cameroon, China, and Qatar, effectively requiring firms to break either the law of the United States and the European Union or the law of their hosts.[33] The Dodd-Frank law and the EU law assert their primacy in this situation.

In July 2013, the US District Court for the District of Columbia ruled in favor of the oil companies, accepting the industry's argument that the payment reports should go to the SEC privately and not be made public.[34] The court sent the regulations back to the SEC for revision. How they may be revised and what if any impact the court ruling may have for developments in the European Union, Canada, and elsewhere are unclear at this writing. Large US firms such as ExxonMobil, Chevron, and ConocoPhilips would still be covered under the stricter EU laws, as they are listed on European stock exchanges.

Similar arguments about transparency can be made with respect to the behavior of bankers, insurers, investors, and international financial institutions. To cite one example, the China National Petroleum Corporation (CNPC) was subject to a 2007 suit in Canada alleging insider trading infractions with regard to its takeover of Petro-Kazakhstan (Shankleman n.d.).[35]

Bribery of public officials is broadly illegal throughout the world under the 1977 Foreign Corrupt Practices Act (FCPA), which US authorities have applied extraterritorially; the counterpart 1997 Convention on Combating Bribery of Foreign Public Officials in International Business Transactions of the Organization for Economic Cooperation and Development (OECD); and similar national and regional laws passed since (Danielsen and Kennedy 2011).[36] The OECD Anti-Bribery Convention has been ratified by all members of the OECD as well as six nonmember countries (Argentina, Brazil, Bulgaria,

---

33. Peter Rees, ET–Extraterritoriality–Alien or Friend, speech at the KPMG Forensic Annual Law Lecture, September 25, 2012, www.shell.com/global/aboutshell/media/speeches-and-webcasts /2012/rees-kpmg-forensic-law-lecture-250912.html (accessed on July 24, 2013).

34. Ed Crooks, "Oil Groups Win U.S. Court Case on Disclosure," *Financial Times*, July 2, 2013.

35. CNPC was accused of malfeasance in Kazakhstan. It voluntarily revealed payments as part of Mongolia's EITI implementation.

36. To cite a few examples, in February 2009, the US Justice Department reached a $579 million settlement with Kellogg Brown and Root (KBR) and Halliburton under FCPA in connection to bribery in Nigeria involving contracts to build a liquefied natural gas plant. In 2012, the Japanese firm Marubeni paid $54.6 million in fines relating to bribery in Nigeria between 1995 and 2004 on behalf of a four-firm consortium that included KBR. Despite the size of the contracts in question ($6 billion), the penalty ($51 million) barely exceeded the bribe price. Although the intensity of enforcement has picked up in recent years, the pattern of enforcement (or lack thereof) has led some analysts to question whether the law has any significant deterrent effect (Weismann 2008). See Hughes and Hubbard (2012) for details on these and other corruption cases.

Colombia, Russia, and South Africa).[37] Enforcement is based on national law, with a peer review mechanism to encourage diligence.[38]

Anticorruption activity is not confined to OECD codes. Disparate countries, from Cambodia to the United Arab Emirates, have enhanced their anticorruption efforts. Nigeria threatened to issue an Interpol warrant for the arrest of former US Vice President Dick Cheney for his alleged role in bribery when he was CEO of the Halliburton Corporation (the company eventually agreed to settle the case by paying a fine).

The oil and gas sector appears to be especially prone to bribery (Weismann 2008, Sanyal 2012). There is some statistical evidence that US officials impose proportionately heavier fines for violations committed in low-income countries, possibly compensating for weak prosecutorial capacity in these jurisdictions (Choi and Davis 2012). Whether employees of state-owned enterprises and sovereign wealth funds count as "foreign officials" under the FCPA is an unresolved issue that may take on greater salience in the future (Rose 2012).[39]

Given this context, US producers (or producers subject to the application of US law through any of these channels) presumably would be less reluctant to support strictures that would level the playing field with respect to less legally constrained rivals. The trend is clearly toward ratcheting up disclosure requirements for a broad swath of producers. For example, all four of China's major oil companies have foreign operations, and all are listed on the New York Stock Exchange (therefore subject to the FCPA). Many of China's major extractive firms are joint ventures with Western multinationals such as Total, BP, and BHP Billiton and thus included in these operations by extension, although as Theodore Moran (2012) observes, there are significant gaps with respect to coverage of non-Western producers.[40] Growing legal liability may encourage

---

37. The OECD convention appears to be notably weaker than the FCPA, permitting corporate donations to foreign political candidates that could be interpreted as a bribery mechanism, for example (Weismann 2008). One is reminded of the extraordinary level of post–oil discovery political campaign expenditures in Ghana, discussed in chapter 3.

38. For example, Britain's 2010 Bribery Act goes farther than the FCPA. The law makes it illegal to receive a bribe or bribe private officials, but it also contains an adequate preventive measures provision that would appear to make it marginally easier for a defendant to insulate itself legally from the profit-maximizing malfeasance of its employees and agents (Rose-Ackerman 2010, Danielsen and Kennedy 2011).

39. Until recently, another, more controversial channel through which producers could become entangled in the US legal system was through litigation under the 1789 Alien Tort Claims Act (ATCA). Under this law, non-US citizens (but not US citizens) can file suit against US or foreign corporations as long as they are subject to US jurisdiction (by doing business in the United States, for example), for practices anywhere in the world that violate US law or the "law of nations" (Hufbauer 2009). US and non-US multinational corporations were sued under ATCA for selling computers and software to the apartheid-era South African government for use in implementing apartheid. However, the 2013 US Supreme Court ruling in *Kiobel v. Shell Petroleum* would appear to close this avenue by establishing "a presumption against extraterritoriality."

40. Moran (2012, 2013b) observes that a number of major Russian, Chinese, and Indian oil and

non-Western producers to take transparency concerns more seriously, even if the domestic political consensus at home is not there yet. (See box 6.1 on Chinese misadventures in Africa.)[41]

The pattern of Chinese foreign investments suggests that such concerns may be warranted. Jill Shankleman (n.d) compares the distribution of assets of the major Chinese oil companies with those of the three largest US companies (ExxonMobil, Chevron, and Conoco). Apart from three countries under US sanctions at the time (Sudan, Myanmar, and Iran) where the US firms were prohibited from operating, only Chinese firms were operating in Iraq, Syria, Uzbekistan, and Turkmenistan, all of which were in principle contestable.[42] Although this pattern could reflect the competitive advantage of politically connected state-owned firms in countries with very weak business-enabling environments over less politically influential private firms (see chapter 5), it is just as likely that it reflects lower risk aversion in multiple dimensions by the Chinese. As one observer put it, "Beijing no longer seeks to export communism or actively undermine the liberal international order, but it can and does offer autocrats and governments somewhere to run when they fall out with the West" (Halper 2010c, location 1500).[43] Yet even an analyst as generally critical of Chinese behavior as Matthew Chen (2006, 53) concluded that when it came to EITI and other multilateral good governance initiatives, "it is far better to have Chinese [national oil companies] to be part of the process than to have no voice or vote."

---

mining companies do not list in New York or Hong Kong and thus would not be subject to EITI via those channels. The regulations also do not apply to foreign issuers of American depositary receipts, such as Lukoil and Gazprom.

41. Shankleman (n.d.) reports that there are now loosely defined corporate social responsibility requirements in company law, State-Owned Assets Supervision and Administration Commission of the State Council (SASAC) guidelines, and stock exchange rules. The Chinese Exim Bank has issued guidelines on environmental and social standards (which in essence instruct Chinese enterprises to meet local and international protocols). But Chinese firms have few if any specialists in these areas and little awareness of "resource curse" issues or the justification for EITI.

42. For more on Chinese investments in so-called pariah states, see Kleine-Ahlbrandt and Small (2008) and International Crisis Group (2008).

43. For example, in 2009 when the Guinean military government was facing the threat of sanctions by both Western powers and the African Union following the overthrow of a democratically elected government and the massacre of unarmed demonstrators, China, which was interested in gaining access to Guinean resources, particularly bauxite, offered billions of dollars in loans, equivalent to more than 200 percent of Guinea's GDP (Tom Burgis and William Wallis, "Guinea Regime Eyes China Offer of Lifeline," *Financial Times*, October 12, 2009). Mamadi Kaba, the president of the Guinean branch of the African Assembly for human rights, observed that "the Chinese are perceived as supporting the junta and against the will of the people. Guineans are convinced that there will never be development unless there is a lot more democracy. So the American support [in isolating the military regime] is much more important" (Adam Nossiter, "Guinea Trumpets Deal with Chinese" *New York Times*, October 15, 2009).

Box 6.1 The new kids on the block

Apart from concerns about its ability to undercut Western-led good governance initiatives, China is undergoing the ritual hazing of new investors in foreign countries. The entry of China (and to a more modest extent Russia) has enabled a government like Nigeria to extract better terms on oil concessions from incumbent producers such as ExxonMobil, Royal Dutch Shell, and Chevron, although skepticism about what share of those rents will trickle down is warranted.[1] The week that Chinese president Hu Jintao visited Nigeria, militants from the Movement for the Emancipation of the Niger Delta (MEND) warned the Chinese government and its oil companies "to steer well clear of the Niger Delta," detonating a car bomb to underscore the point (Shankleman n.d., 61). During subsequent negotiations, MEND noted that Chinese "entry into the oil industry in Nigeria will be a disaster for oil-bearing communities. Our take on the Chinese is that we see them as locusts who will ravage any farmland in minutes.... Existing [oil companies operating there] are no better, except sometimes they adhere to standards under the right conditions."[2] Indeed, Nigerian officials expressed concern that the tendency of Chinese producers to import more expatriate labor than their Western counterparts could exacerbate tensions in oil-producing regions, generating grievances but also providing many targets for kidnapping and extortion.

Similar issues have arisen in the Democratic Republic of the Congo. An agreement between the two governments limited the Chinese share of the workforce at a joint venture of two state-owned firms to 20 percent. Such restrictions have not been extended to the activities of smaller, private Chinese firms. Put off by what they perceive as unreliable and even lazy local labor, the Chinese enterprises have offered Chinese miners two-year contracts at $1,000 a month plus food and accommodation (Komesaroff 2008). But many of these companies pulled out overnight in 2009, leaving wages unpaid and local officials fuming. When asked by a reporter if they would be welcomed back, Moïse Katumbi, the governor of Katanga province, responded "No, no, no. Not as long as I am governor. Katanga is not a jungle. They worked as if it was a jungle."[3]

---

1. See the following articles by Tom Burgis in the *Financial Times*: "Chinese Seek a Huge Stake in Nigerian Oil" and "Nigeria Feels Pull from East and West," September 29, 2009; "Oil Groups Battle Plans for Nigerian Overhaul," October 12, 2009; and "Groups Dig Deep for Nigerian Leases," December 14, 2009. See also William Wallis, "Chinese Investment Has Put Africans in the Driving Seat," *Financial Times*, January 27, 2010. China is not alone in this regard. The entry of Russian producer Gazprom into the Nigerian market also alarmed European producers.

2. Tom Burgis, "Militants Criticize China's Plans to Tap Nigerian Oil," *Financial Times*, September 29, 2009.

3. Barney Jopson, "Chinese Copper Entrepreneurs Flee DR Congo," *Financial Times*, February 19, 2009.

Conflict Minerals

During a roughly three-month period in 1994, an estimated 500,000 or more Rwandans—roughly 10 percent of the population, largely ethnic Tutsis—were slaughtered. There were many causes for the genocide, but apart from ethnic tensions, Rwanda was under considerable economic stress. As observed in chapter 2, the country, along with neighboring Burundi, was among the few economies where the bulk of export commodities had experienced secular price declines for centuries.

In response to the upheaval, a Tutsi-led insurgency, based in neighboring Uganda, overthrew the Rwandan government later that year. Elements of the deposed Hutu-dominated government, along with Hutu ethnic militias, fled to Eastern Zaire (now the Democratic Republic of the Congo). The militias used refugee camps in Zaire as a base from which to launch cross-border incursions into Rwanda. In 1996, Rwandan government forces and Tutsi militias destroyed the camps, resulting in some Hutu fighters retreating further into Zaire.

The Rwandans joined forces with several preexisting Zairian rebel groups operating in eastern Zaire under the banner of the Alliance of Democratic Forces for the Liberation of Congo-Zaire (ADFL). The Congolese insurgency sparked the widest interstate conflict in Africa's history, eventually drawing in nine countries, and directly affected the lives of 50 million people. Human rights abuses were pervasive: Common tactics included recruitment of child soldiers and mass rape. It has been estimated that between 1998 and 2007, 5.4 million people may have died from direct and indirect causes associated with the war, making it the deadliest conflict since World War II (International Rescue Committee 2007).

Backed by several neighboring countries, including Rwanda, the insurgents, led by Laurent Kabila, marched across Zaire, seized the capital Kinshasa in 1997, and overthrew long-time dictator Mobutu Sese Seko. The country was rechristened the Democratic Republic of the Congo, similar to its name at independence (Republic of the Congo), before Mobutu renamed it Zaire.

A second phase of the civil war began in 1998, ostensibly in response to poor governance and corruption under Kabila but heightened by ethnic and personal rivalries within the ADFL. Kabila was assassinated in 2001 and replaced by his son, Joseph. A series of peace accords, beginning in 1999, and the deployment of a UN peacekeeping mission theoretically ended the civil war, but the writ of the central government does not hold in eastern Congo, and the region is plagued by competing insurgencies, militias, and criminal groups. Although M23, an allegedly Rwanda- and Uganda-backed rebel movement, is at the center of the current travails, the military in the Democratic Republic of the Congo confronted 27 different domestic armed groups in 2012 (ACLED 2013).

The endurance of the conflict and the involvement of numerous outside forces are directly linked to the concentration of mineral deposits in the region.

The conflict led to an NGO campaign, subsequent legislation in the United States, and guidelines by the OECD to attempt to create a Kimberley-like certification process for certain minerals exported from the Democratic Republic of the Congo and adjacent countries. These minerals, used in electronic devices such as cell phones and laptops, are thought to constitute a major source of funding for armed groups in eastern Congo, funding atrocities against civilians, including forced mining labor, forced child labor, debt bondage, peonage (forced labor by state officials on the basis of sham criminal proceedings), coerced sex work, forced marriage, and the recruitment and deployment of child soldiers (Cook 2012).

Much like the Kimberley Process, legislation on conflict minerals had its origin in an NGO campaign, the Enough Project, which began in 2007. It pursued a strategy of mobilizing Western consumers to pressure electronics firms over the inputs used in their devices. The consumer electronics sector is even more diverse than diamonds or oil. According to Laura Seay (2012), the most responsive firm was Hewlett-Packard. The Enough Project also gave high marks to Motorola, Intel, Nokia, Microsoft, and Dell. The absence of Asian firms is striking.

Like the KPCS, the legislation attempts to leverage the reputational concerns of private firms as a means of choking off finance to human rights-abusing groups while at the same time promoting legitimate mining. The Conflict Minerals Trade Act was introduced in 2009 by Senator Sam Brownback (R-KS) in the US Senate and Representative Jim McDermott (D-WA) along with 56 cosponsors, including Representative Frank Wolf (R-VA), in the House. The legislation passed the Senate but stalled in the House.[44] As in the case of the Energy Security through Transparency Act, when the Dodd-Frank bill came up for consideration, Brownback and Wolf were able to get their proposal inserted as an amendment. The bill was approved and signed into law by President Obama with the Conflict Minerals Trade Act included as Section 1502 of the Dodd-Frank bill.[45]

Section 1502 requires that companies regulated by the SEC publicly report whether they obtained any of four minerals (listed below) from the Democratic Republic of the Congo or adjacent countries. If they can establish that their products do not incorporate minerals mined in a way that directly or indirectly finances the activities of nonstate armed groups in the Democratic Republic of the Congo or surrounding countries, they are permitted to label their products "conflict-free." They must publicly report to the SEC products that incorporate conflict minerals and also submit public reports to the SEC describing

---

44. Before the US legislation, the KPCS was the inspiration for a 2006 protocol to prevent illegal exploitation of conflict minerals signed by the International Conference on the Great Lakes Region (ICGLR), an 11-member coalition of African states (Roxane Horton, "For Kimberley Process, Next Challenge Is Broadening the Mandate on Conflict Diamonds," *World Politics Review*, December 6, 2012).

45. See Cook (2012) for a highly informative review of the legislation and associated issues.

the measures undertaken with respect to due diligence regarding sourcing and chain of custody of potential conflict minerals, together with a certified, independent, SEC-compliant audit. Violations are subject to penalties imposed by the SEC.

Section 1502 provisions could ultimately affect more than 6,000 firms across a wide array of industrial sectors.[46] The US Chamber of Commerce, the National Association of Manufacturers, and the Business Roundtable claim to support the goals of the legislation but have mounted a legal effort to overturn the implementing regulations, which they argue put an undue financial burden on their members. Yet at the same time the industry lobbies were opposing the initiative in the courts, Intel's CEO, Brian Krzanich, announced that the firm had achieved a "critical milestone" of conflict minerals–free microprocessors and used this accomplishment as a marketing point.[47]

Parallel to the US effort, the OECD developed noncompulsory guidelines ("Due Diligence Guidance for Responsible Supply Chains of Minerals from Conflict-Affected and High Risk Areas"). The government of the Democratic Republic of the Congo adopted a national certification system based on the OECD guidelines, pilot implementation of which has been supported by the US Agency for International Development (USAID).

Four minerals are identified in the legislation (which allows the State Department to expand the list if necessary):

- columbite-tantalite, also known as coltan, a corrosion-resistant conductor of heat and electricity, used in capacitors for cell phones, automobile electronics, computers, and digital cameras;

- cassiterite (tin oxide), another corrosion-resistant conductor, used in a variety of products, including electronics goods;

- wolframite (tungsten ore), used in a variety of industrial applications requiring hard, high-density, high-melting point products as well as in some semiconductors and cell phone parts; and

- gold, which has a variety of uses, including jewelry.

Sometimes these metals are collectively known as the 3Ts (tantalite or tantalum, tin, and tungsten) or, if gold is included, 3TGs (Cook 2012). Although they constitute a significant portion of the economy of the eastern Democratic Republic of the Congo, there are alternative sources of supply for

---

46. Katrina Manson, "The Quest for Clean Hands," *Financial Times*, December 19, 2012. According to Global Witness, as of September 2013, nearly 3,000 firms had established conflict minerals compliance programs.

47. "Intel Says Chips Are 'Conflict-Mineral' Free," VOA News, January 7, 2014, www.voanews.com/content/intel-says-chips-are-conflict-mineral-free/1825308.html (accessed on January 9, 2014); Carey L. Biron, "Despite Legal Attacks, Conflict Minerals Ban Gets Stronger," Inter Press Service, January 8, 2014, www.ipsnews.net/2014/01/despite-legal-attacks-conflict-minerals-ban-gets-stronger (accessed on January 8, 2014).

the 3Ts, such as significant deposits in Australia, the United States, and Brazil (Seay 2012, USGS 2012b).

To the consternation of many observers, including a number of NGOs, the final implementing regulations issued in August 2012 did not mandate the adoption of the OECD due diligence guidelines, instead adopting weaker requirements, essentially identifying the OECD guidelines as sufficient but not necessary (Global Witness 2012b). The rules also allow companies to list mineral origins as "undeterminable," essentially side-stepping the whole certification process for two years (up to four years in the case of small firms), and they exempt certain categories of firms. The SEC puts compliance costs at $4 billion, well above its original estimate of $71 million but well below the $9 billion to $16 billion price tag estimated by the National Association of Manufacturers before the release of the final implementation rules.[48]

Given the short life of the legislation (and the multiyear effective phase-in created by the "undeterminable" provision), the benefits are difficult to discern. As the legislation and several associated private initiatives moved forward, a de facto partial boycott emerged as some firms simply stopped sourcing from the Democratic Republic of the Congo. In 2010, President Joseph Kabila banned mining in two key eastern Congo provinces, which one observer claims contributed to the militarization of mines in the region (Seay 2012). Although the ban was lifted the following year, by that point Section 1502 was on the horizon. The predictable result was a shift in procurement toward Chinese firms less sensitive to these concerns (a UN Group of Experts reported that the boycott had forced producers to sell to Chinese entities "that do not require tags or evidence of due diligence"), as well as a fall in price that the UN group argued "increased economic hardship and [led to] more smuggling and general criminalization of the minerals trade. The ban also has had a severely negative impact on provincial government revenues, weakening governance" (quoted in Cook 2012, 12). (See box 6.1.)[49] As part of its guidelines, the OECD initiated pilot projects on upstream and downstream implementation that ran from August 2011 to November 2012; it released reports on these projects in January 2013 (OECD 2013a, 2013b). As might be expected, both reports document initial skepticism and confusion, which abated over time as learning occurred and attitudes shifted. The downstream report notes that "the SEC Final Rule was regarded by pilot participants as providing a disincentive to companies sourcing from the region, because those companies that do source from the region will have to conduct due diligence, write a conflict minerals report, get an independent audit and prepare a public disclosure document to

---

48. Katrina Manson, "The Quest for Clean Hands," *Financial Times*, December 19, 2012.

49. From North Kivu province, the *Financial Times'* Katrina Manson reported that "only five provincial trading houses were still exporting in September [2012], down from 29 in 2010. All supplied Chinese buyers. 'The Chinese are the only ones who are left,' says Nguba Zirimwabagobo, an out of work minerals trader. 'They impose a nothing price because the Americans no longer buy from the Congo'" ("The Quest for Clean Hands," *Financial Times*, December 19, 2012).

the SEC, while others who decide not to source from the Great Lakes Region altogether will not have to undertake such endeavors" (OECD 2013a, 12).

However, the UN Experts Group concluded that following the signing of Dodd-Frank "a higher proportion than before of tin, tungsten, and tantalum mined in the DRC was not funding conflict" and that efforts such as the Conflict Minerals Act and the OECD guidelines were "reducing conflict financing, promoting good governance in the DRC mining sector, and preserving access to international markets for impoverished artisanal miners...[who are] among the prime sources of recruitment of armed groups in the DRC" (quoted in Cook 2012, 13). The OECD upstream report concluded that "the impact of 3T mining on conflict has been significantly reduced [and] the recent escalation of violence in the Kivus has heightened awareness of the need to carry out due diligence in conflict-affected and high-risk areas" (OECD 2013b, 8).

As in the case of conflict diamonds, the key to conflict minerals is conflict. The existence of abundant point-source resources did not create conflict in the Democratic Republic of the Congo, but it has enabled the conflict to continue at a higher level of intensity than it otherwise would have. The issue is whether better management of these resources could attenuate conflict by depriving the fire of oxygen and whether better management could contribute to better long-term developmental outcomes.

The conflict minerals initiatives appears to face some high hurdles. First, the operation of a tagging and chain of custody system in what amounts to a failed state, where state militaries and other armed groups play a significant role in production, would appear problematic on its face. To the extent that there are alternative sources of supply, one has to expect that legal liability will steer Western producers away from the Democratic Republic of the Congo, encouraging investment by illiberal producers—not the result proponents sought. One potential response would be to extend the rules to all sources of supply globally, but this seems exceedingly unlikely.

Second, the United States is currently the only major country adhering to these rules. Because of the breadth of the industrial sectors potentially involved, compulsory government policy will be commensurately more important, as the likelihood of a coherent comprehensive private sector response is remote. If Section 1502 becomes the embryo of a broader international effort, as the OECD's work suggests it might, effectiveness could increase. In this respect, given the much broader array of industrial firms potentially involved in conflict minerals, the absence of China and other non-OECD governments is an enormous weakness. The same is true of governance initiatives supported by the G-8 but based in developing countries. The June 2013 Leaders' Communiqué voiced support for EITI, OECD-led measures, and the International Conference on the Great Lakes Regional Certification Mechanism (ICGLRC), an initiative by 11 African states to discipline mining companies through a process of mine inspections and certifications. Mines found not to be compliant can be "red flagged," requiring them to cease production for a period of six months. Although this program may encourage compliance, it grants host-country governments discretion over implementation, and its independent audit process is very weak. The ICGLRC has the potential to be just another mechanism for promoting graft: If mines can be red carded by a member country without external validation, the mechanism could be implemented for a host of reasons that have little to do with conditions in the mine.

Finally, something like DDI has to be developed to address the long-term needs of artisanal miners. Seay (2012) observes that the original legislation introduced by Representative McDermott contained such provisions, but they were dropped when the legislation was inserted into Dodd-Frank. Although USAID is operating some programs, they are small and not generously funded. And unlike the diamonds case, where De Beers took the lead on a number of DDI issues, in the case of conflict minerals there is not a dominant firm that internalizes the industry's externalities in the same way.

In short, if one regards the existing law statically, it may have some positive effects, but it is unlikely to fully address the challenges of the Democratic Republic of the Congo. If one regards it as a start, there is more room for hope.

Diamonds and 3TGs may not be the end of the story. Rubies and other semiprecious stones have played a role in conflict in Myanmar. Emeralds played a role in Colombia. In both cases, political settlements to attenuate conflict appear to be moving forward. But at some point in the future, it is a virtual certainty that minerals will once again be implicated in large-scale civil strife—if not as the ultimate motivator, then certainly as a factor prolonging conflict.

Conclusion

One response to the potential problems associated with the extraction of point-source minerals has been multilateral good governance schemes, including the Kimberley Process for diamonds, the EITI (originally focused on oil but subsequently broadened to a wider array of commodities), and recent initiatives directed at conflict minerals.

The three initiatives share some fundamental commonalities. All are responses to campaigns initiated by Western, indeed, anglophone, NGOs, which in turn were responses to political upheavals in low-income countries. The fact that political conflict preceded these campaigns cannot be overemphasized. Valuable point-source minerals did not create conflict, but they acted as enablers, extending the duration and heightening the intensity of the conflict. These initiatives may be able to contribute to the attenuation of conflict even if they are not the fundamental source of conflict per se.

All of these campaigns initially targeted Western consumers and, by extension, Western politicians, in an attempt to leverage the reputational concerns of major corporations to good ends. Shaming via transparency was expected to elicit desired changes in the behavior of the firms. The effectiveness, narrowly construed, of the resulting policies is likely to be conditioned on the following factors:

- the extent to which the campaign can target easily identifiable or branded consumer products;

- industry concentration, which concentrates reputational risk and facilitates an industry response;

- the alignment of producer and consumer interests in the dominant powers;

- the relative importance of large Western producers sensitive to Western consumer sentiment and, by extension, the political response of Western governments versus the importance of small or non-Western firms less sensitive to these considerations; and

- geological and other considerations that affect the ubiquity of alternative supply sources, the technical ability to implement certification procedures, and so forth.

Of the three initiatives considered, there is a fairly clear ranking, with the KPCS most amenable to improved governance and 3TG/Section 1502 least likely to be effective.

In the case of diamonds, it is notable that the United States is a pure consumer; there are no US producers.[50] Canada, which is emerging as a producer, supported the KPCS to protect the reputation of its nascent industry. Western Europe has a diamond-processing industry, but it is not a producer, so competitiveness concerns were not a major issue in the dominant powers. In the cases of EITI and conflict minerals, the United States and the European Union are home to producers with "level playing field" concerns. Policy has been more tentative, reflecting a balancing of interests by the political system.

Looking forward, given the waning relative influence of the Western populations and associated producers that have led these efforts, a key issue is how to draw in non-Western publics, which may make or break these and similar future efforts. The Chinese, Indian, and Arab markets are too large to be ignored in this regard. The Dubai Diamond Exchange, for example, went from negligible trading when it was established in 2005 to $39 billion turnover in 2011. A former chief executive accused it of turning a blind eye toward conflict diamonds.[51]

Both participants in existing schemes and activists contemplating future initiatives will need to devise ways of inculcating a conflict-free norm—and government behavior—in these emerging consumer countries. Doing so may not be easy. As Hongying Wang and Erik French (2013) show, as a matter of policy, China deliberately punches under its weight in the international system

---

50. The only active diamond mine in the United States is in Crater of Diamonds State Park, near Murfresboro, Arkansas, which functions primarily as a tourist attraction.

51. Dubai has been particularly key in Zimbabwe's diamond trade. See Simeon Kerr and Andrew England, "Mugabe Back in the Money as Dubai Provides a Lifeline for Zimbabwe's Gems," *Financial Times*, April 6, 2013.

of government, providing noticeably less in terms of personnel, financial, and ideational inputs than even the other BRICs. And as chapter 4 notes, the oil-rich Arab economies are underglobalized in terms of their footprint in international institutions.

The role as investors is particularly important in this regard. Chinese oil firms quickly moved in after a Canadian firm, Talisman Energy, was forced to withdraw from the Sudan because of human rights concerns associated with the Sudanese government's policy in Darfur. China won an oil concession in Angola by offering a loan package comparable to the one provided by the IMF but without the transparency strings attached (Karl 2007). Chinese commentators argue that there is no consensus as to what constitutes good governance (Brenthurst Foundation et al. 2007). Publicly traded Western companies fear being disadvantaged by disclosure requirements in competition with nonlisted and state-owned Chinese enterprises, which are less susceptible to shaming. Beijing continues to emphasize its commitment to the principle of noninterference in the internal affairs of other countries, arguing that human rights are a sovereignty issue and that "in some cases democratization was destabilizing. Accordingly, the international community should not push Africa to democratize too quickly."[52] After years of policy conditionality, many African elites welcome the relatively hands-off approach of the Chinese.

A deeper issue is whether these initiatives are likely to generate better development outcomes in the long run. The impact of transparency on outcomes is indirect and conditioned on a number of political and institutional factors, such as the existence of a free press or a robust civil society, which although possibly positively affected by such initiatives, is not under the control of the agencies implementing these schemes. This is not to say that these efforts are worthless: actions that deprive participants in horrendous conflicts of the resources to prolong fighting and thereby encourage a political settlement are worthy, regardless of whether they contribute to significantly improved economic performance. Achieving those deeper goals will require additional policy interventions.

Indeed, given the indirect linkage between transparency and long-run development outcomes, it is worth considering whether those outcomes are more closely tied to the financial terms of extraction rather than transparency per se. As Gavin Hilson and Roy Maconachie (2009) observe, the contracts governing mineral extraction in sub-Saharan Africa have been highly favorable to foreign investors. Recalibrating those contracts might do more for development, particularly in peaceful, non-conflict-ridden countries, than transparency initiatives. In this regard, the emergence of new investors may shift negotiating leverage from incumbent producers to host-country governments. The governments of the Democratic Republic of the Congo and Nigeria, for example, were able to renegotiate existing concessions on more favorable terms after the entry of

---

52. Ibid., page 3.

Chinese and South Korean producers (Komesaroff 2008).[53] Whether these more favorable terms result in greater expenditures on public goods or larger foreign bank accounts for government officials is an open question.

In short, how one evaluates the success of these measures is a function of the criteria against which they are judged. With respect to the issues of internal political stability discussed in chapter 3, there is evidence that they have made positive contributions. With respect to the economic performance issues discussed in chapter 2, the evidence is more elusive.

---

53. Katrina Manson, "Land of Wasted Opportunity Slips Further," *Financial Times*, February 9, 2012.

7

Conclusion

Countries whose wealth derives heavily from the exploitation of point-source natural resources, such as mined commodities, tend to be poorer and less democratic than more balanced or diversified economies whose wealth is based on the accumulation of human and physical capital. Correlation is not the same as causality, however. Are countries poor and undemocratic because of something intrinsic about the nature of resource endowments and their exploitation? Or are they poor because of underlying institutional weaknesses that impede the development of stable politics and implicitly force them into simple extraction rather than more complex activities?

Analysis suggests that through a variety of channels—terms of trade effects, revenue volatility and a tendency toward procyclical macroeconomic policies, resource pulls, and Dutch disease—economic dependence on the exploitation of point-source resources has a long-run negative effect on economic performance. These problems appear to be particularly acute for poor countries. That is the bad news. The good news is that there are policy tools to address these challenges, including industrial policies; policies to hedge risk, curb revenue instability, and offset the tendency toward procyclical policies; and exchange rate policies, some of which are more promising than others. Achieving success depends on implementation, and these resource curse problems are the most severe in poor countries—precisely the countries with the least technical and financial capacity to respond.

The most useful contribution the global community could make—via multilateral development banks, bilateral aid programs, or private initiatives—would be to provide technical and financial assistance to support institution building and the accumulation of human capital. Improved governance may not be a sufficient condition for addressing the resource curse, but it is surely a necessary one.

Unfortunately, the politics of resource-centric countries are unusually conflictual and unstable. Although disentangling the influence of various factors is difficult, it appears that the centrality of point-source resources, particularly oil, is associated with authoritarianism. Resource rents permit governments to abjure normal taxes, severing the link between paying taxes and demanding accountability ("no representation without taxation"). They allow leaders to buy off potential challengers and, if cooption does not work, invest in instruments of repression.

These effects are unfortunate even beyond their direct implications for political liberties. Resource-dependent states tend to have low state capacity, partly because the availability of resource rents reduces the need to develop robust institutions and practices. Weak institutions and lack of democratic accountability contribute to poor governance. In this light, it is not surprising that democracies exhibit a tendency to accumulate human capital at a more rapid rate than authoritarian countries and exhibit somewhat stronger economic performance as well (Acemoglu et al. 2014). For these reasons, strengthening institutional capacity (including democratic accountability) and encouraging the accumulation of human capital in the most severely affected poor states should be at the top of the international agenda.

The existence of resource rents also acts as a magnet for potential challengers; low state capacity, despite investments in repression, may imply difficulties in fending off challengers. Indeed, some commodities characterized by high value-to-weight ratios and locally concentrated production (gemstones, oil, cocaine, and opium, for example) are particularly "lootable." The result is unusually conflict-ridden and unstable politics.

Taken together, these two strands of argument—one demonstrating the impact on economic performance posed by commodities production, the other outlining an association between resource dependence and a set of undesirable political corollaries—are self-reinforcing. Addressing the economic aspects of the resource curse requires considerable state capacity; the weakness of policymaking further contributes to a worsening of economic outcomes, fueling even more conflict.

Unfortunately, the domestic political and economic implications are not the end of the story. One manifestation of state weakness and unstable politics is involvement in undesirable transborder phenomena, such as terrorism, drug trafficking, illegal migration, and human trafficking. Exposure to these maladies understandably upsets the neighbors, at times drawing them in. The diamond-financed West African civil wars, which eventually induced military intervention by the United States and United Kingdom, are cases in point.

Fighting is not limited to internal conflicts: There is evidence that oil exporters are more bellicose in their external relations than otherwise comparable countries. But even if they do not actually engage in armed conflicts with their neighbors, resource-centric polities tend not to be well integrated into the institutions of global governance. This lack of integration has real implications for adherence to international norms in areas such as human rights, potentially weakening these fragile international governance regimes for all participants. Oil exporters can more easily bust economic sanctions, either as the target (they have something valuable others want) or as defecting participant suppliers. Oil endows exporting countries with a freer hand with which to pursue their aims, an effect that is accentuated by high prices.

The obvious response is to deflate commodity prices and thereby reduce the financial—and by extension, political—influence of these revisionist oil producers, by reducing the consumption of these commodities or increasing supply from alternative sources. Reducing the consumption of hydrocarbons would have beneficial knock-on effects on the environment and climate change. However appealing to economists a carbon tax might be, the prospects for implementing one in large consuming countries like the United States or China, much less on a global level, appear dim.

If reducing demand is unlikely, what about expanding supply? The reemergence, via new discoveries and technological breakthroughs, of North America as a major producer of hydrocarbons, if not putting downward pressure on world prices, at least holds the prospect of dampening price increases over the next couple of decades and, barring some calamity, moderating the influence of revisionist oil exporters.

China's reaction has been quite different. As one might expect from the country that has become the world's largest importer, China has emerged as a major investor in extraction around the world, not only in oil but in a wide range of commodities. And although it appears to be "resource seeking" in its foreign direct investment (FDI), trying to sew up guaranteed sources of supply, and increasingly provides aid disproportionately to countries with significant mineral endowments, it is not the case that this pursuit of resources extends to arms transfers, much less invasion of countries with significant reserves—at least not yet.

As with any investment in specific assets, Chinese extractive enterprises operating in foreign countries face extraordinarily high costs to adjusting to host-country policy changes, and thus face strong incentives to meddle in their domestic politics (Alt et al. 1996). The Chinese "hands-off" approach to domestic policy extends only to the point where policy decisions affect the viability of Chinese investments. Moreover, a reciprocal policy of noninterference—courting Chinese FDI by adopting a hands-off approach to host-country oversight—is an increasingly untenable proposition.

Recent events in Myanmar and Zambia highlight the potential for conflict between host and investor countries, even when investor countries are at least rhetorically committed to noninterference. China has surpassed Thailand as the top source of FDI in Myanmar, with much of this investment targeted at extractives and controversial hydropower projects. In 2011, President Thein Sein decided to suspend work on the controversial Chinese-funded Myitsone Dam project, located in Kachin state, which subjected Chinese investments to a greater degree of political scrutiny. In 2013, China played a very active role in pushing the government of Myanmar to negotiate with the Kachin Independence Organization (KIO), a separatist group fighting for autonomy in a region through which Chinese pipelines flow. China's involvement in the domestic affairs of Myanmar is not entirely driven by its investments in extractives, but it is colored by them. Myanmar's post-2010 Western engagement and courtship of investment, which has expanded rapidly since economic sanctions were lifted in 2012, must be understood in the context of growing Chinese influence in Southeast Asia and a desire by Myanmar to reduce its economic dependence on the region's emerging superpower.

Between 2000 and 2011, China provided nearly $3 billion in development finance to Zambia, with an additional finance coming in the form of FDI (Strange et al. 2013a). Most of this FDI has been targeted at Zambia's copper mining industry, which accounted for roughly 10 percent of GDP and 50 percent of exports in 2010 (Hart Group 2013). China's engagement with Zambia extends back to the 1970s, when Chinese official development finance (ODF) facilitated the construction of the TAZARA railway. At the time, TAZARA was the largest Chinese ODF project ever, part of the geopolitical maneuvering between China and the Soviet Union for influence in the developing world that occurred after the Sino-Soviet split. More recently, relations have become strained over conflicts between Zambian miners and management at Chinese-owned mines. According to Human Rights Watch, Chinese mine management routinely fails to undertake adequate safety measures and provide miners with protective gear (Human Rights Watch 2013). Fifty-one Zambian workers were killed in an explosion at a Chinese-owned copper mine in Chambishi in 2005. In 2010, mine security fired on miners protesting at the Chinese-owned Collum coal mine, injuring 13. Two years later, Collum was back in the news after Zambian miners killed a Chinese manager over a pay dispute.

These incidents became highly politicized. Both the Chambishi accident and the Collum mine incident became focal points in a broader discussion about whether Chinese investment in and ownership of Zambian mineral resources was good for Zambia. In 2006, then opposition leader (and current president) Michael Sata accused the government of selling out Zambia to Chinese interests and promised to offer diplomatic recognition to Taiwan if elected.[1] His campaign was built around pledges to more closely monitor foreign-owned firms operating in Zambia, holding them accountable for both safety issues and the hiring of non-Zambian workers. In 2011, Sata was elected president. Collum was among the first companies to be targeted. In February 2013, the Zambian government revoked all three of its mining permits; the

---

1. China countered that it would suspend diplomatic relations with (and investment in) Zambia were this to occur. See "Tough Election Race in Zambia," *Al Jazeera*, September 30, 2006; "Zambia's 'King Cobra,'" BBC News, September 29, 2006.

Zambian Ministry of Mines stepped in to manage them until another investor could be found.[2]

The emerging story in Myanmar and Zambia is one in which the promises of unconditional Chinese investment and development assistance run headlong into domestic politics. In Myanmar, these politics revolve around the complex bilateral relationship between two nondemocratic countries with a shared interest in their troubled border region. In Zambia, democratic processes have led toward a resource governance regime in which worker safety and positive economic spillovers are increasingly viewed as necessary conditions for welcoming foreign investment. China may not be in the business of attaching policy-oriented strings to its investments (with the notable exception of policy toward Taiwan), but domestic constituencies in host countries may be.

The domestically driven move toward more responsible extractive industries, in Zambia and elsewhere, is mirrored in the realm of global governance. Over the past decade, a number of international good governance initiatives, including the Kimberley Process Certification Scheme (KPCS) for diamonds, the Extractive Industries Transparency Initiative (EITI), and the US-led effort to establish Kimberley-like processes in the area of conflict minerals—all sharing common roots in human rights campaigns by Western NGOs—have been put forward to promote improved transparency and disclosure as a means of promoting better long-term development outcomes. Given their origins and "name and shame" tactics, it is not a coincidence that these initiatives have targeted primarily poor, weak states, not major resource producers such as Russia or the Gulf states, where deficiencies in transparency and adherence to human rights can also be found. As previously discussed, their effectiveness has varied depending on such factors as the structure of the industry and the interests of the dominant Western powers. The growing importance of Chinese, Middle Eastern, and Indian consumers, investors, and producers, who are less sensitive to the concerns of Western NGOs and governments, threatens to undercut these efforts. At this point, China does not appear to be actively undercutting these initiatives; it is worth devoting effort to drawing China and other emerging powers more fully into them.

These sorts of initiatives alone will not deliver development or solve the resource curse. Doing so will require complementary measures, such as the Diamond Development Initiative and the broadening of EITI to increase transparency and accountability both upstream (tendering, bidding, and procurement) and downstream (expenditures), as is being done through EITI++. But these international good governance efforts have achieved some success with respect to internal political stability. And if one believes that improving internal governance is key to addressing the traditional economic concerns,

---

2. Regardless of ownership/management, mining is an inherently hazardous enterprise. A massive fire broke out at the facility in July, in part because it had been dormant for several months after the cancellation of the mining licenses.

they are worthy of support even if their economic impact is not immediately evident.

In essence, this narrative is a cautionary tale: High dependence on the production of these resources generates economic and political difficulties that cannot be completely ameliorated. Indeed, the economic and political challenges feed on each other and are felt most acutely in the poorest countries. The West should promote good governance initiatives at both the local and international level and try to induce China and other new players to participate in these efforts. But as long as commodity prices remain high, it should be prepared for both more assertive, possibly even revisionist behavior from some producer states, and civil turmoil, with potential cross-border spillovers in some of the others. From the standpoint of the United States and other Western countries, these broader foreign policy externalities or spillovers justify pushing the regulatory approach beyond the usual norm.

What Is to Be Done?

So what is to be done? The resource curse is a disease that presents a variety of symptoms.

It is critical to map potential solutions to the particular malady, as the economic, domestic political, and interstate aspects of the resource challenge will require different responses. We focus here on narrow issues of economic management at the national level, beginning with specialization in products with declining secular terms of trade. We then consider microeconomic and macroeconomic approaches to managing revenue instability before moving on to political considerations. (Complementary multilateral approaches are reviewed in chapter 6.)

If the issue is specialization in products with declining secular terms of trade and the source of the decline is not increased productivity in the exportable activity, one response is to diversify out of these products.[3] Doing so is easier said than done, however. Diversification can be costly. Alan Gelb (2012) persuasively argues that the policies and institutions that help a country manage its resource wealth are also key to successful diversification. So the question is how to build such institutions in the context of a resource-centric economy? Significant investment in human capital appears to be the characteristic that separates countries that have been successful in diversifying away from heavy reliance on extractive industries from those that have not. Indeed, Claudio Bravo-Ortega and José De Gregorio (2007) find that the positive impact of natural resource abundance on growth rises with the stock of human capital.

The countries most heavily specialized in products with secularly declining prices tend to be poor, perhaps tautologically so. Our analysis suggests that

---

3. The structure of this discussion follows the excellent survey of these issues by Jeffrey Frankel (2012b).

multilateral aid agencies should put particular emphasis on technical assistance in institution building and investment in education in their programs in these countries. In this sense, dependence on commodities with declining terms of trade can be viewed as a symptom of deeper problems that are institutional in nature rather than as the disease itself.

Beyond these sorts of generic policies, it is likely that some kind of industrial policy to overcome the inertia of history and encourage diversification will be necessary. The track record of selective intervention policies is mixed, depending on both the policy specifics and the setting in which policies are applied (Noland and Pack 2003). Political economy considerations—mainly the ability to avoid political capture by favored sectors—are critical, lending further circularity to the reasoning: The likelihood of success in dealing with resource curse issues is contingent on the quality of domestic governance.

Similar arguments apply to the issue of resource pull issues exerting an undesired influence on the composition of output, specifically retarding the development of nonresource sectors. One response is that the resource curse is simply a fact of life and that in the absence of an obvious market failure, countries should simply accept their fate. Alternatively, policymakers may believe that such a response consigns them to a suboptimal long-run pattern of specialization along the lines of models sketched out by Eugene Grossman and Elhanan Helpman (1991) and others. From this perspective, the obvious response is industrial policy that promotes non-resource-based activities. The problem is that it is hard to identify successful examples of industrial promotion in resource-centric economies, other than the promotion of downstream activities such as fertilizer production or aluminum smelting in Gulf oil states on the basis of very low input costs. The more successful examples of selective intervention in East Asia appear to be in part the product of unique resource-scarce factor endowments: Conventional trade theory would have led one to expect the early emergence of and strong specialization in manufacturing activities (Leamer 1987). The promotion of manufacturing activities in these East Asian economies was essentially "leaning with the wind" (Noland and Pack 2003).

But at least with respect to the narrower, declining terms of trade problem, the results presented in table 2.2 do not suggest that this problem is a major global issue. At 45 percent, Guyana appears to be the only country whose exports are significantly concentrated in commodities with secularly declining prices, although at roughly 20 percent the issue is nontrivial for Malawi and Belize (Malawi is also 40 percent specialized in tobacco, which has secularly rising prices). Even at 15 percent one could argue that the situation is a significant impediment to a small open economy like Sri Lanka. The point is that when one argues for industrial policy for diversification purposes, the argument really applies to a limited number of countries that are probably best evaluated on a case-by-case basis. Of course, the more general resource pull argument for diversification is potentially applicable to a wider range of countries, but in a less compelling fashion.

Microeconomic Approaches to Managing Instability

If the issue is not declining prices or resource pulls but rather revenue instability, microeconomic and macroeconomic tools can be brought to bear. We start with microeconomic approaches, examining first internal controls undertaken at the national level and then attempts at international coordination. But before getting into the specifics, it is worth restating that not all commodity price volatility is bad. Some price volatility may be revenue stabilizing, as illustrated in figure 2.3. The concern is with revenue instability, not price volatility per se.

One response to price volatility, pursued mainly in Africa with respect to commodities such as coffee and cocoa, has been to establish national commodity-marketing boards. The idea is that the rgovernment stabilizes the domestic price paid to local producers, setting the local price above world prices when the world price is low and below world prices when the world price is high. In theory, the marketing board accumulates stocks when world prices are low and divests its inventory when world prices are high.

In reality, the local price is always set below the world price, effectively taxing the mainly peasant producers. As a matter of historical record, revenues collected by governments do not appear to have been spent in ways that produced significant development gains. In many instances, farmers protected themselves from state predation via smuggling, facilitated by arbitrary borders that often divide populations of the same ethnic group. If, for example, the Ghanaian national cocoa marketing board offers a price lower than the national cocoa boards in Togo or Côte d'Ivoire, producers smuggle their cocoa out of Ghana. Togolese and Ivoirian producers exhibit similar behavior, smuggling their product into Ghana if the Ghanaian price is high relative to the prices offered by national cocoa boards in their countries. One consequence is that official production statistics for each of these three adjacent producers exhibit greater volatility than official production across the three countries aggregated together. As a consequence of such problems, the marketing board approach has been largely discredited and abandoned.

A related approach is to simply tax production or profits, particularly in mining, where the producer may be a foreign multinational. One issue is the appropriate level of tax on a nonrenewable resource. Although there is a considerable body of theoretical economic literature on this issue, actual taxation policies do not appear to be driven principally by theory. Rather, at least with regard to foreign producers, taxation policies appear to significantly reflect the negotiating ability of the parties, including the ability of producers, sometimes using extralegal means, to separate the personal self-interests of the host country's negotiators from the broader interests of the state. In their review of contracts governing mineral extraction in sub-Saharan Africa, Gavin Hilson and Roy Maconachie (2009) conclude that the contracts have been highly favorable to foreign investors.

A natural response is for successor governments to attempt to renegotiate contracts, as is currently occurring in Mongolia with respect to the Oyu Tolgoi copper mine (Moran 2013a) and in Indonesia with the implementation of a new mining law.[4] The prospect of such ex post renegotiation obviously discourages investment in projects with large sunk costs. It also undermines the credibility of the government to precommit to countercyclical fiscal policies, such as a commodity stabilization fund or a sovereign wealth fund that targets a certain export price, accumulates windfall revenues, and segregates these revenues from other government revenue. The problem is one of credibility or time consistency uncertainty as to whether taxes (explicit or implicit) will be cut (or maintained) on the downswing.[5] Producer confidence that taxes imposed during booms will be eased during busts may be undercut by distrust between the local or host government if the producers are foreign multinational corporations.

Conversely, if the extractive sector is politically influential, it may be able to obtain subsidies. (This phenomenon should not be underestimated with respect to the use of industrial policy to promote diversification. During the heyday of Japan's industrial policy, roughly 90 percent of on-budget subsidies went to coal mining and farming, not supercomputers or biotechnology.) Often the result is accumulating stockpiles. Sometimes these stockpiles are justified on national security grounds, as in the case of the US strategic petroleum reserve, but in this case the stabilization rationale is diluted or abandoned entirely.[6]

Yet another approach to stabilization is consumer price controls (Frankel 2012b), which many developing countries impose on fuel and staple foods. If the country is an exporter of the commodity in question, export controls are generally needed in order to ensure the availability of domestic supply. These controls stabilize export revenues locally by restraining exports during periods of high world prices. If the country is a consumer of the commodity, when local prices are below world prices either the

---

4. Marcus Noland, "Proposed Export Ban in Indonesia," RealTime Economic Issues blog, December 18, 2013, Peterson Institute for International Economics, www.piie.com/blogs/realtime/?p=4177 (accessed on January 9, 2014).

5. Pauline Jones Luong and Erika Weinthal (2001, 2010) argue that the structure of ownership (the degree of state ownership and control and the role, if any, of foreigners) determines the nature of the fiscal regime. Christa Brunnschweiler (2009) and Stacy Closson (2012) argue that although the structure of ownership matters, neither the econometric nor the case study evidence indicates that impact is as clear-cut or decisive as Luong and Weinthal claim.

6. In terms of security, Daniel Ahn (2007) finds that the United States would need a vastly larger reserve (at least 10 times its current level) to deter an embargo by the Organization of Petroleum Exporting Countries (OPEC). For the world as a whole, the reserve would need to be at least one year's consumption. As for stabilization, Blake Clayton (2012) reviews the 2011 experience when members of the International Energy Agency executed a coordinated release of stocks in response to the Libya crisis. He finds that the impact on prices had completely dissipated within two weeks. He concludes that although such reserves may be useful in offsetting very narrow spikes, they are unlikely to be of much help for longer-run stabilization purposes.

product must be rationed across households or the government must make up the shortfall by importing stocks and subsidizing domestic consumption through the government budget. However, these policies, which are commonly applied to basic foodstuffs and fuel, are less directly relevant for many mined commodities whose export does not trade off against domestic consumption.

Such interventions by both exporter and importer governments increase the volatility of world prices, with exporting governments capping supply on the world market when prices are high and importing governments contributing to excess demand. There have been proposals to constrain such behavior in the World Trade Organization's Doha Development Round negotiations, but little or no progress has been made.

One area where governments have tried to work together is cartels, the most famous of which is OPEC. There is considerable disagreement as to the extent to which OPEC has succeeded in raising or stabilizing prices; analytically, it is probably best thought of as an oligopoly with a single dominant member (Saudi Arabia) and multiple fringe producers. Price dynamics are basically determined by Saudi Arabia's aggressiveness and cartel cohesion, as in the aftermath of the 1973 Arab-Israeli War and subsequent Saudi willingness to drive down prices to punish cheaters who exceeded their quotas (see figure 3.1). The growth of non-OPEC member producers may have weakened the cartel in recent years, although if the market functions less through explicit quotas and more through Saudi price leadership behavior, the fundamental market dynamic will continue. Other attempts to cartelize commodities (coffee, tin, rubber, and natural gas) have failed (Gilbert 1996).

Risk-Sharing Approaches

Given the generally poor track record of stabilization schemes, another approach has been to use financial techniques, including indexed price provisions in contracts with foreign producers, hedging in futures markets, and commodity price–indexed debt to limit revenue volatility.[7]

With regard to the first approach, pricing of contracts between host governments and foreign producers sometimes suffers from the same dynamic inconsistency problem noted with respect to taxation: When world prices change significantly, the government wants to renegotiate the contract, and uncertainty over the government's credibility with respect to its commitments discourages investment. David Johnston (2007) provides a detailed overview of the structure of oil contracts around the world and the characteristics that make them "regressive" or "progressive" with respect to whether the "government take" falls or rises as the price increases. His review suggests that few existing contracts are indexed to take account of significant changes in prices. Given the degree of commodity price volatility observed in recent years, it

---

7. Lessard and Williamson (1985) is an accessible introduction to this literature.

would seem that governments would want to insist that contracts contain provisions with respect to future prices.

They could also use commodities futures and options markets to hedge risks, which would reduce the pressure to renegotiate contracts every time prices rose significantly. The downside of hedging through the futures market is that it requires the government or state-owned enterprise (SOE) to actively forecast price movements. Except for rare cases like Saudi Arabia, where production can sway world prices, there is no reason to believe that finance ministers or SOE treasurers are uniquely prescient forecasters. The approach is also of limited use in that the maximum maturities traded in these markets are typically short.

Additional problems can arise when futures are used so aggressively that hedging veers into speculation. A case in point is the experience of the partially state-owned Ashanti Goldfields in Ghana, which aggressively sold forward half of its reserves. When the price of gold unexpectedly spiked in September 1999, the firm faced $570 million of losses on its hedge book and margin calls from its creditors.[8] The firm never recovered from its near-bankruptcy experience; in 2004, it merged with South Africa's AngloGold. More generally, as Jeffrey Frankel (2012b, 30) observes, policymakers and managers who use hedging instruments prudently and reduce losses in bad times are unlikely to be lionized, but "will be excoriated for having sold out the national patrimony when the world price rises."

Perhaps a more provident approach to diminishing revenue instability, applicable to both local producers and the government, would be to denominate or index debt in terms of commodity prices.[9] The usual explanation for the relative rarity of such instruments is the reluctance of investors to hold them. But industrial users of these commodities, such as utilities in the case of oil or gas, have a counterpart interest in hedging risk, and speculators have beliefs regarding the future direction of prices. An alternative that might be more attractive to investors to whom stability in nominal payment streams is attractive but still preserves some of the risk mitigation characteristics of an indexed bond would be a constant real payment floating rate note (Lessard and Williamson 1985).

A crude second-best approach would be to borrow in the currency of a country exposed to a similar set of commodity-related price risks (Lessard and Williamson 1985). An oil exporter like Nigeria or Venezuela might want to borrow in Norwegian kronor (or more realistically US dollars or British pounds), whereas an oil importer might want to borrow in the currency of another oil importer (such as Japan, for instance).

---

8. Raymond Taylor, "Ashanti: A Hedge Too Far," February 23, 2002, www.modernghana.com v/news/110762/1/ashantia-hedge-too-far.html (accessed on July 27, 2013).

9. Trade-linked bonds are another variant. The principal advantage is that they align borrowers' obligations with their ability to pay. Disadvantages include moral hazard concerns that countries accumulating large debts might be tempted to discourage exports through a variety of means (Lessard and Williamson 1985).

Macroeconomic Approaches to Managing Instability

Both monetary and fiscal policy can be brought to bear to ameliorate macro-economic difficulties created by commodity revenue instability. We start with the more general case of using fiscal policy tools to fight instability and then discuss exchange rate policy responses to Dutch disease.

Fiscal Policy Approaches

Governments, be they democratic or authoritarian, have a natural tendency to run procyclical fiscal policies, overspending during booms and contracting during busts. The greater macroeconomic volatility of commodity-centric economies is both a cause and a consequence of this phenomenon. This bias toward spending in turn raises issues of intergenerational equity, particularly when current economic activity is based on an exhaustible resource. Robert Solow (1974) argues that the revenue streams generated by produced capital broadly defined and depletable resources could be thought of as substitutable; one way to generate a sustainable long-run consumption trajectory would be to accumulate capital at such a rate that the returns from capital offset the expected exhaustion of the resource stock. This insight has been reified in the "Hartwick rule," which states that all resource rents should be invested for the benefit of future generations (Hartwick 1977). A number of approaches have been developed to dampen the tendency toward overspending and generate a more sustainable consumption path.[10]

Concerns regarding procyclical bias are reinforced by perceptions that some expenditures are wasteful, stemming from the investment of resource rents in patronage networks and "white elephants"—poorly designed investment projects with negative social surpluses but clear constituency-based political economies (Robinson and Torvik 2005; Acemoglu, Ticchi, and Vindigni 2011)—rather than productive, market-sustaining public goods. Proposals for adoption of fiscal policy rules (including the possibility of earmarking expenditures for particular programs), the creation of natural resource or sovereign wealth funds, and direct distribution of resource rents via cash transfers/dividends to the public ("oil to cash") can be interpreted as both improving the quality of investment and supporting greater political accountability for the use of natural wealth. In this view, resource rents can be specifically channeled to improving human capital and durable infrastructure. Investments in human capital have clear (and positive) ramifications for future economic growth (see chapter 3); investments in infrastructure provide economic stimulus in the short term and help create large social surpluses over the long term.

---

10. For a discussion of such tradeoffs in the context of Brazil, see Fajnzylber, Lederman, and Oliver (2013).

Fiscal Policy Rules

Fiscal policy rules are relatively easy to formulate but exceedingly difficult to implement, as policymakers face intense demands for spending during boom periods. Rabah Arezki and Kareem Ismail (2013) find little evidence that such rules constrain spending. The key issue is not the rules per se but the credibility of the precommitment mechanism.

The outstanding example of a successful fiscal policy rule (at least for the time being; nothing is forever) is the copper-centric economy of Chile. In 2006, Chile initiated a number of fiscal reforms, including the establishment of a pension reserve fund, a social and economic stabilization fund (successor to the copper stabilization fund), and a budget surplus target of 1 percent (subsequently reduced to simple balance) (Frankel 2012b). The innovation of the Chilean approach was to set specific conditions with respect to the GDP output gap and the 10-year price of copper under which the budget constraint could be relaxed and then delegate assessment of these two conditions to a technocratic panel. The government would be permitted to run a deficit if there were a recession and the price of copper fell below its 10-year historical average. If the economy were not in recession and the price of copper was not low, any surpluses would be directed into the pension and stabilization funds (corresponding roughly to long- and short-run safety net requirements) and a sovereign wealth fund.

In 2008, the government came under intense pressure to scrap the rule when copper prices spiked and the budget surplus reached nearly 9 percent of GDP. But the following year, the copper price collapsed, and the government had ample reserves with which to implement a countercyclical fiscal policy.

What seems to have set the Chilean experience apart is not the specifics of the fiscal rules but rather the legal delegation of key technical decisions to a relatively political insulated panel of technocrats—backed by the leadership of the Bachelet government. The obvious parallel is to central bank independence. Ultimately, the sustainability of such a system is a function of the professional competency of the technocrats and particularly the depth of consensus within the political leadership regarding sticking with a system even if it generates unpopular short-term outcomes.

Although fiscal rules can limit the procyclicality of spending, the actual composition of spending is left up to the politicians. Arezki and Ismail (2013) find that although such rules in general may not constrain aggregate spending significantly, they generate potentially perverse outcomes by reducing public investment during busts without commensurate increases during booms, as politicians prioritize spending on public consumption over investment.

An even more fundamental challenge is the central role that the allocation of resource rents plays in the maintenance of political power in many resource-centric economies and the consequent reluctance of the leaderships to submit to any kind of constraint on the level or composition of spending.

One potential way of getting at this problem is to earmark expenditures for particular programs that have public support, in an effort to build accountability. Bowing to public pressure for greater investment in schools, public health, and infrastructure, in 2013 the Brazilian Congress passed a law that earmarks 100 percent of oil royalties for expenditure in education and health care.[11] Under this model, resource rents can be specifically channeled to improving human capital and durable infrastructure. Such an approach may not reflect textbook public finance, but it may generate more durable public support than theoretically preferable policies and underline the key point that escaping the resource curse requires not just management of production and revenue but focus on expenditure for long-run development. In the multilateral context, downstream expenditure is one of the emphases coming out of EITI++.

Natural Resource and Sovereign Wealth Funds

Natural resource funds (NRFs) and sovereign wealth funds (SWFs) are a proliferating way of managing resource revenues (Truman 2010). The basic idea is that resource revenues are segregated from and controlled independently of the normal fiscal process.

NRFs are special government funds that typically consist of savings funds and automatic budget stabilizers. The savings portion is lauded both for reducing inflationary pressure in the economy by removing liquidity and for being more consistent with long-range investment decisions that promote intergenerational equity.

Closely related to NRFs are SWFs, which are state-owned investment funds that pursue higher return on investment through investment in real assets, derivatives, and hedge funds. The budget-stabilizing function helps diminish the impact of commodity price volatility on government revenues and expenditures by smoothing expenditures over the commodity cycle.

These vehicles are sometimes criticized for politicizing investment decisions or contributing to exchange rate manipulation. In this discussion, we set aside such concerns and focus on the impact on macroeconomic stabilization at the national level. For expository simplicity, we use the term SWF to refer to this whole class of state-controlled investment vehicles.

Key issues in the establishment of an SWF include its specific legal form, whether it is held in an onshore or offshore depository institution, and how the qualifications of the custodian is specified and the custodian selected. The fund needs rules on investment policy, selection and oversight of portfolio managers, and the magnitude and composition of spending. A critical issue is whether the government should be able to borrow against the fund. The operation of the fund has to be subject to some kind of accountability, oversight,

---

11. Under the law, 75 percent will be dedicated to education and 25 percent to health care. "Brazil Leader Hails Law Marking Oil Funds for Services," Agence France Presse, August 20, 2013.

and auditing process. The largest funds appear to be operated by Abu Dhabi, Norway, and Saudi Arabia (Truman 2010).[12]

In 2007, out of growing concern about the activities of these funds, which had become major players in financial markets, a group of countries convened under the auspices of the International Monetary Fund (IMF) as the International Working Group on SWFs (IWGSWF). The following year, the group released a code of 30 generally accepted principles and practices, commonly referred to as the Santiago Principles, covering three areas: legal framework, objectives, and coordination with macroeconomic policies; institutional framework and governance structure; and investment and risk management framework (Truman 2010). Compliance has been mixed; the biggest shortfalls appear to be with respect to investment principles and internal ethical standards (Bagnall and Truman 2011).

SWFs face the same problem that fiscal rules do—namely, how to constrain the behavior of incumbent politicians who may not wish to be constrained. Macartan Humphreys and Martin Sandbu (2007, 194) argue that to be successful, "(1) withdrawal decisions should be regulated in part by clear rules rather than general guidelines, (2) key decisions should be made by bodies representing the interests of diverse political constituencies, and (3) there should be high levels of transparency regarding their status and operation—in particular there should be a unified budgetary process and public reporting of payments, holdings, and investments." The last point has to be balanced against the interests of portfolio managers in maintaining a certain degree of confidentiality (Bell and Faria 2007).

One advantage that SWFs have over fiscal rules is that they impose a modicum of international peer pressure. Similarly, EITI may contribute to more transparency in revenue flows and thus support better-functioning SWFs.

Are SWFs effective in moderating macroeconomic instability? Ghiath Shabsigh and Nadeem Ilahi (2007) examine the experiences of 15 oil producers, some with SWFs, some without. They find a robust negative relationship between the existence of an SWF on the one hand and money supply growth and inflation on the other. The statistical evidence is less categorical with respect to the relationship between SWFs and the real exchange rate. Beyond the simple macroeconomic effects, Stella Tsani (2013) finds that the establishment of a resource fund is positively associated with government effectiveness, control of corruption, and rule of law, a result she interprets causally. This result is potentially important, as it suggests that the approach supports the strengthening of domestic institutions broadly and is not simply a mechanism for addressing macroeconomic instability. It is also striking that the particular aspects of governance that resource funds appear to positively affect are also robustly associated with superior long-run growth performance (Givens

---

12. Norway has shown particular zeal in advocating for SWFs for resource-centric developing countries. See Ekeli and Sy (2012) for a discussion of the Norwegian experience.

2013). These aggregate cross-country results are suggestive, but more research needs to be conducted to identify the channels through which these desirable effects are obtained and the preconditions (effective professional bureaucracy, for example) on which successful outcomes depend.

The viability of fiscal rules and SWFs rests squarely on the degree to which fund managers and government bureaucrats can be relied upon to make wise investments in the first place and credibly commit themselves to not raiding the kitty when it is politically expedient to do so (Moss and Majerowicz 2013). "Politically expedient" can mean "politically attractive," as when Hugo Chávez used his country's SWF to funnel arms to Central America and shore up support at home, "politically necessary," as when Azerbaijan's Ilham Aliyev tapped his country's SWF to support conflict with Armenia, or "a matter of regime life and death," as when Chadian president Idris Deby raided the Chadian NRF in order to better equip the Chadian army, which was under heavy attack from Sudanese-backed rebels, in 2005 and 2006. For credible commitments to be made, the government must have an efficient, meritocratic bureaucracy that is insulated from political pressure and constrained by credible checks on executive authority (Weinthal and Luong 2006). Norway, New Zealand, Chile, and Alaska's Permanent Fund may meet this standard (Bagnall and Truman 2013), but the vast majority of emerging resource exporters do not or will not. Tsani's (2013) results on the impact of resource funds on governance are suggestive, but until the precise mechanisms through which these effects operate are better understood, SWFs and earmarking are likely to function best where they are needed least.

It bears mentioning that Western governments with comparatively strong checks on government borrowing from earmarked funds have demonstrated an inability to foreswear said action when pressed. The lion's share of Ireland's contribution to financing its joint EU-IMF bailout in 2010 (€10 billion of €17.5 billion) came directly from its national pension reserve fund. This payout left the fund with €4.9 billion at the end of 2010, amounting to a two-thirds drawdown in a single year. SWFs are not a panacea, but at least they can be anchored in international norms and practices that may bolster their domestic political viability.

Direct or Lump-Sum Distribution

If the government cannot be trusted to invest resource rents wisely, what about the public? Direct disbursement of resource rents via cash transfers or dividend checks has been floated as an alternate policy solution for avoiding the pernicious political economies associated with government oversight and investment of these funds.[13] The "oil-to-cash" plan rests on two premises.

---

13. Such a lump-sum disbursement approach has been advocated for Nigeria (Sala-i-Martin and Subramanian 2003), Iraq (Birdsall and Subramanian 2004), Uganda (Gelb and Majerowicz 2011), and all other commodity producers (Moss and Majerowicz 2013).

First, governments cannot be trusted to invest resource rents wisely. Second, bottom-up approaches to development, which emerge organically from the private sector, produce better outcomes than large, government-financed top-down approaches. Advocates of lump-sum distribution or "cash for oil" argue that receiving payments will incentivize the citizenry to demand transparency and accountability. The example normally invoked by advocates is the Alaskan Permanent Fund.

The proposal is beguiling in its simplicity but not without its drawbacks: The administrative costs are nontrivial, and the potential for negative macroeconomic consequences (inflation, exchange rate volatility, capital flight, rapid expansion of the domestic banking sector absent adequate oversight) exists. Moreover, most variants of this proposal do not explicitly address the issue of intergroup equity.

The first problem is that the administrative demands of direct distribution are significant. Censuses are often a source of tension and conflict in multiethnic societies, particularly in societies such as Côte d'Ivoire or Myanmar, where population movement across borders has been fluid and ascertaining who is a citizen, particularly among ethnic or religious minorities, is complicated and contentious. The informational demands of a direct distribution system are much higher than for a census, and, given the pecuniary stakes, likely to be even more prone to fraud and incitement to conflict. Alan Gelb and Caroline Decker (2011) argue that biometric techniques can be employed to deter fraud and abuse, but such systems may be beyond the administrative capacity of some of the relevant states, at least without external technical and financial assistance.

Moreover many new and emerging producers are ethnically and religiously divided, and as most minerals are point-source resources, their production and the negative externalities thereof are concentrated geographically. Even a well-implemented system in a multiethnic society could give rise to conflict if one or more groups are perceived as obtaining an unequal share. If dividends are provided equally across the board, grievances related to equity are likely to persist, as benefits will be diffuse but costs concentrated. A dividend that provides equal benefits to residents of the Niger Delta and Abuja is unlikely to be viewed—at least by Niger Delta residents—as equitable. Indeed, the issue of who should receive what share could itself become an issue if the process of extraction generates negative externalities (ground water pollution, for example). Demands for larger shares could be particularly contentious if the residents of the region are an ethnic minority, as in the Niger Delta example.

In the absence of well-functioning product markets and financial systems, distribution of the money could give rise to inflation, undesirable exchange rate effects, and balance of payments crises. A policy would act as a stimulus to the financial services industry, particularly in countries where a majority of the population does not have access to the formal banking sector. In the long run, expansion of formal banking and the creation of collateral as a by-product could more generally democratize finance. In the short run, it would not be unreasonable to expect some mishaps in the banking sector, as the regulatory apparatus proved incapable of managing a sudden expansion of the sector.

Perhaps the most fundamental objection is that lump-sum distribution would deprive the state of funds needed for public goods. Here the Alaska example falls flat. For most of the history of the Alaska Permanent Fund, state representatives held senior positions on the congressional Appropriations Committee. Through political influence and outright earmarks, they steered wildly disproportionate federal investment to Alaska. It is only a slight exaggeration to argue that the inflow of federal revenues allowed Alaska to redirect state funds that would have otherwise been spent on the provision of public goods to the Permanent Fund. For the resource-centric countries under consideration, the provision of public goods via a higher-level jurisdictional entity is not a relevant option.

Productive government spending (as might be obtained through a fiscal rule) can dominate external saving (through an SWF, for example) for a credit-constrained, capital-scarce economy (Berg et al. 2012). The historical record of public investment in resource-centric economies is not good, however, possibly because of declining investment efficiency, as it is scaled up in boom times (Heinrich 2011, Berg et al. 2012).

Advocates of direct distribution are correct that governance in these countries is often highly problematic. On a case-by-case basis, it may be advisable to distribute some of the revenue directly (to elicit the desirable transparency and accountability incentives) without entirely defunding the state. Moreover, it may be possible to combine the process of distribution with some other goal, such as child immunization or school attendance, to generate a positive externality (Ross 2007). How far to push the direct distribution approach over other alternatives depends very much on specific local conditions.

Each of these proposals—fiscal rules, SWFs, and direct distribution—has merits and drawbacks. They should not necessarily be perceived as competitors. Depending on specifics, some judicious mixture of all three (an SWF, earmarks for particular programs, and dividend payments) may be ideal. However, none of these interventions really establishes the preconditions for the development of stronger economic and political institutions, which are much more foundational to economic development than any specific policy intervention. Historically, these institutions developed in response to the need for sovereigns to bargain with society over revenue (Bates and Lien 1985, North and Weingast 1989). If state ownership of mineral resources provides the state with easy access to revenue, this fiscal contract is likely to either not develop at all (in legacy exporters like the Gulf states) or erode over time (in new and emerging exporters). The role of private ownership of resources is discussed below.

Exchange Rate Policy

Like fiscal expenditures, cross-border capital flows tend to be procyclical in resource-rich economies, giving rise to Dutch disease. Governments can use monetary policy, in the form of exchange rate policy and capital controls, to mitigate the adverse impact on traded-goods activity outside the resource sector.

One way of increasing saving during booms is for the monetary authority to increase official reserves by intervening in the foreign exchange market. If the principal goal is to smooth consumption over time (not stabilizing the nominal exchange rate), this approach is generally considered suboptimal, as the proceeds are normally invested in low-yielding instruments such as US Treasury bills. If the exchange market intervention is not sterilized, the policy could lead to excessive growth of the money supply and inflation.

If an independent SWF exists, one possibility would be for the central bank to sell its foreign exchange to it. However, if the SWF is not truly independent or can be raided by the executive, the funds may not be saved (Frankel 2012b).

Another alternative would be for the government to pay down existing debt, liberalize any controls on capital outflows by its residents, and introduce capital controls on capital inflows, starting with short-term flows. These instruments are relatively crude for managing the exchange rate, with a checkered history in practice. Olivier Jeanne, Arvind Subramanian, and John Williamson (2012) advocate the imposition of a countercyclical Pigouvian tax on debt inflows to tamp booms and cushion the severity of busts. They argue that imposing such a tax on short-term and foreign debt would affect the forms of inflow with the least growth-promoting effect. The calibration of such taxes is notoriously difficult, but Frederick van der Ploeg and Steve Poelhekke (2008) find some evidence that among commodity exporters, some capital account restrictions have dampened real exchange rate volatility sufficiently to be growth promoting.

A complementary and more direct approach to alleviating Dutch disease would be to explicitly factor its mitigation into exchange rate policy. Inflation targeting has become the conventional wisdom approach to monetary policy in most circumstances, but the approach is not robust to changes in the terms of trade, which, in the case of commodity-centric economies, can be profound.

Some commodity exporters (Chile and Mexico) have allowed their exchange rates to float freely; others (the Gulf Cooperation Council countries and Ecuador) have maintained strict pegs. Most commodity exporters have pursued some kind of intermediate exchange rate management policy (Frankel 2012a, 2012b). The issue is whether transparent nominal targets can be identified that stabilize the real exchange rate.

The most direct approach would be to set the exchange rate in terms of the price of the country's exportable good.[14] In the case of an oil exporter, if the dollar price of oil rose by 1 percent, the country's currency would rise by 1 percent against the dollar. The problem is that given the volatility of

---

14. A similar proposal for a grain-backed dollar was put forward by populists in the United States in the late 19th century as an alternative to the deflationary impact of adherence to the gold standard (Goodwyn 1976).

commodity prices, such a simple rule would generate excessive volatility in the exchange rate (Frankel 2012a).

A milder variant would be to include the price of the exportable good as part of a basket of currencies against which the local currency is pegged.[15] This approach could be made more sophisticated by targeting export prices more broadly, increasing the range of commodities included in the pegging function, or even including exports and nontradables but excluding imports (Frankel 2012a, 2012b). These improvements in macroeconomic nuance would come at the expense of simple transparency and forcefulness in anchoring market participants' expectations. A government pursuing a product price targeting strategy would need to devote significant effort to collecting and publicly disseminating these price series.

Political Economy Considerations

Many of the aforementioned policy interventions have been well understood for decades. Implementation has lagged the technical understanding of the problems. Thus, in some senses, the foundations of the resource curse are found in the incentives of political leaders and bureaucrats in resource-rich regimes. The political and institutional issues raised in chapter 3 go beyond questions about how to maintain competitive exchange rates, for instance. They point to more fundamental questions about the relationship between the state and the extractive sector and how this relationship affects the basic institutions that govern economic transactions and provide market-sustaining public goods.

Private ownership is proposed as an alternative to state ownership of mineral resources. Under private ownership, resource rents are captured by the government through licensing fees or taxation of corporate income. Private ownership of these resources creates the necessary preconditions for a fiscal contract: the asymmetry of resources and capabilities between society, which has a comparative advantage in generating an economic surplus, and the state, which has a comparative advantage in the provision of market-sustaining goods. In order for society to generate the surplus, some public goods must be provided. The state has a natural comparative advantage in the production of these public goods but lacks an independent resource base to fund its activities. This situation gives the state an incentive to develop a capable bureaucracy for extracting revenue from society and society an incentive to demand responsible behavior on the part of the government (Weinthal and Luong 2006). From this exchange, strong legal and representative institutions are more likely to emerge. Thus, one of the prescriptions for avoiding the resource curse may be for states to get out of the mineral industry entirely, focusing

---

15. Soon after the US invasion, Frankel proposed that Iraq adopt a basket peg with equal weights placed on the US dollar, the euro, and the price of oil ("A Crude Peg for the Iraqi Dinar," *Financial Times,* June 13, 2003).

instead on taxing the industry and providing it with the public goods necessary to facilitate production and export.

Before delving into the public versus private ownership issue in detail, it is important to note that just placing mineral resources in private hands may not ensure that stronger political and revenue-generating institutions develop. The incentives to develop capable bureaucracies to extract revenue are roughly proportional to the degree of difficulty in levying taxes. Point-source resources are easy to tax because of two factors relating to their geographic concentration. First, producers can be identified, monitored, and coerced relatively easily (Tanzi 1991). Second, the territorial concentration of production and labor constitutes a natural tax handle, or bottleneck, in the production of a good, which makes evasion inherently more difficult (Musgrave 1969). Convenient tax handles do not promote the development of highly capable bureaucracies. For most of the second half of the 20th century, developing countries relied heavily on port and excise taxes rather than corporate or individual income taxes to fund general government expenditures; doing so did not generally lead to stronger, more capable bureaucracies, even when it did lead to high tax/GDP ratios. The technologies of production in the resource sector suggest that bureaucracies in resource-rich countries will not develop the same way they did in regions where capital was less highly specific, such as Northern Europe in the early modern era (Bates and Lien 1985), irrespective of the nature of ownership (public or private). The threat of expropriation/reappropriation is, therefore, omnipresent.

For countries considering the structure of resource ownership, Erika Weinthal and Pauline Jones Luong (2006) advocate for private domestic ownership. Such ownership may be feasible for countries with adequate expertise in mineral exploration and exploitation and an accumulated stock of physical capital, but what about countries with little or no indigenous expertise and investment capital?

One reason why Weinthal and Luong's proposal has not received more attention has to do with the performance of the central case around which it was originally based: Russia. Their article charts the privatization of the oil sector in Russia in the 1990s, noting that privatization had the effect of both making the Russian oil sector more competitive and establishing independent economic actors, like former Yukos head Mikhail Khodorkovsky, who could press the Russian government for continued economic reforms and greater political transparency. Khodorkovsky's subsequent prosecution and incarceration, the bankrupting of Yukos, and the reconsolidation of the Russian state's position in the Russian oil market (half the country's crude output, 45 percent of domestic refining, according to the Fitch Group [2013]) show how privatization in the extractive sector can be undone.

Macartan Humphreys, Jeffrey Sachs, and Joseph Stiglitz (2007) point out that the increasing capital intensity and complexity of oil exploration mean that few, if any, new producers will be able to entirely go it alone in oil exploration and production. Partnerships with multinational companies will be the norm rather than the exception. How best, then, to manage these partnerships, especially when information asymmetries between multinational companies—with deep knowledge of the industry and global commodity markets—and host governments are likely to be large? How can host countries get the best possible deal, and how can this deal be structured so as to minimize the potential that undue influence is exerted by foreign actors, especially illiberal consumers or investors, which could erode the emergent good governance institutions and norms in the host country?

One solution may be to court greater foreign involvement in the form of encouraging partnerships between Western and non-Western entities for joint exploration and development. Examples are already abundant: Uganda's Albertine Rift deposits are being jointly developed by Total SA (France), Tullow PLC (United Kingdom), and CNOOC Ltd. (China); Royal Dutch Shell (Netherlands-UK) and CNOOC Ltd. are partnering to explore two offshore blocks in Gabon; and Kazakhstan's KazMunaiGaz is partnering with both Western and Chinese firms to develop the Kashagan field in the Caspian Sea.[16]

Joint partnerships are attractive to host countries for two reasons. First, they promote greater transparency. In a single firm–host government arrangement, the multinational corporation has little incentive to make private information public, and the costs of monitoring the terms of the agreement fall entirely on the host-country government and civil society, which is nascent in many new and emerging producers. Multifirm arrangements introduce additional parties with pecuniary incentives to verify claims by both the government and other multinational corporations. These incentives are true both generally and specifically with respect to Western partners. Western civil society groups have driven good governance initiatives in the extractive sector, as argued in chapter 6. The involvement of Western firms in developing mineral resources, even with minority stakes, draws the attention of these watchdog groups and offloads some of the costs of monitoring compliance with both international law and the specific terms of agreements with host countries onto interested third parties. Although some governments may not view this enhanced scrutiny as a good thing, for governments seeking to minimize the political effects of the resource curse, it is likely to help. Moreover, this scrutiny is likely to have positive spillovers for domestic civil society in host countries, which can benefit from tapping into broader, more financially established activist networks, often with issue-specific technical expertise.

Second, joint partnerships dilute the political influence of the multinational corporation's home-country government by pitting its interests against the interests of other major powers. The 1953 CIA- and MI6-backed ouster of Mossadeq in Iran, which followed his decision to nationalize the Iranian oil

16. As of September 2013, the entities were ENI S.p.A (Italy), ExxonMobil (United States), Total SA (France), Royal Dutch Shell, ConocoPhillips (United States), Inpex (Japan), and state-owned CNPC (China) ("Western Oil Firms Pay Kazakhstan's Oil Field Investment Bill," *Telegraph*, May 28, 2012; "China Buys into Giant Kazakh Oilfield for $5 Billion," Reuters, September 7, 2013).

industry at the expense of Anglo-Persian Oil Company (later BP), is but one example of the potential dangers associated with hosting major power investment in strategic resources. It is hard to imagine a similar situation playing out in a country hosting both Western and Chinese investments. For this reason, host-country governments may find that joint Western-non-Western partnerships provide them with greater insurance against multinational corporation meddling in domestic affairs and, paradoxically, more policy autonomy. This benefit may be more salient for countries, like Kazakhstan, that border major powers.

Final Thoughts

This book began with an account of a kitchen table conversation about an oil discovery in Ghana. Similar conversations have taken place in households across the developing world with increasing frequency. Demand for primary commodities has spurred massive investment in exploration and resource development, resulting in a host of new developing countries, including Ghana, either poised to enter or already among the family of major mineral exporters. Are those discoveries a blessing or curse? Oil is being pumped in ever larger volumes off the Ghanaian coast, and luxury hotels are springing up in Accra, the capital. But the city's thoroughfares remain filled with poor hawkers trying to sell everything from drinking water to newspapers, apparel, and household wares to passing motorists. Coastal fishermen who ply their trade in tiny wooden vessels complain that their catches are down since drilling and exploitation began. Of the $287 million in oil revenue the Ghanaian government spent in 2012, almost 20 percent was spent on administrative departments (Africa Centre for Energy Policy 2013), raising fears that corruption, patronage, and self-dealing are on the rise. Chinese investment in the oil and gold industry has brought in billions in much-needed FDI and ODF but also wildcat Chinese gold prospectors, hundreds of whom have been detained, deported, or otherwise forced to leave the country. To date, this situation has not resulted in significant diplomatic conflict. With growing investment in extractives, however, the potential for tension is omnipresent. Whether the country is able to maintain its young and fragile democracy and harness its newly discovered bounty to benefit all of its citizens remains an open question—one that many countries will face in the coming decades.

Appendices

Appendix A
Determinants of Official Chinese Development Finance, 2000–11

Official development finance (ODF) includes "official development assistance (ODA)-like," "other official flows (OOF)-like," and "vague official finance." The term "-like" relates to the attempt by AidData researchers to fit Chinese development assistance, which is not recorded and catalogued according to the Organization for Economic Cooperation and Development (OECD) Development Assistance Committee (DAC) standards (Strange et al. 2013b). ODA-like refers to loans from donor country governments intended to promote economic development on concessional terms. "Other official flows" come from governments but do not meet ODA criteria.[1] They could be loans that do not have a grant element of more than 25 percent, or they could be "official bilateral transactions, whatever their grant element, that are primarily export facilitating in purpose" (OECD 2010, quoted in Bräutigam 2011a, 757). These flows often take the form of export credits to promote the purchase of Chinese goods. "Vague official finance" is finance that appears to be either ODA-like or OOF-like, "but for which there is insufficient information to assign the flows to either the ODA-like or OOF-like category" (Strange et al.

---

1. This category includes "grants with a representational or commercial purpose (i.e., grants that do not have a primary objective of promoting economic development or welfare in the recipient country); loans from a Chinese government institution that do not have any apparent grant element (commercial loans based on Libor or Libor plus a margin) or a grant element that does not exceed 25 percent; and export credits from a Chinese government institution to a recipient institution" (Bräutigam 2011a, 206). OOF activities also include "short-term credits to Chinese exporters (export sellers' credits) to help them finance foreign sales, and...longer-term credits to foreign buyers to assist in the export of Chinese goods and services" (Bräutigam 2011a, 206). "OOF also includes lines of credit that the Chinese government provides to a Chinese enterprise (state owned or not state owned) to do business overseas" (Strange et al. 2013b, 28).

2013b, 17). We regress Chinese ODF on our two key variables of interest—the Polity score and various measures of a country's mineral wealth—and a sparse set of controls (table A.1). We split the sample into two periods, 2000–05 and 2006–11, and provide summed and log-transformed regressions for the two periods.

The Polity score proxies democracy. To measure mineral wealth, we include stock measures of mineral capital. These measures—of oil reserves, natural gas reserves, and mineral reserves and of oil, natural gas, and minerals combined—are taken from the World Bank's Measuring Capital for the 21st Century Project. They represent the present discounted value of economic profits over the life of the resource (World Bank 2006, 147).[2] The minerals category includes bauxite, copper, gold, iron ore, lead, nickel, phosphate, silver, tin, and zinc.

We include controls for population and level of development (real GDP per capita). Population proxies both need for aid—ceteris paribus, more aid should flow to countries with larger populations, as they need more resources to develop—and the potential size of the domestic market, as Chinese aid is also believed to be market seeking. Real GDP per capita proxies recipient need, with poorer countries expected to receive more development financing.

We also include a control for whether the country extends diplomatic recognition to Taiwan. Previous studies highlight China's use of aid to further its One China policy of denying diplomatic recognition to Taiwan's government (Bräutigam 2009, Halper 2010a, Dreher and Fuchs 2013). For each model, we use ordinary least squares regression with Huber-White robust standard errors. (For an extended discussion of results, see chapter 5.)

---

2. The value of the resource stock is calculated as $v_t = \pi_t q_t \left(1 + \frac{1}{r^*}\right)\left(1 - \frac{1}{(1+r^*)^T}\right)$, where π is the unit rent, q is the volume of production, r is the social discount rate, and T is the lifetime of the resource (World Bank 2006, 148).

Table A.1 Determinants of Chinese official development finance (ODF), 2000–11

Variable	(1) ln Chinese ODF, 2000–05	(2) ln Chinese ODF, 2000–05	(3) ln Chinese ODF, 2000–05	(4) ln Chinese ODF, 2000–05	(5) ln Chinese ODF, 2006–11	(6) ln Chinese ODF, 2006–11	(7) ln Chinese ODF, 2006–11	(8) ln Chinese ODF, 2006–11
ln population	-0.587 (0.639)	-0.163 (0.531)	0.054 (0.477)	-0.31 (0.594)	0.423** (0.164)	0.686*** (0.177)	0.793*** (0.199)	0.499*** (0.175)
ln GDP per capita	-0.969 (0.991)	-0.526 (0.886)	-0.311 (0.871)	-0.686 (0.937)	-0.177 (0.328)	0.105 (0.276)	0.202 (0.313)	-0.092 (0.321)
Polity score	-0.056 (0.241)	-0.149 (0.221)	-0.149 (0.182)	-0.11 (0.237)	0.068 (0.052)	-0.008 (0.060)	0.005 (0.054)	0.023 (0.052)
Taiwan recognition	-15.930*** (3.613)	-18.649*** (2.136)	-18.711*** (1.624)	-17.382*** (3.311)	-17.864*** (0.886)	-19.471*** (0.844)	-19.356*** (0.817)	-18.582*** (0.754)
ln oil, natural gas, and mineral wealth, 2000	0.167 (0.139)				0.079*** (0.025)			
ln oil wealth, 2000		0.005 (0.073)				-0.011 (0.027)		
ln natural gas wealth, 2000			-0.054 (0.081)				-0.038 (0.038)	
ln mineral wealth, 2000				0.093 (0.132)				0.064** (0.026)
Constant	27.712** (12.230)	23.244** (10.865)	19.943* (10.326)	24.544* (12.318)	16.129*** (3.118)	13.079*** (2.768)	11.405*** (3.387)	15.371*** (3.175)
Observations	43	43	43	43	45	45	45	45
R-squared	0.588	0.551	0.554	0.563	0.933	0.921	0.923	0.93

Note: Robust standard errors in parentheses. *** $p<0.01$, ** $p<0.05$, * $p<0.1$.

Appendix B
Determinants of Arms Transfers to African Countries, 2000–11

Arms transfers refer to actual deliveries of major conventional weapons (SIPRI 2013). In order to compare arms transfers across countries for which unit costs may vary widely for similar weapons systems, the Stockholm International Peace Research Institute (SIPRI) uses a common unit, called the trend indicator value (TIV). TIV is based on known production costs for common weapons systems. It compares transfers on the basis of their contribution to recipient-state military capacity rather than the dollar amount of the transfer. The variable captures sales, in-kind military aid, and aid tied to purchases of donor-country arms.[1]

We regress total arms inflows, Chinese arms transfers, and US arms transfers on three variables of interest—the Polity score, the Physical Integrity Rights Index, and various measures of a country's mineral wealth—and a sparse set of controls. The Polity score proxies democracy. The Physical Integrity Rights Index proxies human rights conditions, measuring "the rights not to be tortured, summarily executed, disappeared, or imprisoned for political beliefs"

---

1. The results are presented summed and log-transformed across the two periods 2000–05 and 2006–11. For regression tables and expanded discussion, see appendix A. The units for arms transfers are TIV, constructed by SIPRI. "These prices are based upon the average unit costs for core conventional weapons. Weapons for which the cost is unknown are compared with core weapons based upon size and performance characteristics (weight, speed, range, and payload); type of electronics, loading or unloading arrangements, engine, tracks or wheels, armament and materials; and finally the era in which the weapon was produced. SIPRI then calculates the volume of transfers to, from, and between all end-users using the TIV/price and the number of weapon systems or subsystems delivered in a given year. The quantitative data provide a common unit for measuring trends in the flow of arms to particular countries and regions over time—in effect it is a price index" (de Soysa and Midford 2012, 846, footnote 10).

(Cingranelli and Richards 2010b). The index ranges from 0 (no government respect for these rights) to 8 (full government respect for these rights). We include stock measures of mineral capital, as in appendix A. We include an additional control, conflict intensity, to proxy "need" for arms shipments. Conflict intensity refers to the scale of domestic armed conflict; higher values indicate more violence and should generate more government demand for military resources (Gleditsch et al. 2001). As in appendix A, we split the sample into two periods, 2000–05 and 2006–11. For each model, we use ordinary least squares regression with Huber-White robust standard errors (tables B.1 and B.2). (For an extended discussion of results, see chapter 5.)

Table B.1 Total, US, and Chinese arms transfers to African countries, 2000–05

Variable	(1) ln total arms inflows, 2000–05	(2) ln US arms transfers, 2000–05	(3) ln Chinese arms transfers, 2000–05	(4) ln total arms inflows, 2000–05	(5) ln US arms transfers, 2000–05	(6) ln Chinese arms transfers, 2000–05
ln population	1.105*** (0.187)	0.605** (0.282)	0.308 (0.254)	1.094*** (0.202)	0.539* (0.275)	0.389 (0.246)
ln GDP per capita	1.070*** (0.224)	0.703** (0.316)	0.287 (0.255)	1.126*** (0.232)	0.682** (0.310)	0.451* (0.249)
Polity score	–0.076 (0.048)	–0.064 (0.056)	–0.076 (0.055)	–0.069 (0.053)	–0.052 (0.056)	–0.079 (0.060)
Human rights	0.214 (0.166)	0.161 (0.210)	0.223 (0.250)	0.114 (0.156)	0.096 (0.185)	0.099 (0.234)
Conflict intensity	1.423*** (0.395)	–0.109 (0.798)	0.610 (0.938)	1.257*** (0.396)	–0.217 (0.745)	0.407 (0.982)
ln oil, natural gas, and mineral wealth, 2000	0.036 (0.025)	0.025 (0.020)	0.041* (0.022)			
ln oil wealth, 2000				0.016 (0.020)	0.027 (0.021)	–0.007 (0.024)
ln natural gas wealth, 2000						
ln mineral wealth, 2000						
Constant	–16.591*** (2.482)	–11.014** (4.463)	–5.734 (3.543)	–16.050*** (2.703)	–9.795** (4.313)	–6.478* (3.437)
Observations	43	43	43	43	43	43
R-squared	0.712	0.385	0.227	0.700	0.390	0.186

(continues on next page)

153

Table B.1   Total, US, and Chinese arms transfers to African countries, 2000–05 *(continued)*

Variable	(7) ln total arms inflows, 2000–05	(8) ln US arms transfers, 2000–05	(9) ln Chinese arms transfers, 2000–05	(10) ln total arms inflows, 2000–05	(11) ln US arms transfers, 2000–05	(12) ln Chinese arms transfers, 2000–05
ln population	1.146***	0.446**	0.414*	1.133***	0.628**	0.335
	(0.198)	(0.218)	(0.236)	(0.179)	(0.282)	(0.249)
ln GDP per capita	1.181***	0.578*	0.478*	1.103***	0.739**	0.301
	(0.246)	(0.316)	(0.257)	(0.226)	(0.312)	(0.241)
Polity score	−0.076	−0.070	−0.074	−0.078	−0.065	−0.079
	(0.053)	(0.057)	(0.060)	(0.048)	(0.057)	(0.055)
Human rights	0.109	0.106	0.097	0.202	0.139	0.235
	(0.159)	(0.176)	(0.234)	(0.170)	(0.202)	(0.230)
Conflict intensity	1.249***	−0.212	0.406	1.399***	−0.147	0.626
	(0.412)	(0.629)	(0.961)	(0.391)	(0.794)	(0.906)
ln oil, natural gas, and mineral wealth, 2000						
ln oil wealth, 2000						
ln natural gas wealth, 2000	0.002	0.056	−0.014			
	(0.023)	(0.042)	(0.038)			
ln mineral wealth, 2000				0.035	0.020	0.050**
				(0.025)	(0.020)	(0.023)
Constant	−16.797***	−8.248**	−6.884*	−16.947***	−11.261**	−6.148*
	(2.889)	(3.689)	(3.424)	(2.447)	(4.542)	(3.586)
Observations	43	43	43	43	43	43
R-squared	0.696	0.418	0.188	0.712	0.38	0.249

Note: Robust standard errors in parentheses. *** $p<0.01$, ** $p<0.05$, * $p<0.1$.

Table B.2 Total, US, and Chinese arms transfers to African countries, 2006–11

Variable	(1) ln total arms inflows, 2006–11	(2) ln US arms transfers, 2006–11	(3) ln Chinese arms transfers, 2006–11	(4) ln total arms inflows, 2006–11	(5) ln US arms transfers, 2006–11	(6) ln Chinese arms transfers, 2006–11
ln population	0.882*** (0.260)	0.559* (0.304)	0.366 (0.268)	0.827*** (0.251)	0.472* (0.277)	0.423 (0.256)
ln GDP per capita	0.798*** (0.274)	0.530** (0.254)	0.264 (0.252)	0.744** (0.276)	0.420* (0.219)	0.347 (0.276)
Polity score	0.044 (0.044)	−0.034 (0.049)	0.034 (0.050)	0.068 (0.043)	−0.012 (0.047)	0.029 (0.052)
Human rights	0.268 (0.252)	0.056 (0.222)	0.044 (0.285)	0.165 (0.244)	0.043 (0.199)	−0.024 (0.279)
Conflict intensity	2.327*** (0.586)	−0.560 (0.620)	0.455 (0.754)	2.001*** (0.599)	−0.702 (0.591)	0.357 (0.770)
ln oil, natural gas, and mineral wealth, 2005	0.071*** (0.021)	0.019 (0.014)	0.036 (0.022)			
ln oil wealth, 2005				0.075*** (0.022)	0.044* (0.023)	0.009 (0.025)
ln natural gas wealth, 2005						
ln mineral wealth, 2005						
Constant	−13.914*** (3.507)	−8.690* (4.409)	−5.191 (3.861)	−12.116*** (3.281)	−7.087* (4.070)	−5.604 (3.840)
Observations	45	45	45	45	45	45
R-squared	0.641	0.336	0.221	0.656	0.388	0.190

(continues on next page)

Table B.2 Total, US, and Chinese arms transfers to African countries, 2006–11 *(continued)*

	(7) ln total arms inflows, 2006–11	(8) ln US arms transfers, 2006–11	(9) ln Chinese arms transfers, 2006–11	(10) ln total arms inflows, 2006–11	(11) ln US arms transfers, 2006–11	(12) ln Chinese arms transfers, 2006–11
ln population	0.919*** (0.278)	0.422 (0.259)	0.337 (0.262)	0.908*** (0.261)	0.522* (0.297)	0.376 (0.277)
ln GDP per capita	0.949*** (0.333)	0.473** (0.217)	0.308 (0.267)	0.855*** (0.272)	0.490** (0.238)	0.288 (0.251)
Polity score	0.025 (0.053)	−0.037 (0.047)	0.025 (0.049)	0.022 (0.046)	−0.040 (0.046)	0.023 (0.050)
Human rights	0.089 (0.235)	−0.028 (0.224)	−0.058 (0.279)	0.252 (0.225)	0.091 (0.208)	0.038 (0.280)
Conflict intensity	2.247*** (0.602)	−0.502 (0.556)	0.440 (0.731)	2.541*** (0.653)	−0.393 (0.650)	0.570 (0.786)
ln oil, natural gas, and mineral wealth, 2005						
ln oil wealth, 2005						
ln natural gas wealth, 2005	0.026 (0.045)	0.036 (0.036)	0.022 (0.039)			
ln mineral wealth, 2005				0.072** (0.027)	0.041** (0.017)	0.038 (0.027)
Constant	−13.706*** (3.955)	−6.561* (3.852)	−4.423 (3.835)	−14.286*** (3.378)	−8.388* (4.277)	−5.348 (3.914)
Observations	45	45	45	45	45	45
R-squared	0.580	0.350	0.196	0.637	0.370	0.222

Note: Robust standard errors in parentheses. *** $p<0.01$, ** $p<0.05$, * $p<0.1$.

References

Aaronson, Susan Ariel. 2011. Limited Partnership: Business, Government, Civil Society, and the Public in the Extractive Industries Transparency Initiative (EITI). *Public Administration and Development* 31, no. 1: 50-63.

Acemoglu, Daron, and James A. Robinson. 2006. De Facto Political Power and Institutional Persistence. *American Economic Review* 96, no. 2: 326-30.

Acemoglu, Daron, Simon Johnson, and James A. Robinson. 2001. The Colonial Origins of Comparative Development: An Empirical Investigation. *American Economic Review* 91, no. 5: 1369-401.

Acemoglu, Daron, Simon Johnson, and James A. Robinson. 2002. *An African Success Story: Botswana.* CEPR Discussion Paper No. 3219. London: Centre for Economic Policy Research.

Acemoglu, Daron, Davide Ticchi, and Andrea Vindigni. 2011. Emergence and Persistence of Inefficient States. *Journal of the European Economic Association* 9, no. 2: 177-208.

Acemoglu, Daron, Suresh Naidu, Pascual Restrepo, and James A. Robinson. 2014. *Democracy Does Cause Growth.* NBER Working Paper 20004. Cambridge, MA: National Bureau of Economic Research.

ACLED (Armed Conflict Location and Event Dataset). 2013. *Conflict Trends No. 10: Real-Time Analysis of African Political Violence.* January. Available at www.acleddata.com/wp-content/uploads/2013/01/ACLED-Conflict-Trends-Report_No-10_January-2013.pdf.

ADB (African Development Bank). 2009. *Maximizing the Benefits from Africa's Oil and Gas Resources.* Abidjan.

Africa Centre for Energy Policy. 2013. *How a Good Law May Not Stop Oil Money from Going Down the Drain.* Accra.

Ahn, Daniel P. 2007. *The U.S. Strategic Petroleum Reserve and Cartel Deterrence.* Working Paper. Available at http://papers.ssrn.com/sol3/papers.cfm?abstract_id=2025228 (accessed on February 6, 2014).

Aleksynska, Mariya, and Olena Havrylchyk. 2013. FDI from the South: The Role of Institutional Distance and Natural Resources. *European Journal of Political Economy* 29, no. 1: 38-53.

Alesina, Alberto, and David Dollar. 2000. Who Gives Foreign Aid to Whom and Why? *Journal of Economic Growth* 5, no. 1: 33-63.

Alexeev, Michael, and Robert Conrad. 2009. The Elusive Curse of Oil. *Review of Economics and Statistics* 91, no. 3: 586-98.

Alexeev, Michael, and Robert Conrad. 2011. The Natural Resource Curse and Economic Transition. *Economic Systems* 35: 445-61.

Alt, James E., Jeffrey Frieden, Michael J. Gilligan, Dani Rodrik, and Ronald Rogowski. 1996. The Political Economy of International Trade: Enduring Puzzles and an Agenda for Inquiry. *Comparative Political Studies* 29, no. 6: 689-717.

Al-Ubaydli, Omar. 2012. Natural Resources and the Tradeoff between Authoritarianism and Development. *Journal of Economic Behavior & Organization* 81, no. 1: 137-52.

Amnesty International. 2006. *People's Republic of China: Sustaining Conflict and Human Rights Abuses: The Flow of Arms Accelerates*. Amnesty International Background Report 17/030/2006. London: Amnesty International.

Andersen, Jørgen Juel, and Michael L. Ross. 2014. The Big Oil Change: A Closer Look at the Haber-Menaldo Analysis. *Comparative Political Studies* (forthcoming).

Arezki, Rabah, and Kareem Ismail. 2013. Boom-Bust Cycle, Asymmetrical Fiscal Response and the Dutch Disease. *Journal of Development Economics* 101, no. C: 256-67.

Arezki, Rabah, Thorvaldur Gylfason, and Amadou Sy, eds. 2012. *Beyond the Resource Curse: Policies to Harness the Power of Natural Resources*. Washington: International Monetary Fund.

Arezki, Rabah, Catherine A. Pattillo, Marc Quintyn, and Min Zhu. 2012. *Commodity Price Volatility and Inclusive Growth in Low-Income Countries*. Washington: International Monetary Fund.

Asiedu, Elizabeth. 2006. Foreign Direct Investment in Africa: The Role of Natural Resources, Market Size, Government Policy, Institutions and Political Instability. *World Economy* 29, no. 1: 63-77.

Auty, Richard M. 1993. *Sustaining Development in Mineral Economies*. London: Routledge.

Axelrod, Robert, and Robert O. Keohane. 1985. Achieving Cooperation under Anarchy: Strategies and Institutions. *World Politics* 38, no. 1: 226-54.

Bagnall, Allie E., and Edwin M. Truman. 2011. *IFSWF Report on Compliance with the Santiago Principles: Admirable but Flawed Transparency*. Policy Brief 11-14. Washington: Peterson Institute for International Economics.

Bagnall, Allie E., and Edwin M. Truman. 2013. *Progress on Sovereign Wealth Fund Transparency and Accountability: An Updated SWF Scoreboard*. Policy Brief 13-19. Washington: Peterson Institute for International Economics.

Barbieri, Katherine, and Omar M. G. Keshk. 2012. Correlates of War Project Trade Data Set Codebook, Version 3.0. Available at http://correlatesofwar.org.

Barma, Naazneen H., Kai Kaiser, Tuan Minh Le, and Lorena Viñuela. 2012. *Rents to Riches: The Political Economy of Resource-Led Development*. Washington: World Bank.

Barro, Robert J. 1991. Economic Growth in a Cross-Section of Countries. *Quarterly Journal of Economics* 106, no. 2: 407-43.

Barro, Robert J. 2001. Human Capital and Growth. *American Economic Review* 91, no. 2: 12-17.

Barro, Robert J. 2012. *Convergence and Modernization Revisited*. NBER Working Paper 18295. Cambridge, MA: National Bureau of Economic Research.

Bates, Robert H., and Da-Hsiang Donald Lien. 1985. A Note on Taxation, Development, and Representative Government. *Politics & Society* 14, no. 1: 53-70.

Baum, Matthew A., and David A. Lake. 2003. The Political Economy of Growth: Democracy and Human Capital. *American Journal of Political Science* 47, no. 2: 333-47.

Behrman, Jere R. 1984. The Importance of Supply and Demand Variations in Earnings Instability: Comment. *Economic Development and Cultural Change* 33, no. 1: 167-70.

Bell, Joseph C., and Teresa Maurea Faria. 2007. Critical Issues for a Revenue Management Law. In *Escaping the Resource Curse*, ed. Macartan Humphreys, Jeffrey D. Sachs, and Joseph E. Stiglitz. New York: Columbia University Press.

Benes, Jaromir, Marcelle Chauvet, Ondra Kamenik, Michael Kumhof, Douglas Laxton, Susanna Mursula, and Jack Selody. 2012. *The Future of Oil: Geology vs. Technology*. IMF Working Paper WP/12/109. Washington: International Monetary Fund.

Berg, Andrew, Rafael Portillo, Shu-Chun S. Yang, and Luis-Felipe Zanna. 2012. *Public Investment in Resource-Abundant Developing Countries*. IMF Working Paper WP/12/274. Washington: International Monetary Fund.

Bernauer, Thomas, Anna Kalbhenn, Vally Koubi, and Gabriele Spilker. 2010. A Comparison of International and Domestic Sources of Global Governance Dynamics. *British Journal of Political Science* 40, no. 3: 509-38.

Besley, Timothy, and Torsten Persson. 2009. The Origins of State Capacity: Property Rights, Taxation, and Politics. *American Economic Review* 99, no. 4: 1218-44.

Bevan, David, Paul Collier, and Jan Gunning. 1999. *The Political Economy of Poverty, Equity and Growth: Nigeria and Indonesia*. New York: Oxford University Press.

Bhattacharyya, Sambit, and Roland Hodler. 2010. Natural Resources, Democracy and Corruption. *European Economic Review* 54, no. 4: 608-21.

Birdsall, Nancy, and Arvind Subramanian. 2004. Saving Iraq from Its Oil. *Foreign Affairs* (July/August): 77-89.

Blattman, Christopher, and Edward Miguel. 2010. Civil War. *Journal of Economic Literature* 48, no. 1: 3-57.

Bloom, David E., David Canning, and Jaypee Sevilla. 2004. The Effect of Health on Economic Growth: A Production Function Approach. *World Development* 32, no. 1: 1-13.

Bob, Clifford. 2005. *The Marketing of Rebellion: Insurgents, Media, and International Activism*. New York: Cambridge University Press.

Bohn, Henning, and Robert T. Deacon. 2000. Ownership Risk, Investment, and the Use of Natural Resources. *American Economic Review* 90, no. 3 (June): 526-49.

Boschini, Anne, Jan Pettersson, and Jesper Roine. 2012. The Resource Curse and Its Potential Reversal. *World Development* 43: 19-41.

Boyce, John R., and J. C. Herbert Emery. 2011. Is a Negative Correlation between Resource Abundance and Growth Sufficient Evidence That There Is a "Resource Curse"? *Resources Policy* 36, no. 1: 1-13.

BP (British Petroleum). 2012. *BP Statistical Review of World Energy* (June). Available at http://bp.com/statisticalreview.

BP (British Petroleum). 2013. *BP Statistical Review of World Energy* (June). Available at http://bp.com/statisticalreview.

Bräutigam, Deborah. 2008. *China's African Aid: Transatlantic Challenges*. Washington: International Development Program, School of International Service, American University.

Bräutigam, Deborah. 2009. *The Dragon's Gift: The Real Story of China in Africa*. Oxford: Oxford University Press.

Bräutigam, Deborah. 2011a. Aid "with Chinese Characteristics": Chinese Aid and Development Finance Meet the OECD-DAC Regime. *Journal of International Development* 23, no. 5. Available at http://deborahbrautigam.files.wordpress.com/2013/04/2011-aid-with-chinese-characteristics.pdf.

Bräutigam, Deborah. 2011b. Chinese Development Aid in Africa: What, Where, Why and How Much? In *China Update 2011*, ed. Jane Golley and Ligang Song. Canberra: Australian National University.

Bravo-Ortega, Claudio, and José De Gregorio. 2007. The Relative Richness of the Poor? Natural Resources, Human Capital, and Economic Growth. In *Natural Resources: Neither Curse nor Destiny*, ed. Daniel Lederman and William F. Maloney. Stanford, CA: Stanford University Press and Washington: World Bank.

Brenthurst Foundation, Chinese Academy of Social Sciences, Council on Foreign Relations, and Leon H. Sullivan Foundation. 2007. Africa-China-U.S. Trilateral Dialogue. Washington: Council on Foreign Relations. Available at www.cfr.org/content/publications/attachments /Trilateral_Report.pdf (accessed on January 10, 2008).

Brock, Philip L. 1991. Export Instability and the Economic Performance of Developing Countries. *Journal of Economic Dynamics and Control* 15, no. 1: 129–47.

Brooks, Stephen G. 2007. *Producing Security: Multinational Corporations, Globalization, and the Changing Calculus of Conflict*. Princeton, NJ: Princeton University Press.

Brunnschweiler, Christa. 2009. *Oil and Growth in Transition Countries*. ETH Working Paper 09/108. Zurich: Center of Economic Research at Eidgenossische Technische Hochschule.

Brunnschweiler, Christa, and Erwin Bulte. 2008. The Resource Curse Revisited and Revised: A Tale of Paradoxes and Red Herrings. *Journal of Environmental Economics and Management* 55, no. 3: 248–64.

Brunnschweiler, Christa, and Erwin Bulte. 2009. Natural Resources and Violent Conflict: Resource Abundance, Dependence, and the Onset of Civil Wars. *Oxford Economic Papers* 61, no. 4: 651–74.

Bueno de Mesquita, Bruce, and Alastair Smith. 2009. A Political Economy of Aid. *International Organization* 63, no. 2: 309–40.

Bueno de Mesquita, Bruce, and Alastair Smith. 2010. Leader Survival, Revolutions, and the Nature of Government Finance. *American Journal of Political Science* 54, no. 4: 936–50.

Buys, Piet, Uwe Deichmann, Craig Meisner, Thao Ton That, and David Wheeler. 2009. Country Stakes in Climate Change Negotiations: Two Dimensions of Vulnerability. *Climate Policy* 9, no. 3: 288–305.

Caceres, Carlos, and Leandro Medina. 2012. *Measures of Fiscal Risk in Hydrocarbon-Exporting Countries*. IMF Working Paper WP/12/260. Washington: International Monetary Fund.

Campbell, Greg. 2002. *Blood Diamonds*. Boulder, CO: Westview Press.

Canuto, Otaviano, and Matheus Cavallari. 2012. Natural Capital and the Resource Curse. *Economic Premise* 83. Washington: World Bank.

Carmody, Padraig. 2011. *The New Scramble for Africa*. New York: Polity.

Carter, Colin A., Gordon C. Rausser, and Aaron Smith. 2011. Commodity Booms and Busts. *Annual Review of Resource Economics* 3, no. 1: 87–118.

Cederman, Lars-Erik, Nils B. Weidmann, and Kristian Skrede Gleditsch. 2011. Horizontal Inequalities and Ethnonationalist Civil War: A Global Comparison. *American Political Science Review* 105, no. 3: 478–95.

Center for International Development. 2010. *The Atlas of Economic Complexity*. Cambridge, MA: Harvard University. Available at www.atlas.cid.harvard.edu/explore/tree_map/export/lby /all/show/2010 (accessed on November 21, 2013).

Centre for Natural Resource Governance. 2013. *A Tale of Two Countries: A Comparison of Botswana's and Zimbabwe's Diamond Industries*. Available at www.ddiglobal.org/login/Upload /A-Comparison-of-Botswana-and-Zimbabwe-Diamond-Sectors.pdf (accessed on January 9, 2014).

Cerra, Valerie, and Sweta Chaman Saxena. 2008. Growth Dynamics: The Myth of Economic Recovery. *American Economic Review* 98, no. 1: 439–57.

Chaudhry, Kiren Aziz. 1989. The Price of Wealth: Business and State in Labor Remittance and Oil Economies. *International Organization* 43, no. 1: 101–45.

Checkel, Jeffrey T. 2005. International Institutions and Socialization in Europe: Introduction and Framework. *International Organization* 59, no. 4: 801–26.

Chen, Matthew E. 2007. Chinese National Oil Companies and Human Rights. *Orbis* (Winter): 41–54.

Cherif, Reda. 2013. The Dutch Disease and the Technological Gap. *Journal of Development Economics* 101: 248–55.

Choi, Seung-Whan. 2010. Beyond Kantian Liberalism: Peace through Globalization? *Conflict Management and Peace Science* 27, no. 3: 272–95.

Choi, Stephen J., and Kevin E. Davis. 2012. *Foreign Affairs and Enforcement of the Foreign Corrupt Practices Act.* Public Law and Legal Theory Research Paper Series Working Series No. 12-35. New York: New York University School of Law.

Cingranelli, David L., and David L. Richards. 2010a. The Cingranelli and Richards (CIRI) Human Rights Data Project. *Human Rights Quarterly* 32, no. 2: 395–418.

Cingranelli, David L., and David L. Richards. 2010b. Short Variable Descriptions for Indicators in the Cingranelli-Richards (CIRI) Human Rights Dataset, version 11.22.10. Available at www.humanrightsdata.org/documentation/ciri_variables_short_descriptions.pdf.

Clayton, Blake. 2012. *Lessons Learned from the 2011 Strategic Petroleum Reserve Release.* Working Paper. New York: Council on Foreign Relations.

Cline, William. 2012. *Projecting China's Current Account Surplus.* Policy Brief 12-7. Washington: Peterson Institute for International Economics.

Closson, Stacy. 2012. Challenging the Consensus on the Oil Curse. *International Studies Review* 14, no. 2: 346–48.

Colgan, Jeff D. 2010. Oil and Revolutionary Governments: Fuel for International Conflict. *International Organization* 64, no. 3: 661–94.

Colgan, Jeff D. 2011. Oil and Resource-Backed Aggression. *Energy Policy* 39, no. 3: 1669–76.

Colgan, Jeff D. 2012. Measuring Revolution. *Conflict Management and Peace Science* 29, no. 4: 444–67.

Colgan, Jeff D. 2013. *Petro-Aggression: When Oil Causes War.* New York: Cambridge University Press.

Collier, Paul. 1999. On the Economic Consequences of Civil War. *Oxford Economic Paper* 51, no. 1: 168–83.

Collier, Paul. 2006. African Security: What the Statistics Suggest. In *African Security, Commodities, and Development.* London: Royal United Services Institute.

Collier, Paul, and Anke Hoeffler. 2004. Greed and Grievance in Civil War. *Oxford Economic Paper* 56, no. 4: 563–95.

Collier, Paul, Lani Elliot, Håvard Hegre, Anke Hoeffler, Nicholas Sambanis, and Marta Reynal-Querol. 2003. *Breaking the Conflict Trap: Civil War and Development Policy.* Oxford: Oxford University Press.

Cook, Nicolas. 2003. *Diamonds and Conflict: Background, Policy, and Legislation.* Washington: Congressional Research Service, Library of Congress.

Cook, Nicolas. 2012. *Conflict Minerals in Central Africa: U.S. and International Responses.* Washington: Congressional Research Service, Library of Congress.

Coppedge, Michael, John Gerring, David Altman, Michael Bernhard, Steven Fish, Allen Hicken, Matthew Kroenig, Staffan I. Lindberg, Kelly McMann, Pamela Paxton, Holli A. Semetko, Svend-Erik Skaaninga, Jeffrey Staton, and Jan Teorella. 2011. Conceptualizing and Measuring Democracy: A New Approach. *Perspectives on Politics* 9, no. 2: 247–67.

Corden, W. M., and J. Peter Neary. 1982. Booming Sector and De-Industrialization in a Small Open Economy. *Economic Journal* 92: 825–48.

Cramer, Christopher. 2003. Does Inequality Cause Conflict? *Journal of International Development* 15, no. 4: 397–412.

Cuddington, John T. 2010. Long-Term Trends in the *Real* Real Prices of Primary Commodities: Inflation Bias and the Prebisch-Singer Hypothesis. *Resources Policy* 35: 72–76.

Cuddington, John T., and Daniel Jerrett. 2008. *Super Cycles in Real Metals Prices?* IMF Staff Paper 55: 541–65. Washington: International Monetary Fund.

Cuddington, John T., and Grant Nülle. 2013. Variable Long-Term Trends in Mineral Prices: The Ongoing Tug-of-War between Exploration, Depletion, and Technological Change. *Journal of International Money and Finance* (forthcoming).

Cuddington, John T., Rodney Ludema, and Shamila A. Jayasuriya. 2007. Prebisch-Singer Redux. In *Natural Resources: Neither Curse nor Destiny*, ed. Daniel Lederman and William F. Maloney. Stanford, CA: Stanford University Press and Washington: World Bank.

Danielsen, Dan, and David Kennedy. 2011. *Busting Bribery: Sustaining the Global Momentum of the Foreign Corrupt Practices Act*. New York: Open Society Foundations.

Darby, Sefton. 2009. *The Case for Company-by-Company Reporting of Data in the Extractive Industries Transparency Initiative*. Available at http://caspianrevenuewatch.org/images/RWI_EITI _AggDisaggReporting_Darby.pdf (accessed on July 24, 2013).

Dawe, David. 1996. A New Look at the Effects of Export Instability on Investment and Growth. *World Development* 24, no. 12: 1905–14.

DeMeritt, Jacqueline H. R., and Joseph K. Young. 2013. A Political Economy of Human Rights: Oil, Natural Gas, and State Incentives to Repress. *Conflict Management and Peace Science* 30, no. 2: 99–120.

de Soysa, Indra, and Paul Midford. 2012. Enter the Dragon! An Empirical Analysis of Chinese versus US Arms Transfers to Autocrats and Violators of Human Rights, 1989–2006. *International Studies Quarterly* 56, no. 4: 843–56.

de Soysa, Indra, Erik Gartzke, and Tove Grete Lie. 2011. Oil, Blood, and Strategy: How Petroleum Influences Interstate Conflict. Photocopy.

de Soysa, Indra, and Krishna Chaitanya Vadlamannati. 2011. Does Being Bound Together Suffocate, or Liberate? The Effects of Economic, Social, and Political Globalization on Human Rights, 1981–2005. *Kyklos* 64, no. 1: 20–53.

Deutsch, Karl W. 1961. Social Mobilization and Political Development. *American Political Science Review* 55, no. 3: 493–514.

Diamond Development Initiative. 2005. *Report on the Proceedings of the DDI Conference*. Ottawa. Available at www.ddiglobal.org/contentDocuments/accra%20report-engl.pdf (accessed on April 1, 2014).

Dobbs, Richard, Jeremy Oppenheim, Adam Kendall, Fraser Thompson, Martin Bratt, and Fransje van der Marel. 2013. *Reverse the Curse: Maximizing the Potential of Resource-Driven Economies*. McKinsey Global Institute. Available at www.mckinsey.com/insights/energy_resources _materials/reverse_the_curse_maximizing_the_potential_of_resource_driven_economies (accessed on January 9, 2014).

Downing, Brian. 1992. *Military Revolution and Political Change: Origins of Democracy and Autocracy in Early Modern Europe*. Princeton, NJ: Princeton University Press.

Downs, Erica, and Suzanne Maloney. 2011. Getting China to Sanction Iran: The Chinese-Iranian Oil Connection. *Foreign Affairs* 90: 15–21.

Dreher, Axel. 2006. Does Globalization Affect Growth? Evidence from a New Index of Globalization. *Applied Economics* 38, no. 10: 1091–110.

Dreher, Axel, and Andreas Fuchs. 2013. Rogue Aid? The Determinants of China's Aid Allocation. Photocopy.

Dreher, Axel, Martin Gassebner, and Lars H. R. Siemers. 2012. Globalization, Economic Freedom, and Human Rights. *Journal of Conflict Resolution* 56, no. 3: 516–46.

Dreher, Axel, Noel Gaston, and Pim Martens. 2008. *Measuring Globalisation: Gauging Its Consequences.* New York: Springer.

Dreher, Axel, Rainer Thiele, and Peter Nunnenkamp. 2008. Does US Aid Buy UN General Assembly Votes? A Disaggregated Analysis. *Public Choice* 136, no. 1: 139–64.

Dube, Oendrila, and Juan Vargas. 2013. Commodity Price Shocks and Civil Conflict: Evidence from Colombia. *Review of Economic Studies* 80, no. 4: 1384–421.

Easterly, William, and Ross Levine. 2003. Tropics, Germs, and Crops: How Endowments Influence Economic Development. *Journal of Monetary Economics* 50, no. 1: 3–39.

Ekeli, Thomas, and Amadou N. R. Sy. 2012. The Economics of Sovereign Wealth Funds: Lessons from Norway. In *Beyond the Resource Curse: Policies to Harness the Power of Natural Resources*, ed. Rabah Arezki, Thorvaldur Gylfason, and Amadou Sy. Washington: International Monetary Fund.

Engerman, Stanley L., and Kenneth L. Sokoloff. 1997. Factor Endowments, Institutions, and Differential Paths of Economic Growth among New World Economies: A View from Economic Historians of the United States. In *How Latin America Fell Behind*, ed. Steven Haber. Stanford, CA: Stanford University Press.

Ernst & Young. 2012. *Building Bridges: Ernst & Young's 2012 Attractiveness Survey for Africa.* Available at http://emergingmarkets.ey.com/wp-content/uploads/downloads/2012/05/attractiveness _2012_africa_v16.pdf.

Erten, Bilge, and José Antonio Ocampo. 2012. Super-Cycles of Commodity Prices since the Mid-Nineteenth Century. DESA Working Paper No. 110 (February). UN Department of Economic and Social Affairs. Available at www.un.org/esa/desa/papers/2012/wp110_2012. pdf (accessed on January 8, 2014).

Even-Zohar, Chaim. 2005. Background Paper on Macroeconomic Issues. Diamond Development Initiative, Ottawa. Available at www.pacweb.org/e/images/stories/documents/ddi-macro %20paper%202005-08.pdf (accessed on January 10, 2008).

FAO (Food and Agriculture Organization). 2012. *State of Food Insecurity in the World.* Rome.

Fajnzylber, Pablo, Daniel Lederman, and Julia Oliver. 2013. Presalt Oil Discoveries and the Long-Term Development of Brazil. *Economic Premise* 113. Washington: World Bank.

Farah, Douglas. 2004. *Blood from Stones: The Secret Financial Network of Terror.* New York: Broadway Books.

Fearon, James D. 2004. Why Do Some Civil Wars Last So Much Longer than Others? *Journal of Peace Research* 41, no. 3: 275–301.

Fearon, James D., and David D. Laitin. 2003. Ethnicity, Insurgency, and Civil War. *American Political Science Review* 97, no. 1: 75–90.

Feenstra, Robert C., Robert Inklaar, and Marcel P. Timmer. 2013. The Next Generation of the Penn World Table. Groningen Growth and Development Centre, University of Groningen. Available at www.ggdc.net/pwt (accessed on November 22, 2013).

Feld, Lars P., and Stefan Voigt. 2003. Economic Growth and Judicial Independence: Cross-Country Evidence Using a New Set of Indicators. *European Journal of Political Economy* 19, no. 3: 497-527.

Fitch Group. 2013. *Russian Oil and Gas Industry: Rising State Ownership, Less Volatility, Higher Country Risks.* New York.

Frankel, Jeffrey A. 2012a. How Can Commodity Exporters Make Fiscal and Monetary Policy Less Procyclical? In *Beyond the Resource Curse: Policies to Harness the Power of Natural Resources,* ed. Rabah Arezki, Thorvaldur Gylfason, and Amadou Sy. Washington: International Monetary Fund.

Frankel, Jeffrey A. 2012b. *The Natural Resource Curse: A Survey.* Harvard Environmental Economics Program Discussion Paper 10-21. Cambridge, MA: Kennedy School, Harvard University.

Friedman, Thomas L. 2006. The First Law of Petropolitics. *Foreign Policy* 154, no. 3: 28-36.

GAO (Government Accountability Office). 2006. *Conflict Diamonds.* Washington.

Gartzke, Erik. 2007. The Capitalist Peace. *American Journal of Political Science* 51, no. 5: 166-91.

Gelb, Alan. 2012. Economic Diversification in Resource-Rich Countries. In *Beyond the Resource Curse: Policies to Harness the Power of Natural Resources,* ed. Rabah Arezki, Thorvaldur Gylfason, and Amadou Sy. Washington: International Monetary Fund.

Gelb, Alan, and Caroline Decker. 2011. *Identification for Development: The Biometrics Revolution.* CGD Working Paper 315. Washington: Center for Global Development.

Gelb, Alan, and Stephanie Majerowicz. 2011. *Oil for Uganda—or Ugandans? Can Cash Transfers Prevent the Resource Curse?* CGD Working Paper 261. Washington: Center for Global Development.

Ghosn, Faten, Glenn Palmer, and Stuart Bremer. 2004. The MID3 Data Set, 1993-2001: Procedures, Coding Rules, and Description. *Conflict Management and Peace Science* 21, no. 2: 133-54.

Gilbert, Christopher L. 1996. International Commodity Agreements: An Obituary Notice. *World Development* 24, no. 1: 1-19.

Gillies, Alexandra. 2010. Reputational Concerns and the Emergence of Oil Sector Transparency as an International Norm. *International Studies Quarterly* 54: 103-26.

Givens, David. 2013. Defining Governance Matters: A Factor Analytic Assessment of Governance Institutions. *Journal of Comparative Economics* 41, no. 4: 1026-53.

Gleditsch, Nils Petter, Peter Wallensteen, Mikael Eriksson, Margareta Sollenberg, and Håvard Strand. 2001. Armed Conflict 1946-2001: A New Dataset. *Journal of Peace Research* 39, no. 5: 615-37.

Glezakos, Constantine. 1973. Export Instability and Economic Growth: A Statistical Verification. *Economic Development and Cultural Change* 21, no. 4, part 1: 670-78.

Glezakos, Constantine. 1983. Export Instability and Economic Growth: A Misinterpretation of the Evidence from the Western Pacific Countries. *Journal of Development Economics* 12: 229-36.

Glezakos, Constantine. 1984. Export Instability and Economic Growth: Reply. *Economic Development and Cultural Change* 32, no. 3: 615-23.

Global Witness. 1999. *Crude Awakening: The Oil and Banking Industries in Angola's Conflict.* New York. Available at www.globalwitness.org/sites/default/files/pdfs/A%20Crude%20Awakening.pdf.

Global Witness. 2010. *Return of the Blood Diamond: The Deadly Race to Control Zimbabwe's New-Found Diamond Wealth.* Washington: Global Witness Publishing Inc.

Global Witness. 2012a. *Financing a Parallel Government?* Washington: Global Witness Publishing Inc.

Global Witness. 2012b. *Global Witness Comment on SEC Conflict Minerals Rule* (August 29). Washington: Global Witness Publishing Inc.

Goodwin, Jeff. 2001. *No Other Way Out: States and Revolutionary Movements, 1945-1991.* New York: Cambridge University Press.

Goodwyn, Laurence. 1976. *Democratic Promise: The Populist Movement in America.* New York: Oxford University Press.

Grant, Andrew J., and Ian Taylor. 2004. Global Governance and Conflict Diamonds: The Kimberley Process and the Quest for Clean Gems. *Round Table* 93, no. 375: 385-40.

Greenhill, Brian. 2010. The Company You Keep: International Socialization and the Diffusion of Human Rights Norms. *International Studies Quarterly* 54, no. 1: 127-45.

Gregory, R. G. 1976. Some Aspects of Growth in the Mineral Sector. *Australian Journal of Agricultural Economics* 20: 71-91.

Grilli, Enzo R., and Maw Cheng Yang. 1988. Commodity Prices, Manufactured Goods Prices, and the Terms of Trade of Developing Countries. *World Bank Economic Review* 2: 1-48.

Grimm, Sven. 2011. *Transparency of Chinese Aid: An Analysis of the Published Information on Chinese External Aid Flows.* Stellenbosch, South Africa: Centre for Chinese Studies at Stellenbosch University.

Grossman, Eugene, and Elhanan Helpman. 1991. *Innovation and Growth in the Global Economy.* Cambridge, MA: MIT Press.

Guidolin, Massimo, and Eliana La Ferrara. 2005. *Diamonds Are Forever, Wars Are Not. Is Conflict Bad for Private Firms?* Federal Reserve Bank of St. Louis Working Paper Series 2005-004B. Available at http://research.stlouisfed.org/wp/2005/2005-004.pdf (accessed on August 21, 2006).

Gurses, Mehmet. 2009. State-Sponsored Development, Oil and Democratization. *Democratization* 16, no. 3: 508-29.

Gylfason, Thorvaldur. 2001. Natural Resources, Education, and Economic Development. *European Economic Review* 45, no. 4: 847-59.

Haber, Stephen, and Victor Menaldo. 2011. Do Natural Resources Fuel Authoritarianism? A Reappraisal of the Resource Curse. *American Political Science Review* 105, no. 1: 1-24.

Hafner-Burton, Emilie. 2009. *Forced to Be Good: Why Trade Agreements Boost Human Rights.* Ithaca, NY: Cornell University Press.

Haggard, Stephan, Jennifer Lee, and Marcus Noland. 2012. Integration in the Absence of Institutions: China-North Korea Cross-Border Exchange. *Journal of Asian Economics* 113, no. 2: 130-45.

Haggard, Stephan, and Marcus Noland. 2012. *Networks, Trust, and Trade: The Microeconomics of China–North Korea Integration.* Working Paper 12-8. Washington: Peterson Institute for International Economics.

Haggard, Stephan, and Lydia Tiede. 2011. The Rule of Law and Economic Growth: Where Are We? *World Development* 39, no. 5: 673-85.

Halper, Stefan. 2010a. Beijing's Coalition of the Willing. *Foreign Policy* (July/August): 100-102.

Halper, Stefan. 2010b. The Beijing Consensus: How China's Authoritarian Model Will Dominate the 21st Century. Speech to the World Affairs Council, Seattle, Washington, April 22.

Halper, Stefan. 2010c. *The Beijing Consensus: How China's Authoritarian Model Will Dominate the 21st Century.* New York: Basic Books. Kindle edition.

Hamilton, James D. 2008. *Understanding Crude Oil Prices.* NBER Working Paper 14492. Cambridge, MA: National Bureau of Economic Research. Available at www.nber.org/papers/w14492.pdf.

Hart Group. 2013. *Zambia Extractive Industry Transparency Initiative (EITI): Final Reconciliation Report.* Oxfordshire, UK.

Hartwick, John. 1977. Intergenerational Equity and the Investing of Rents from Exhaustible Resources. *American Economic Review* 67, no. 5: 972-74.

Harvey, Charles, and Stephen R. Lewis Jr. 1990. *Policy Choice and Development Performance in Botswana*. New York: St. Martin's Press.

Harvey, David I., Neil M. Kellard, Jakob B. Madsen, and Mark E. Wohar. 2010. The Prebisch-Singer Hypothesis: Four Centuries of Evidence. *Review of Economics and Statistics* 92, no. 2: 367-77.

Harvey, David I., Neil M. Kellard, Jakob B. Madsen, and Mark E. Wohar. 2012. Erratum: The Prebisch-Singer Hypothesis: Four Centuries of Evidence. (*Review of Economics and Statistics* 92 (2010): 367-77). Available at http://ssrn.com/abstract=2202900 (accessed on January 8, 2014).

Harvey, David I., Neil M. Kellard, Jakob B. Madsen, and Mark E. Wohar. 2013. *Trends and Cycles in Real Commodity Prices: 1650–2010*. Available at www.nottingham.ac.uk/~lezdih/commod.pdf (accessed on July 24, 2013).

Haufler, Virginia. 2010. Disclosure as Governance: The Extractive Industries Transparency Initiative and Resource Management in the Developing World. *Global Environmental Politics* 10, no. 3: 53-73.

Heger, Lindsay, and Idean Salehyan. 2007. Ruthless Rulers: Coalition Size and the Severity of Civil Conflict. *International Studies Quarterly* 51, no. 2: 385-403.

Hegre, Håvard, and Nicholas Sambanis. 2006. Sensitivity Analysis of Empirical Results on Civil War Onset. *Journal of Conflict Resolution* 50, no. 4: 508-35.

Heinrich, Andreas. 2011. Challenges of a Resource Boom: Review of the Literature. *Forschungsstelle Osteuropa Bremen Arbeitspapiere und Materialien* Nr. 114. Bremen, Germany: Forschungsstelle Osteuropa an der Universität Bremen.

Hendrix, Cullen S. 2010. Measuring State Capacity: Theoretical and Empirical Implications for the Study of Civil Conflict. *Journal of Peace Research* 47, no. 3: 273-85.

Hendrix, Cullen S. 2011. *Markets vs. Malthus: Food Security and the Global Economy*. Policy Brief 11-12. Washington: Peterson Institute for International Economics.

Hendrix, Cullen S. 2014 (forthcoming). *Oil Prices and Conflict Behavior in Oil-Exporting States*. Working Paper. Washington: Peterson Institute for International Economics.

Herbst, Jeffrey, and Greg Mills. 2006. Diamonds and Development. In *African Security, Commodities, and Development*. London: Royal United Services Institute.

Hibbs Jr., Douglas A., and Ola Olsson. 2004. Geography, Biogeography, and Why Some Countries Are Rich and Others Are Poor. *Proceedings of the National Academy of Sciences* 101, no. 10: 3715-20.

Hilson, Gavin, and Roy Maconachie. 2009. "Good Governance" and the Extractive Industries in Sub-Saharan Africa. *Mineral Processing and Extractive Metal Review* 30: 52-100.

Hufbauer, Gary Clyde. 2009. *The Alien Tort Statute of 1789: Time for a Fresh Look*. Policy Brief 09-9. Washington: Peterson Institute for International Economics.

Hughes and Hubbard. 2012. *FCPA/Anti-Bribery Alert Summer 2012*. Washington.

Human Rights Watch. 1999. *The Price of Oil: Corporate Responsibility and Human Rights Violations in Nigeria's Oil Producing Communities*. New York. Available at www.hrw.org/reports/1999/nigeria/nigeria0199.pdf.

Human Rights Watch. 2005. *Rivers and Blood: Gun, Oil and Power in Nigeria's River State*. Briefing Paper. New York. Available at www.bebor.org/wp-content/uploads/2012/09/HRW-Rivers-and-Blood-Report.pdf.

Human Rights Watch. 2013. *Zambia: Safety Gaps Threaten Copper Miners*. Available at www.hrw.org/news/2013/02/20/zambia-safety-gaps-threaten-copper-miners.

Humphreys, Macartan, Jeffrey D. Sachs, and Joseph E. Stiglitz, eds. 2007. *Escaping the Resource Curse*. New York: Columbia University Press.

Humphreys, Macartan, and Martin E. Sandbu. 2007. The Political Economy of Natural Resource Funds. In *Escaping the Resource Curse,* ed. Macartan Humphreys, Jeffrey D. Sachs, and Joseph E. Stiglitz. New York: Columbia University Press.

IEA (International Energy Agency). 2012. *World Energy Outlook.* Paris.

IEA (International Energy Agency). 2013. *World Energy Outlook.* Paris.

Iimi, Atsushi. 2006. *Did Botswana Escape from the Resource Curse?* IMF Working Paper 06/138. Washington: International Monetary Fund. Available at www.imf.org/external/pubs/ft /wp/2006/wp06138.pdf (accessed on August 21, 2006).

IISS (International Institute for Strategic Studies). 2011. *The FARC Files: Venezuela, Ecuador, and the Secret Archives of "Raúl Reyes."* London.

IMF (International Monetary Fund). 2013. Primary Commodity Index Charts. Available at www. imf.org/external/np/res/commod/index.aspx (accessed on February 2, 2013).

Information Office of the State Council of China. 2011. *China's Foreign Aid.* Beijing.

Information Office of the State Council of China. 2013. *The Diversified Employment of China's Armed Forces.* Beijing.

Inglehart, Ronald. 1997. *Modernization and Postmodernization: Cultural, Economic, and Political Change in 43 Societies.* Princeton, NJ: Princeton University Press.

International Crisis Group. 2008. China's First for Oil. *Asia Report* no. 153 (June 9).

International Rescue Committee. 2007. *Mortality in the Democratic Republic of the Congo.* Available at www.rescue.org/sites/default/files/migrated/resources/2007/2006-7_congomortalitysurvey .pdf.

Isham, Jonathan, Michael Woolcock, Lant Pritchett, and Gwen Busby. 2005. The Varieties of the Resource Experience: Natural Resource Export Structures and the Political Economy of Ecnomic Growth. *World Bank Economic Review* 19, no. 2: 141-74.

Jacks, David S., Kevin H. O'Rourke, and Jeffrey G. Williamson. 2012. *Commodity Price Volatility and World Market Integration Since 1700.* NBER Working Paper 14748. Cambridge, MA: National Bureau of Economic Research. Available at www.nber.org/papers/w14748 (accessed on February 6, 2014).

Jeanne, Olivier, Arvind Subramanian, and John Williamson. 2012. *Who Needs to Open the Capital Account?* Washington: Peterson Institute for International Economics.

Jensen, Nathan M., and Noel P. Johnston. 2011. Political Risk, Reputation, and the Resource Curse. *Comparative Political Studies* 44, no. 6: 662-88.

Johnston, David. 2007. How to Evaluate Fiscal Terms of Oil Contracts. In *Escaping the Resource Curse,* ed. Macartan Humphreys, Jeffrey D. Sachs, and Joseph E. Stiglitz. New York: Columbia University Press.

Jones, Daniel M., Stuart A. Bremer, and J. David Singer. 1996. Militarized Interstate Disputes, 1816-1992: Rationale, Coding Rules, and Empirical Patterns. *Conflict Management and Peace Science* 15, no. 2: 163-212.

Kaiser Associates Economic Development Practice. 2005. *FRIDGE: South African Diamond Valuation Project.* Cape Town: Kaiser Associates.

Karl, Terry Lynne. 1997. *The Paradox of Plenty: Oil Booms and Petro-States.* Berkeley: University of California.

Karl, Terry Lynne. 2007. Ensuring Fairness: The Case for a Transparent Fiscal Social Contract. In *Escaping the Resource Curse,* ed. Macartan Humphreys, Jeffrey D. Sachs, and Joseph E. Stiglitz. New York: Columbia University Press.

Kaufmann, Daniel, Aart Kraay, and Massimo Mastruzzi. 2010. *The Worldwide Governance Indicators: Methodology and Analytical Issues.* World Bank Policy Research Working Paper 5430. Washington: World Bank.

Kenen, Peter B., and Constantine S. Voivodas. 1972. Export Instability and Growth. *Kyklos* 25: 701–803.

Kerner, Andrew, and Jane Lawrence. 2014. What's the Risk? Bilateral Investment Treaties, Political Risk, and Fixed Capital Accumulation. *British Journal of Political Science* 44, no. 1: 107–22.

Kjøk, Åshild, and Lia Brynjar. 2001. *Terrorism and Oil—An Explosive Mixture. A Survey of Terrorist and Rebel Attacks on Petroleum Infrastructure, 1968–1999*. Kjeller, Norway: Norwegian Defense Research Establishment.

Klare, Michael T. 2002. *Resource Wars: The New Landscape of Global Conflict*. New York: Holt Paperbacks.

Klare, Michael T. 2004. *Blood and Oil: The Dangers and Consequences of America's Growing Dependence on Imported Petroleum*. New York: Holt Paperbacks.

Kleine-Ahlbrandt, Stephanie, and Andrew Small. 2008. China's New Dictatorship Diplomacy. *Foreign Affairs* 87, no. 1: 38–56.

Knudsen, Odin, and Andrew Parnes. 1975. *Trade Instability and Economic Development: An Empirical Study*. Lexington, MA: D.C. Heath.

Kolstad, Ivar, and Arne Wiig. 2009. Is Transparency the Key to Reducing Corruption in Resource-Rich Countries? *World Development* 37, no. 3: 521–32.

Kolstad, Ivar, and Arne Wiig. 2012. What Determines Chinese Outward FDI? *Journal of World Business* 47, no. 1: 26–34.

Komesaroff, Michael. 2008. China Eyes Congo's Treasures. *Far Eastern Economic Review* (April): 38–41.

Kugler, Jacek, and A. F. K. Organski. 1989. The Power Transition: A Retrospective and Prospective Evaluation. In *Handbook of War Studies*, ed. Manus Midlarsky. Boston: Unwin Hyman.

Kuralbayeva, Karlygash, and Radoslaw Stefanski. 2013. Windfalls, Structural Transformation and Specialization. *Journal of International Economics* 90, no. 2: 273–301.

Kuziemko, Ilyana, and Eric Werker. 2006. How Much Is a Seat on the Security Council Worth? Foreign Aid and Bribery at the United Nations. *Journal of Political Economy* 114, no. 5: 905–30.

Lake, David A., and Matthew A. Baum. 2001. The Invisible Hand of Democracy: Political Control and the Provision of Public Services. *Comparative Political Studies* 34, no. 6: 587–621.

Lam, N. V. 1980. Export Instability, Expansion, and Market Concentration: A Methodological Interpretation. *Journal of Development Economics* 7: 99–115.

Leamer, Edward E. 1987. Paths of Development in the Three-Factor *n*-Good General Equilibrium Model. *Journal of Political Economy* 95, no. 5: 961–99.

Leamer, Edward E., Hugo Maul, Sergio Rodriguez, and Peter K. Schott. 1999. Does Natural Resource Abundance Increase Latin American Income Inequality? *Journal of Development Economics* 59: 3–42.

Leblang, David. 1996. Property Rights, Democracy, and Economic Growth. *Political Research Quarterly* 49, no. 1: 5–26.

Lederman, Daniel, and William F. Maloney, eds. 2007. *Natural Resources: Neither Curse nor Destiny*. Stanford, CA: Stanford University Press and Washington: World Bank.

Lessard, Donald R., and John Williamson. 1985. *Financial Intermediation Beyond the Debt Crisis*. Washington: Institute for International Economics.

Levi, Margaret. 1988. *Of Rule and Revenue*. Berkeley: University of California Press.

Levi, Margaret. 1997. *Consent, Dissent, and Patriotism*. New York: Cambridge University Press.

Lipset, Seymour Martin. 1955. Some Social Requisites of Democracy: Economic Development and Political Legitimacy. *American Political Science Review* 53, no. 1: 69–105.

Lujala, Päivi. 2010. The Spoils of Nature: Armed Civil Conflict and Rebel Access to Natural Resources. *Journal of Peace Research* 47, no. 1: 15-28.

Lujala, Päivi, Nils Petter Gleditsch, and Elisabeth Gilmore. 2005. A Diamond Curse? Civil War and a Lootable Resource. *Journal of Conflict Resolution* 49, no. 4: 538-62.

Luong, Pauline Jones, and Erika Weinthal. 2001. Prelude to the Resource Curse: Explaining Oil and Gas Development Strategies in the Soviet Successor States and Beyond. *Comparative Political Studies* 34, no. 4: 367-99.

Luong, Pauline Jones, and Erika Weinthal. 2010. *Oil Is Not a Curse: Ownership Structure and Institutions in Soviet Successor States.* Cambridge: Cambridge University Press.

Lutz, Matthias. 1994. The Effects of Volatility in the Terms of Trade on Output Growth: New Evidence. *World Development* 22, no. 12: 1959-75.

MacBean, Alasdair I. 1966. *Export Instability and Economic Development.* Cambridge, MA: Harvard University Press.

Madison, James (as *Publius*). 1799. Federalist Paper #51. *The Federalist: A Collection of Essays Written in Favor of the New Constitution, as Agreed upon by the Federal Convention, September 17, 1787.* New York: John Tiebout.

Magud, Nicolás, and Sebastián Sosa. 2010. *When and Why Worry about Real Exchange Rate Appreciation? The Missing Link between Dutch Disease and Growth.* IMF Working Paper WP/10/271. Washington: International Monetary Fund.

Mankiw, N. Gregory, David Romer, and David N. Weil. 1992. A Contribution to the Empirics of Economic Growth. *Quarterly Journal of Economics* 107, no. 2: 407-37.

Mansfield, Edward D., and Jon C. Pevehouse. 2008. Democratization and Varieties of International Organizations. *Journal of Conflict Resolution* 52, no. 2: 269-94.

Marciano, Sonia, Michael E. Porter, and Alyson Warhurst. 2006. *De Beers: Addressing the New Competitiveness Challenges.* Boston: Harvard Business School Publishing.

Marshall, Monty J., Keith Jaggers, and Ted Robert Gurr. 2011. Polity IV Project: Political Regime Characteristics and Transitions, 1800-2010. Version p4v2010. College Park, MD: University of Maryland.

Martin, Lisa L. 1992. *Coercive Cooperation: Explaining Multilateral Economic Sanctions.* Princeton, NJ: Princeton University Press.

Martin, Lisa L. 1993. Credibility, Costs, and Institutions: Cooperation on Economic Sanctions. *World Politics* 45, no. 3: 406-32.

Marx, Karl. 1859. *A Contribution to the Critique of Political Economy.* Moscow: Progress Publishers.

Matsuyama, Kiminori. 1992. Agricultural Productivity, Comparative Advantage, and Economic Growth. *Journal of Economic Theory* 58: 317-34.

McGuire, Martin C., and Mancur Olson. 1996. The Economics of Autocracy and Majority Rule: The Invisible Hand and the Use of Force. *Journal of Economic Literature* 34, no. 1: 72-96.

Mehlum, Halvor, Karl Moene, and Ragnar Torvik. 2006. Institutions and the Resource Curse. *Economic Journal* 116, no. 508: 1-20.

Menaldo, Victor. 2013. *Not Manna from Heaven After All: The Endogeneity of Oil.* Available at http://ssrn.com/abstract=2008889.

Michel, Serge, and Michel Beuret. 2009. *China Safari: On the Trail of Beijing's Expansion in Africa.* New York: Basic Books.

Miguel, Edward, Shanker Satyanath, and Ernest Sergenti. 2004. Economic Shocks and Civil Conflict: An Instrumental Variables Approach. *Journal of Political Economy* 112, no. 4: 725-53.

Morán, Christián. 1983. Export Fluctuation and Economic Growth: An Empirical Analysis. *Journal of Development Economics* 12: 195-218.

Moran, Theodore H. 2010. *China's Strategy to Secure Natural Resources: Risks, Dangers, and Opportunities*. Policy Analyses in International Economics 92. Washington: Peterson Institute for International Economics.

Moran, Theodore H. 2012. An Assessment of the Requirement that Oil, Gas and Mining Companies Registered with the US Securities and Exchange Commission Publish How Much They Pay to Governments Where They Operate. Photocopy.

Moran, Theodore H. 2013a. *Avoiding the "Resource Curse" in Mongolia*. Policy Brief 13-18. Washington: Peterson Institute for International Economics.

Moran, Theodore H. 2013b. *Reform EITI to Require Compliant Countries to Publish Disaggregated Company-by-Company Revenue Payments*. Available at www.cgdev.org/sites/default/files /Draft%20CGD%20Policy%20Paper%20-%20EITI%20-%20Moran_.pdf (accessed on July 24, 2013).

Moran, Theodore H., Barbara R. Kotschwar, and Julia Muir. 2011. Do Chinese Mining Companies Exploit More? *Americas Quarterly* (Fall): 48-57.

Moran, Theodore H., Barbara R. Kotschwar, and Julia Muir. 2012. *Chinese Investment in Latin American Resources: The Good, the Bad, and the Ugly*. Working Paper 12-3. Washington: Peterson Institute for International Economics.

Morrison, Kevin M. 2009. Oil, Non-Tax Revenue, and the Redistributive Foundations of Regime Stability. *International Organization* 63, no. 1: 107-38.

Moss, Todd, and Stephanie Majerowicz. 2013. *Oil-to-Cash Won't Work Here! Ten Common Objections*. CGD Policy Paper 024. Washington: Center for Global Development.

Moyo, Dambisa. 2012. *Winner Take All: China's Race for Resources and What It Means for Us*. New York: Basic Books. Kindle edition.

Munck, Gerardo L., and Jay Verkuilen. 2002. Conceptualizing and Measuring Democracy: Evaluating Alternative Indices. *Comparative Political Studies* 35, no. 1: 5-34.

Murdoch, James C., and Todd Sandler. 2002. Economic Growth, Civil Wars, and Spatial Spillovers. *Journal of Conflict Resolution* 46, no. 1: 91-110.

Murphy, Martin N. 2007. The Blue, Green, and Brown: Insurgency and Counter-Insurgency on the Water. *Contemporary Security Policy* 28, no. 1: 63-79.

Murray, David. 1978. Export Earnings Instability: Price, Quantity, Supply, Demand? *Economic Development and Cultural Change* 26: 61-73.

Musgrave, Richard A. 1969. *Fiscal Systems*. New Haven, CT: Yale University Press.

Naím, Moisés. 2007. Rogue Aid. *Foreign Policy* (March 1).

Neary, J. Peter, and Sweder van Wijnbergen. 1986. Natural Resources and the Macroeconomy: A Theoretical Framework. In *Natural Resources and the Macroeconomy*, ed. J. Peter Neary and Sweder van Wijnbergen. Cambridge, MA: MIT Press.

Nelson, Joan M. 2007. Elections, Democracy, and Social Services. *Studies in Comparative International Development* 41, no. 4: 79-97.

Noland, Marcus. 1997. Has Asian Export Behavior Been Unique? *Journal of International Economics* 43: 79-101.

Noland, Marcus. 2008a. Explaining Middle Eastern Authoritarianism I: The Level of Democracy. *Review of Middle East Economics and Finance* 4, no. 1: 1-30.

Noland, Marcus. 2008b. Explaining Middle Eastern Authoritarianism II: Democratizing Transitions. *Review of Middle East Economics and Finance* 4, no. 2: 31-40.

Noland, Marcus, and Howard Pack. 2003. *Industrial Policy in an Era of Globalization: Lessons from Asia*. Washington: Institute for International Economics.

Noland, Marcus, and J. Brooks Spector. 2006. *The Stuff of Legends: Diamonds and Development in Southern Africa*. Parktown, South Africa: Business Leadership South Africa.

North, Douglass, and Barry Weingast. 1989. Constitutions and Commitment: The Evolution of Institutions Governing Public Choice in Seventeenth Century England. *Journal of Economic History* 49, no. 4: 803-32.

Nugent, Jeffrey B., and Pan A. Yotopoulos. 1976. *Economics of Development: Empirical Investigations*. New York: Harper and Row.

Nurkse, Ragnar. 1958. Trade Fluctuations and Buffer Policies of Low-Income Countries. *Kyklos* 11, no. 2: 141-54.

OECD (Organization for Economic Cooperation and Development). 2010. International Development Statistics: Other Official Flows. Paris. Available at http://stats.oecd.org.

OECD (Organization for Economic Cooperation and Development). 2012a. *DAC Glossary of Key Terms and Concepts*. Paris.

OECD (Organization for Economic Cooperation and Development). 2012b. *Uranium 2011: Resources, Production and Demand (the Red Book)*. A Joint Report by the OECD Nuclear Energy Agency and the International Atomic Energy Agency. Paris. Available at http://www.oecd-nea.org/ndd/pubs/2012/7059-uranium-2011.pdf.

OECD (Organization for Economic Cooperation and Development). 2013a. *Downstream Implementation of the OECD Due Diligence Guidance for the Responsible Supply Chains of Minerals from Conflict-Affected and High-Risk Areas*. Paris.

OECD (Organization for Economic Cooperation and Development). 2013b. *Upstream Implementation of the OECD Due Diligence Guidance for the Responsible Supply Chains of Minerals from Conflict-Affected and High-Risk Areas*. Paris.

Olsson, Ola. 2006. Diamonds Are a Rebel's Best Friend. *World Economy* 29, no. 8: 1133-50.

Oneal, John R., Bruce Russett, and Michael L. Berbaum. 2003. Causes of Peace: Democracy, Interdependence, and International Organizations, 1885-1992. *International Studies Quarterly* 47, no. 2: 371-93.

Østby, Gudrun. 2008. Polarization, Horizontal Inequalities and Violent Civil Conflict. *Journal of Peace Research* 45, no. 2: 143-62.

Østby, Gudrun, Ragnhild Nordås, and Jan Ketil Rød. 2009. Regional Inequalities and Civil Conflict in Sub-Saharan Africa. *International Studies Quarterly* 53, no. 2: 301-24.

Ottaway, Marina, and Michele Dunne. 2007. *Incumbent Regimes and the "King's Dilemma" in the Arab World: Promise and Threat of Managed Reform*. Carnegie Papers Middle East Program No. 88. Washington: Carnegie Endowment for International Peace.

Özler, Sule, and James Harrigan. 1988. Export Instability and Growth. Department of Economics Working Paper No. 486. Los Angeles: University of California.

Partnership Africa Canada. 2010. *Diamonds and Clubs: The Militarized Control of Diamonds and Power in Zimbabwe*. Ottawa.

Pegg, Scott. 2005. Can Policy Intervention Beat the Resource Curse? Evidence from the Chad-Cameroon Pipeline Project. *African Affairs* 105/418: 1-25.

Peretto, Pietro F. 2012. Resource Abundance, Growth and Welfare: A Schumpeterian Perspective. *Journal for Development Economics* 97, no. 1: 142-55.

Posen, Barry R., Barry Rubin, James M. Lindsay, and Ray Takeyh. 2010. Containment Conundrum: How Dangerous Is a Nuclear Iran? *Foreign Affairs* 89: 160-68.

Powell, Andrew. 1991. Commodity and Developing Countries Terms of Trade: What Does the Long Run Show? *Economic Journal* 101: 1485-96.

Prebisch, Raúl. 1950. The Economic Development of Latin America and Its Principal Problems. *Economic Bulletin for Latin America* 7, no. 1: 1-22.

Rabasa, Angel, and Peter Chalk. 2001. *The Colombian Labyrinth: The Synergy of Drugs and Insurgency and Its Implications for Regional Stability*. Santa Monica, CA: RAND.

Ramasamy, Bala, Matthew Yeung, and Sylvie Laforet. 2012. China's Outward Foreign Direct Investment: Location Choice and Firm Ownership. *Journal of World Business* 47, no. 1: 17-25.

Ramsay, Kristopher K. 2011. Revisiting the Resource Curse: Natural Disasters, the Price of Oil, and Democracy. *International Organization* 65, no. 3: 507-29.

Reuter, Peter, and Edwin M. Truman. 2004. *Chasing Dirty Money: The Fight against Money Laundering.* Washington: Institute for International Economics.

Risse, Thomas, and Kathryn Sikkink. 1999. The Socialization of International Human Rights Norms into Domestic Practices. In *The Power of Human Rights: International Norms and Domestic Change,* ed. Stephen C. Ropp and Kathryn Sikkink. New York: Cambridge University Press.

Roache, Shaun K. 2012. *China's Impact on World Commodity Markets.* IMF Working Paper WP/12/115. Washington: International Monetary Fund.

Robinson, James A., and Ragnar Torvik. 2005. White Elephants. *Journal of Public Economics* 89, no. 2: 197-210.

Robinson, James A., Ragnar Torvik, and Thierry Verdier. 2006. Political Foundations of the Resource Curse. *Journal of Development Economics* 79, no. 2: 447-68.

Rodríguez, Francisco, and Jeffrey D. Sachs. 1999. Why Do Resource-Abundant Economies Grow More Slowly? *Journal of Economic Growth* 4: 277-303.

Rodrik, Dani, Arvind Subramanian, and Francesco Trebbi. 2004. Institutions Rule: The Primacy of Institutions over Geography and Integration in Economic Development. *Journal of Economic Growth* 9, no. 2: 131-65.

Rogoff, Kenneth, and Carmen Reinhart. 2003. *FDI to Africa: The Role of Price Stability and Currency Instability.* IMF Working Paper 03/10. Washington: International Monetary Fund.

Root, Hilton L. 1989. Tying the King's Hands. *Rationality and Society* 1, no. 2: 240-58.

Rose, Paul. 2012. *State Capitalism and the Foreign Corrupt Practices Act.* Working Paper Series No. 176. Columbus, OH: Ohio State University Moritz College of Law.

Rose-Ackerman, Susan. 2010. *The Law and Economics of Bribery.* John M. Olin Center for Studies in Law, Economics, and Public Policy Research Paper 408. New Haven, CT: Yale Law School.

Ross, Michael L. 2001. Does Oil Hinder Democracy? *World Politics* 53, no. 3: 325-61.

Ross, Michael L. 2004a. How Do Natural Resources Influence Civil War? Evidence from Thirteen Cases. *International Organization* 58, no. 1: 35-67.

Ross, Michael L. 2004b. What Do We Know about Natural Resources and War? *Journal of Peace Research* 41, no. 3: 337-56.

Ross, Michael L. 2004c. Does Taxation Lead to Representation? *British Journal of Political Science* 34, no 2: 229-49.

Ross, Michael L. 2006. A Closer Look at Oil, Diamonds, and Civil War. *Annual Review of Political Science* 9: 265-300.

Ross, Michael L. 2007. How Mineral Rich States Can Reduce Inequality. In *Escaping the Resource Curse,* ed. Macartan Humphreys, Jeffrey D. Sachs, and Joseph E. Stiglitz. New York: Columbia University Press.

Ross, Michael L. 2012. *The Oil Curse: How Petroleum Wealth Shapes the Development of Nations.* Princeton, NJ: Princeton University Press.

Ross, Michael L., and Erik Voeten. 2011. Unbalanced Globalization in the Oil Exporting States. Photocopy.

Rueschemeyer, Dietrich, Evelyne Huber Stephens, and John D. Stephens. 1992. *Capitalist Development and Democracy.* Chicago: University of Chicago.

Russett, Bruce, John R. Oneal, and David R. Davis. 1998. The Third Leg of the Kantian Tripod for Peace: International Organizations and Militarized Disputes, 1950-85. *International Organization* 52, no. 3: 441-67.

Sachs, Jeffery D. 2007. How to Handle the Macroeconomics of Oil Wealth. In *Escaping the Resource Curse*, ed. Macartan Humphreys, Jeffrey D. Sachs, and Joseph E. Stiglitz. New York: Columbia University Press.

Sachs, Jeffrey D., and Andrew M. Warner. 1997. *Natural Resource Abundance and Economic Growth*. Cambridge, MA: Harvard University.

Sachs, Jeffrey D., and Andrew M. Warner. 2001. The Curse of Natural Resources. *European Economic Review* 45, no. 5-6: 827-38.

Sala-i-Martin, Xavier, Gernot Doppelhofer, and Ronald I. Miller. 2004. Determinants of Long-run Growth: A Bayesian Averaging of Classical Estimates (BACE) Approach. *American Economic Review* 94, no. 4: 813-35.

Sala-i-Martin, Xavier, and Arvind Subramanian. 2003. *Addressing the Natural Resource Curse: An Illustration from Nigeria*. IMF Working Paper WP/03. Washington: International Monetary Fund. Available at http://ideas.repec.org/p/nbr/nberwo/9804.html (accessed on January 10, 2008).

Sampson, Anthony. 1991. *The Seven Sisters: The Great Oil Companies and the World They Shaped*. New York: Bantam.

Sanyal, Rajib. 2012. Patterns in International Bribery: Violations of the Foreign Corrupt Practices Act. *Thunderbird International Business Review* 54, no. 3: 299-309.

Sapsford, David. 1985. The Statistical Debate on the Net Terms of Trade between Primary Commodities and Manufactures: A Comment and Some Additional Evidence. *Economic Journal* 95: 781-88.

Savvides, Andreas. 1984. Export Instability and Economic Growth: Some New Evidence. *Economic Development and Cultural Change* 32, no. 3: 607-14.

Schenk C. J., T. A. Cook, R. R. Charpentier, R. M. Pollastro, T. R. Klett, M. E. Tennyson, M. A. Kirschbaum, M. E. Brownfield, and J. K. Pitman. 2009. *An Estimate of Recoverable Heavy Oil Resources of the Orinoco Oil Belt, Venezuela*. US Geological Survey Fact Sheet 2009-3028. Washington: US Geological Survey.

Scott, James C. 1998. *Seeing Like a State: How Certain Schemes to Improve the Human Condition Have Failed*. New Haven: Yale University Press.

Seay, Laura E. 2012. *What's Wrong with Dodd-Frank 1502?* Working Paper 284. Washington: Center for Global Development.

Shabsigh, Ghiath, and Nadeem Ilahi. 2007. *Looking beyond the Fiscal: Do Oil Funds Bring Macroeconomic Stability?* IMF Working Paper WP/07/96. Washington: International Monetary Fund.

Shafer, D. Michael. 1994. *Winners and Losers: How Sectors Shape the Development Prospects of States*. Ithaca, NY: Cornell University.

Shahnawaz, Sheikh, and Jeffrey B. Nugent. 2004. Is Natural Resource Wealth Compatible with Good Governance. *Review of Middle East Economics and Finance* 2, no. 3: 1-33.

Shankleman, Jill. n.d. *Going Global: Chinese Oil and Mining Companies and the Governance of Resource Wealth*. Washington: Woodrow Wilson International Center for Scholars.

Shannon, Megan. 2009. Preventing War and Providing the Peace? International Organizations and the Management of Territorial Disputes. *Conflict Management and Peace Science* 26, no. 2: 144-63.

Simmons, Matthew R. 2005. *Twilight in the Desert: The Coming Saudi Oil Shock and the World Economy*. Hoboken, NJ: John Wiley & Sons.

Simmons, Matthew R. 2007. *Another Nail in the Coffin of the Case against Peak Oil.* White Paper, Simmons & Company International, Houston. Available at www.simmonsco-intl.com (accessed on January 9, 2008).

Singer, H. W. 1950. U.S. Foreign Investment in Underdeveloped Areas: The Distribution of Gains between Investing and Borrowing Countries. *American Economic Review, Papers and Proceedings* 40: 473–85.

SIPRI (Stockholm International Peace Research Institute). 2013. *SIPRI Yearbook 2013: Armaments, Disarmament, and International Security.* London, UK: Oxford University Press.

Smillie, Ian. 2005. *Background Paper on Micro Development Issues.* Ottawa: Diamond Development Initiative.

Smillie, Ian. 2010. *Assessment of the Kimberley Process I Enhancing Formalization of Certification in the Diamond Industry: Problems and Opportunities.* Deutsche Gesellschaft für Internationale Zusammenarbeit (GIZ). Available at www.ddiglobal.org/login/Upload/Ian-Smillie-GIZ -Kimberley-Process-Problems-and-Opportunities-2011.pdf (accessed on January 9, 2014).

Smith, Benjamin. 2004. Oil Wealth and Regime Survival in the Developing World, 1960–1999. *American Journal of Political Science* 48, no. 2: 232–46.

Solow, Robert M. 1956. A Contribution to the Theory of Economic Growth. *Quarterly Journal of Economics* 70, no. 1: 65–94.

Solow, Robert M. 1974. Intergenerational Equity and Exhaustible Resources. *Review of Economic Studies, Symposium on the Economics of Exhaustible Resources* 41: 29–45.

Spar, Debora L. 2006. Continuity and Change in the International Diamond Market. *Journal of Economic Perspectives* 20, no. 3: 195–208.

Spraos, John. 1980. The Statistical Debate on the Net Barter Terms of Trade. *Economic Journal* 90: 107–28.

Strange, Austin M., Vijaya Ramachandran, Julie Walz, Brad Parks, Michael Tierney, Axel Dreher, and Andreas Fuchs. 2013a. *China's "Aid" to Africa: A Media-Based Approach to Data Collection.* Working Paper. Washington: Center for Global Development.

Strange, Austin M., Brian O'Donnell, Daniel Gamboa, Bradley Parks, and Charles Perla. 2013b. AidData's Methodology for Tracking Underreported Financial Flows, version 1.1. Photocopy.

Svedberg, Peter, and John Tilton. 2006. The *Real* Real Price of Nonrenewable Resources: Copper 1870–2000. *World Development* 34, no. 3: 501–19.

Svedberg, Peter, and John Tilton. 2011. Long-Term Trends in the *Real* Real Prices of Primary Commodities: Inflation Bias and the Prebisch-Singer Hypothesis. *Resources Policy* 36, no. 1: 91–93.

Tan, Gerald. 1983. Export Instability, Export Growth, GDP Growth. *Journal of Development Economics* 12: 219–27.

Tanzi, Vito. 1991. *Public Finance in Developing Countries.* Aldershot, NY: Edward Elgar.

Taylor, Ian, and Gladys Mokhawa. 2003. Not Forever: Botswana, Conflict Diamonds and the Bushmen. *African Affairs* 102: 261–83.

Thirlwall, A. P., and J. Bergevin. 1985. Trends, Cycles, and Asymmetry in the Terms of Trade. *World Development* 13: 805–17.

Thompson, William R. 2001. Identifying Rivals and Rivalries in World Politics. *International Studies Quarterly* 45, no. 4: 557–86.

Tilly, Charles. 1975. Reflections on the History of European State-Making. In *The Formation of National States in Western Europe*, ed. Charles Tilly and Gabriel Ardant. Princeton, NJ: Princeton University Press.

Tilton, John E. 2013. The Terms of Trade Debate and the Policy Implications for Primary Product Producers. *Resources Policy* 38: 196–203.

Tørhaug, Magne. 2006. Petroleum Supply Vulnerability Due to Terrorism at North Sea Oil and Gas Infrastructures. In *Protection of Civilian Infrastructure from Acts of Terrorism*, ed. Konstantin V. Frolov and Gregory B. Baecher. Dordrecht: Springer.

Truman, Edwin M. 2010. *Sovereign Wealth Funds: Threat or Salvation?* Washington: Peterson Institute for International Economics.

Tsani, Stella. 2013. Natural Resources, Governance, and Institutional Quality: The Role of Resource Funds. *Resources Policy* 38: 181-95.

Tsui, Kevin K. 2011. More Oil, Less Democracy: Evidence from Worldwide Crude Oil Discoveries. *Economic Journal* 121, no. 551: 89-115.

Ulfelder, Jay. 2007. Natural-Resource Wealth and the Survival of Autocracy. *Comparative Political Studies* 40, no. 8: 995-1018.

UN (United Nations). 1952. *Instability in Export Markets of Underdeveloped Countries*. New York.

UN (United Nations). 2001. *Report of the Panel of Experts on the Illegal Exploitation of Natural Resources and Other Forms of Wealth of the Democratic Republic of Congo*. Report S/2001/357 (April 12). New York.

UN Office on Drugs and Crime. 2012. *World Drug Report*. New York.

USBM (US Bureau of Mines) and USGS (US Geological Survey). 1980. *Principles of a Resource/ Reserve Classification for Minerals*. Geological Survey Circular 831. Washington: Department of the Interior.

USEIA (US Energy Information Administration). 2011. *International Energy Outlook 2011*. Washington.

USEIA (US Energy Information Administration). 2012. *International Energy Outlook 2012*. Washington.

USEIA (US Energy Information Administration). 2013. Sanctions Reduced Iran's Oil Exports and Revenues in 2012. *Today in Energy*. Washington. Available at www.eia.gov/todayinenergy/detail.cfm?id=11011#.

USGS (US Geological Survey). 2000. *Minerals Yearbook, Volume I: Metals and Minerals*. Washington: Department of the Interior.

USGS (US Geological Survey). 2012a. *Mineral Commodity Summaries 2012*. Washington: Department of the Interior.

USGS (US Geological Survey). 2012b. *Minerals Yearbook, Volume I: Metals and Minerals*. Washington: Department of the Interior.

van der Ploeg, Frederick. 2006. *Challenges and Opportunities for Resource Rich Economies*. CEPR Discussion Paper 5688. London: Centre for Economic Policy Research. Available at http://econpapers.repec.org/paper/cprceprdp/5688.htm (accessed on January 10, 2008).

van der Ploeg, Frederick, and Steve Poelhekke. 2008. *Volatility and the Natural Resource Curse*. OxCarre Research Paper no. 2008-03. Oxford: Department of Economics, Oxford University.

van Oranje, Mabel, and Henry Parham. 2009. *Publishing What We Learned*. Available at www.publishwhatyoupay.org.

Verleger, Philip K., Jr. 2012. *Using US Strategic Reserves to Moderate Potential Oil Price Increases from Sanctions on Iran*. Policy Brief 12-6. Washington: Peterson Institute for International Economics.

Vicente, Pedro C. 2010. Does Oil Corrupt? Evidence from a Natural Experiment in West Africa. *Journal of Development Economics* 92, no. 1: 28-38.

Wang, Hongying, and Erik French. 2013. China's Participation in Global Governance from a Comparative Perspective. *Asia Policy* 15: 89-114.

Weil, David N. 2007. Accounting for the Effect of Health on Economic Growth. *Quarterly Journal of Economics* 122, no. 3: 1265-306.

Weingast, Barry R. 1997. The Political Foundations of Democracy and the Rule of Law. *American Political Science Review* 92, no. 2: 245–63.

Weinthal, Erika, and Pauline Jones Luong. 2006. Combating the Resource Curse: An Alternative Solution to Managing Mineral Wealth. *Perspectives on Politics* 4, no. 1: 35–53.

Weismann, Miriam F. 2008. The Foreign Corrupt Practices Act: The Failure of the Self-Regulatory Model of Corporate Governance in the Global Business Environment. *Journal of Business Ethics* 88: 615–61.

Weiss, Daniel J., Jackie Weidman, and Rebecca Leber. 2012. *Big Oil's Banner Year: Higher Prices, Record Profits, Less Oil* (February 7). Washington: Center for American Progress.

Wexler, Pamela. 2006. *An Independent Commissioned Review Evaluating the Effectiveness of the Kimberley Process*. Washington: Global Witness Publishing.

Williamson, John. 2012. Is the Beijing Consensus Dominant? *Asia Policy* 13, no. 1: 1–16.

Wimberley, Laura H. 2007. *Pyrrhic Peace: Governance Costs and the Utility of War*. PhD dissertation, Department of Political Science, University of California, San Diego. Ann Arbor: ProQuest /UMI.

Wong, Chung Ming. 1986. Models of Export Instability and Empirical Tests for Less-Developed Countries. *Journal of Development Economics* 20, no. 2: 263–85.

World Bank. 2006. *Where Is the Wealth of Nations? Measuring Capital for the 21st Century*. Washington.

World Bank. 2011a. *The Changing Wealth of Nations: Measuring Sustainable Development in the New Millennium*. Washington.

World Bank. 2011b. *World Development Report 2011*. Washington.

World Bank. 2013. *World Development Indicators 2013*. Washington.

Wright, Clive. 2004. Tackling Conflict Diamonds: The Kimberley Process Certification Scheme. *International Peacekeeping* 11, no. 4: 697–708.

Yamada, Hiroshi, and Gawon Yoon. 2013. When Grilli and Yang meet Prebisch and Singer: Piecewise Linear Trends in Primary Commodity Prices. *Journal of International Money and Finance* (forthcoming).

Zarate, Juan Carlos. 2005. Testimony before the House Financial Services Committee Subcommittee on Oversight and Investigations, US Congress, Washington, February 16. Available at www.treasury.gov/press/releases/js2256.htm (accessed on August 21, 2006).

Index

diamonds, 45
    high-income American consumers demand
        for, 93
    illegal military involvement in mining, 43
    industrial uses, 92
    primary deposits and political stability, 47
    regulating and tracking system, 99
    in United States, 117
    and violent political conflict, 6
Dodd-Frank Act (US), 39n, 91, 103, 115
    Section 1502, 112-13
    Section 1504, 106
downstream resource-based industry, policies
    to promote, 22
Dubai Diamond Exchange, 117
due diligence rules, on exploration licenses
    allocation, 101
Dutch disease, 20-23, 138, 139
    challenges in economies prone to, 22
Dutch Shell, Bonga platform, attack on, 45n

economic diversity, and conflict, 48
economic growth
    democracy indirect effects on, 28
    natural resources and, 2
economic inequality, and civil conflict, 48
economic integration, mined commodity
    exports and, 52
Ecuador, 58
    total goods exports in commodity basket,
        15t
education, rates of return on, 19
Egypt, food subsidies rollback, 67
Eisenhower, Dwight, 90
EITI, 6, 101-09. See also Extractive Industries
    Transparency Initiative (EITI)
embargos, 55
emeralds, role in conflict, 116
energy
    expenditures on natural gas exploration,
        56
    exploration by weak states, 39
    KOF Index of Political Globalization
        scores for exporters, 65f
    United States' relative decline as importer,
        70
    US foreign policy and, 90
Energy Africa, 53
Energy Security through Transparency Act
    (ESTTA), 106
Enough Project, 112
Equatorial Guinea
    development finance from China, 83t
    EITI and, 104

Ethiopia, development finance from China,
    83t
ethnic diversity, and conflict, 48
European Union, EITI regulations, 106
exchange rate policy, 138-40
exchange rates, 139
    appreciation, 21
exporting states, aspirations of, 5
exports, countries most specialized with
    secularly declining prices, 15t
extraction
    Chinese investment in, 77
    specialization in, 2
Extractive Industries Transparency Initiative
    (EITI), 5, 91, 101-09, 116, 125
    compliant countries, 103n
    components, 103
    market structure, 105
    stakeholder body, 104
ExxonMobil, 29, 40, 51, 57, 77, 106, 107
    EITI and, 105

FARC (Fuerzas Armadas Revolucionarias de
    Colombia), 43
    Chávez support of, 54
Fatal Transactions campaign, 93
financing, for diggers, 99
fiscal policy
    approaches to managing instability, 132
    in commodity-exporting countries, 17
    rules, 133-34
    vs. SWFs, 135
force, international norms regarding use of,
    59
Foreign Corrupt Practices Act (FCPA), 107
foreign exchange market, intervening in, 139
The Foreign Petroleum Policy of the United
    States, 90
foreign producers, contracts between host
    governments and, 130
France
    arms transfers, 86, 87f
    military spending per capita, 61t
    as oil importer, 66
    share of natural capital in total wealth, 11t
Friedman's First Law of Petropolitics, 31, 62
Fuerzas Armadas Revolucionarias de Colom-
    bia (FARC), 43
    Chávez support of, 54
Fund for Peace, Failed States Index, 34

Gabon, 142
    carbon dioxide emissions per capita, 80
    EITI and, 104

Libya, 4, 33
  growth in proven petroleum reserves, 2000-2011, 49t
Luxembourg, share of natural capital in total wealth, 11t

M23 (rebel movement), 111
Macao, China, share of natural capital in total wealth, 11t
macroeconomic approaches to managing instability, 132-43
  direct disbursement of resource rents, 136-37
  direct or lump-sum distribution, 136-38
  exchange rate policy, 138-40
  fiscal policy approaches, 132
  fiscal policy rules, 133-34
  natural resources and sovereign wealth funds, 134-36
  political economy considerations, 140-43
Malawi, 14
  exports, 127
  total goods exports in commodity basket, 15t
Mali, EITI and, 103
Malthusian argument, of exhaustion, 11n
Mauritania, development finance from China, 83t
Mauritius, total goods exports in commodity basket, 15t
Medvedev, Dmitry, rise to power, 64
MEND (Movement for the Emancipation of the Niger Delta), 43, 45n, 110
metal price index, 1980-2013, 3f
metals, prices, 6
microeconomic approaches to managing instability, 128-30
Microsoft, 112
Middle East, demand for diamonds, 98
militarized disputes, 59
  and oil prices, 63f
military spending
  in oil-exporting countries, 32
  per capita 2000-2011, top ten countries, 61t
mined commodities, exports and economic integration, 52
mineral rents
  defined, 52n
  per capita, 52
mineral wealth
  and Chinese ODF, 84
  measuring, 148
  and respect for human rights, 32, 33f

minerals
  certification process, 6
  changes in estimates, 77, 78t
  private ownership vs. state ownership, 140-43
mining
  corporate vs. artisanal, 47
  environmental costs, 42
  mobilization for war, state development and, 35
Mobutu Sese Seko, 111
modernization effect, and democracy, 33
Mongolia
  EITI and, 103
  energy and mineral reserves, 2
  Oyu Tolgoi copper mine, 129
Montreal Protocol, 59
Morales, Evo, 51
Morocco, world rock phosphate reserves, 52
Motorola, 112
Movement for the Emancipation of the Niger Delta (MEND), 43, 45n, 110
Mozambique
  development finance from China, 83t
  energy and mineral reserves, 2
Mugabe, Robert, 96
multilateral aid agencies, proposed emphasis, 127
multinational corporation, political influence of home-country government, 142
Myanmar, 123, 137
  China and, 5, 125
  energy and mineral reserves, 2
  rubies role in conflict, 116
Myitzone Dam project, 123

Namibia, talks on international certification scheme, 94
National Association of Manufacturers, 113
national wealth, share of natural capital in, 19n
nationalization of oil, 29
NATO (North Atlantic Treaty Organization), 4, 66
natural capital, 23
  dependence on, 48, 50
natural gas reserves, changes in estimates, 77, 78t
natural resource exporters, militarized disputes of, 59
natural resource funds (NRFs), 134
natural resource rents
  allocation, and political power, 133
  channeling, 132

Other Publications from the Peterson Institute for International Economics

WORKING PAPERS

14-10 Wages and Labor Market Slack: Making the Dual Mandate Operational David G. Blanchflower and Adam S. Posen

14-11 Managing Myanmar's Resource Boom to Lock in Reforms Cullen S. Hendrix and Marcus Noland

* = out of print

POLICY ANALYSES IN INTERNATIONAL ECONOMICS Series

1 The Lending Policies of the International Monetary Fund* John Williamson
August 1982 ISBN 0-88132-000-5

2 "Reciprocity": A New Approach to World Trade Policy?* William R. Cline
September 1982 ISBN 0-88132-001-3

3 Trade Policy in the 1980s* C. Fred Bergsten and William R. Cline
November 1982 ISBN 0-88132-002-1

4 International Debt and the Stability of the World Economy* William R. Cline
September 1983 ISBN 0-88132-010-2

5 The Exchange Rate System,* 2d ed. John Williamson
Sept. 1983, rev. June 1985 ISBN 0-88132-034-X

6 Economic Sanctions in Support of Foreign Policy Goals* Gary Clyde Hufbauer and Jeffrey J. Schott
October 1983 ISBN 0-88132-014-5

7 A New SDR Allocation?* John Williamson
March 1984 ISBN 0-88132-028-5

8 An International Standard for Monetary Stabilization* Ronald L. McKinnon
March 1984 ISBN 0-88132-018-8

9 The Yen/Dollar Agreement: Liberalizing Japanese Capital Markets* Jeffrey Frankel
December 1984 ISBN 0-88132-035-8

10 Bank Lending to Developing Countries: The Policy Alternatives* C. Fred Bergsten, William R. Cline, and John Williamson
April 1985 ISBN 0-88132-032-3

11 Trading for Growth: The Next Round of Trade Negotiations* Gary Clyde Hufbauer and Jeffrey J. Schott
September 1985 ISBN 0-88132-033-1

12 Financial Intermediation Beyond the Debt Crisis* Donald R. Lessard and John Williamson
September 1985 ISBN 0-88132-021-8

13 The United States-Japan Economic Problem* C. Fred Bergsten and William R. Cline, Oct. 1985, 2d ed. January 1987
ISBN 0-88132-060-9

14 Deficits and the Dollar: The World Economy at Risk* Stephen Marris
Dec. 1985, 2d ed. November 1987
ISBN 0-88132-067-6

15 Trade Policy for Troubled Industries* Gary Clyde Hufbauer and Howard F. Rosen
March 1986 ISBN 0-88132-020-X

16 The United States and Canada: The Quest for Free Trade* Paul Wonnacott, with an appendix by John Williamson
March 1987 ISBN 0-88132-056-0

17 Adjusting to Success: Balance of Payments Policy in the East Asian NICs* Bela Balassa and John Williamson
June 1987, rev. April 1990
ISBN 0-88132-101-X

18 Mobilizing Bank Lending to Debtor Countries* William R. Cline
June 1987 ISBN 0-88132-062-5

19 Auction Quotas and United States Trade Policy* C. Fred Bergsten, Kimberly Ann Elliott, Jeffrey J. Schott, and Wendy E. Takacs
September 1987 ISBN 0-88132-050-1

20 Agriculture and the GATT: Rewriting the Rules* Dale E. Hathaway
September 1987 ISBN 0-88132-052-8

21 Anti-Protection: Changing Forces in United States Trade Politics* I. M. Destler and John S. Odell
September 1987 ISBN 0-88132-043-9

22 Targets and Indicators: A Blueprint for the International Coordination of Economic Policy John Williamson and Marcus Miller
September 1987 ISBN 0-88132-051-X

23 Capital Flight: The Problem and Policy Responses* Donald R. Lessard and John Williamson
December 1987 ISBN 0-88132-059-5

24 United States-Canada Free Trade: An Evaluation of the Agreement* Jeffrey J. Schott
April 1988 ISBN 0-88132-072-2

25 Voluntary Approaches to Debt Relief* John Williamson
Sept. 1988, rev. May 1989
ISBN 0-88132-098-6

26 American Trade Adjustment: The Global Impact* William R. Cline
March 1989 ISBN 0-88132-095-1

27 More Free Trade Areas?* Jeffrey J. Schott
May 1989 ISBN 0-88132-085-4

28 The Progress of Policy Reform in Latin America* John Williamson
January 1990 ISBN 0-88132-100-1

29 The Global Trade Negotiations: What Can Be Achieved?* Jeffrey J. Schott
September 1990 ISBN 0-88132-137-0

30 Economic Policy Coordination: Requiem for Prologue?* Wendy Dobson
April 1991 ISBN 0-88132-102-8

31 The Economic Opening of Eastern Europe* John Williamson
May 1991 ISBN 0-88132-186-9

32 Eastern Europe and the Soviet Union in the World Economy* Susan Collins and Dani Rodrik
May 1991 ISBN 0-88132-157-5

33 African Economic Reform: The External Dimension* Carol Lancaster
June 1991 ISBN 0-88132-096-X

34 Has the Adjustment Process Worked?* Paul R. Krugman
October 1991 ISBN 0-88132-116-8

Subsidies in International Trade* Gary Clyde Hufbauer and Joanna Shelton Erb
1984 ISBN 0-88132-004-8

International Debt: Systemic Risk and Policy Response* William R. Cline
1984 ISBN 0-88132-015-3

Trade Protection in the United States: 31 Case Studies* Gary Clyde Hufbauer, Diane E. Berliner, and Kimberly Ann Elliott
1986 ISBN 0-88132-040-4

Toward Renewed Economic Growth in Latin America* Bela Balassa, Gerardo M. Bueno, Pedro Pablo Kuczynski, and Mario Henrique Simonsen
1986 ISBN 0-88132-045-5

Capital Flight and Third World Debt*
Donald R. Lessard and John Williamson, eds.
1987 ISBN 0-88132-053-6

The Canada-United States Free Trade Agreement: The Global Impact* Jeffrey J. Schott and Murray G. Smith, eds.
1988 ISBN 0-88132-073-0

World Agricultural Trade: Building a Consensus* William M. Miner and Dale E. Hathaway, eds.
1988 ISBN 0-88132-071-3

Japan in the World Economy* Bela Balassa and Marcus Noland
1988 ISBN 0-88132-041-2

America in the World Economy: A Strategy for the 1990s* C. Fred Bergsten
1988 ISBN 0-88132-089-7

Managing the Dollar: From the Plaza to the Louvre* Yoichi Funabashi
1988, 2d ed. 1989 ISBN 0-88132-097-8

United States External Adjustment and the World Economy* William R. Cline
May 1989 ISBN 0-88132-048-X

Free Trade Areas and U.S. Trade Policy*
Jeffrey J. Schott, ed.
May 1989 ISBN 0-88132-094-3

Dollar Politics: Exchange Rate Policymaking in the United States* I. M. Destler and C. Randall Henning
September 1989 ISBN 0-88132-079-X

Latin American Adjustment: How Much Has Happened?* John Williamson, ed.
April 1990 ISBN 0-88132-125-7

The Future of World Trade in Textiles and Apparel* William R. Cline
1987, 2d ed. June 1999 ISBN 0-88132-110-9

Completing the Uruguay Round: A Results-Oriented Approach to the GATT Trade Negotiations* Jeffrey J. Schott, ed.
September 1990 ISBN 0-88132-130-3

Economic Sanctions Reconsidered (2 volumes) Economic Sanctions Reconsidered: Supplemental Case Histories
Gary Clyde Hufbauer, Jeffrey J. Schott, and Kimberly Ann Elliott
1985, 2d ed. Dec. 1990 ISBN cloth 0-88132-115-X
ISBN paper 0-88132-105-2

Economic Sanctions Reconsidered: History and Current Policy Gary C. Hufbauer, Jeffrey J. Schott, and Kimberly Ann Elliott
December 1990 ISBN cloth 0-88132-140-0
ISBN paper 0-88132-136-2

Pacific Basin Developing Countries: Prospects for the Future* Marcus Noland
January 1991 ISBN cloth 0-88132-141-9
ISBN paper 0-88132-081-1

Currency Convertibility in Eastern Europe*
John Williamson, ed.
October 1991 ISBN 0-88132-128-1

International Adjustment and Financing: The Lessons of 1985-1991* C. Fred Bergsten, ed.
January 1992 ISBN 0-88132-112-5

North American Free Trade: Issues and Recommendations* Gary Clyde Hufbauer and Jeffrey J. Schott
April 1992 ISBN 0-88132-120-6

Narrowing the U.S. Current Account Deficit*
Alan J. Lenz
June 1992 ISBN 0-88132-103-6

The Economics of Global Warming
William R. Cline
June 1992 ISBN 0-88132-132-X

US Taxation of International Income: Blueprint for Reform Gary Clyde Hufbauer, assisted by Joanna M. van Rooij
October 1992 ISBN 0-88132-134-6

Who's Bashing Whom? Trade Conflict in High-Technology Industries Laura D'Andrea Tyson
November 1992 ISBN 0-88132-106-0

Korea in the World Economy* Il SaKong
January 1993 ISBN 0-88132-183-4

Pacific Dynamism and the International Economic System* C. Fred Bergsten and Marcus Noland, eds.
May 1993 ISBN 0-88132-196-6

Economic Consequences of Soviet Disintegration* John Williamson, ed.
May 1993 ISBN 0-88132-190-7

Reconcilable Differences? United States-Japan Economic Conflict* C. Fred Bergsten and Marcus Noland
June 1993 ISBN 0-88132-129-X

Does Foreign Exchange Intervention Work?
Kathryn M. Dominguez and Jeffrey A. Frankel
September 1993 ISBN 0-88132-104-4

Sizing Up U.S. Export Disincentives*
J. David Richardson
September 1993 ISBN 0-88132-107-9

NAFTA: An Assessment Gary Clyde Hufbauer and Jeffrey J. Schott, *rev. ed.*
October 1993 ISBN 0-88132-199-0

Adjusting to Volatile Energy Prices
Philip K. Verleger, Jr.
November 1993 ISBN 0-88132-069-2

The Political Economy of Policy Reform
John Williamson, ed.
January 1994 ISBN 0-88132-195-8

Measuring the Costs of Protection in the United States Gary Clyde Hufbauer and Kimberly Ann Elliott
January 1994 ISBN 0-88132-108-7

Trade Policy and Global Poverty
William R. Cline
June 2004   ISBN 0-88132-365-9
Bailouts or Bail-ins? Responding to Financial Crises in Emerging Economies   Nouriel Roubini and Brad Setser
August 2004   ISBN 0-88132-371-3
Transforming the European Economy   Martin Neil Baily and Jacob Funk Kirkegaard
September 2004   ISBN 0-88132-343-8
Chasing Dirty Money: The Fight Against Money Laundering   Peter Reuter and Edwin M. Truman
November 2004   ISBN 0-88132-370-5
The United States and the World Economy: Foreign Economic Policy for the Next Decade
C. Fred Bergsten
January 2005   ISBN 0-88132-380-2
Does Foreign Direct Investment Promote Development?   Theodore H. Moran, Edward M. Graham, and Magnus Blomström, eds.
April 2005   ISBN 0-88132-381-0
American Trade Politics, 4th ed.   I. M. Destler
June 2005   ISBN 0-88132-382-9
Why Does Immigration Divide America? Public Finance and Political Opposition to Open Borders   Gordon H. Hanson
August 2005   ISBN 0-88132-400-0
Reforming the US Corporate Tax   Gary Clyde Hufbauer and Paul L. E. Grieco
September 2005   ISBN 0-88132-384-5
The United States as a Debtor Nation
William R. Cline
September 2005   ISBN 0-88132-399-3
NAFTA Revisited: Achievements and Challenges   Gary Clyde Hufbauer and Jeffrey J. Schott, assisted by Paul L. E. Grieco and Yee Wong
October 2005   ISBN 0-88132-334-9
US National Security and Foreign Direct Investment   Edward M. Graham and David M. Marchick
May 2006   ISBN 978-0-88132-391-7
Accelerating the Globalization of America: The Role for Information Technology   Catherine L. Mann, assisted by Jacob Funk Kirkegaard
June 2006   ISBN 978-0-88132-390-0
Delivering on Doha: Farm Trade and the Poor
Kimberly Ann Elliott
July 2006   ISBN 978-0-88132-392-4
Case Studies in US Trade Negotiation, Vol. 1: Making the Rules   Charan Devereaux, Robert Z. Lawrence, and Michael Watkins
September 2006   ISBN 978-0-88132-362-7
Case Studies in US Trade Negotiation, Vol. 2: Resolving Disputes   Charan Devereaux, Robert Z. Lawrence, and Michael Watkins
September 2006   ISBN 978-0-88132-363-2
C. Fred Bergsten and the World Economy
Michael Mussa, ed.
December 2006   ISBN 978-0-88132-397-9
Working Papers, Volume I   Peterson Institute
December 2006   ISBN 978-0-88132-388-7
The Arab Economies in a Changing World
Marcus Noland and Howard Pack
April 2007   ISBN 978-0-88132-393-1

Working Papers, Volume II   Peterson Institute
April 2007   ISBN 978-0-88132-404-4
Global Warming and Agriculture: Impact Estimates by Country   William R. Cline
July 2007   ISBN 978-0-88132-403-7
US Taxation of Foreign Income   Gary Clyde Hufbauer and Ariel Assa
October 2007   ISBN 978-0-88132-405-1
Russia's Capitalist Revolution: Why Market Reform Succeeded and Democracy Failed
Anders Åslund
October 2007   ISBN 978-0-88132-409-9
Economic Sanctions Reconsidered, 3d ed.
Gary Clyde Hufbauer, Jeffrey J. Schott, Kimberly Ann Elliott, and Barbara Oegg
November 2007
             ISBN hardcover 978-0-88132-407-5
     ISBN hardcover/CD-ROM 978-0-88132-408-2
Debating China's Exchange Rate Policy
Morris Goldstein and Nicholas R. Lardy, eds.
April 2008   ISBN 978-0-88132-415-0
Leveling the Carbon Playing Field: International Competition and US Climate Policy Design
Trevor Houser, Rob Bradley, Britt Childs, Jacob Werksman, and Robert Heilmayr
May 2008   ISBN 978-0-88132-420-4
Accountability and Oversight of US Exchange Rate Policy   C. Randall Henning
June 2008   ISBN 978-0-88132-419-8
Challenges of Globalization: Imbalances and Growth   Anders Åslund and Marek Dabrowski, eds.
July 2008   ISBN 978-0-88132-418-1
China's Rise: Challenges and Opportunities
C. Fred Bergsten, Charles Freeman, Nicholas R. Lardy, and Derek J. Mitchell
September 2008   ISBN 978-0-88132-417-4
Banking on Basel: The Future of International Financial Regulation   Daniel K. Tarullo
September 2008   ISBN 978-0-88132-423-5
US Pension Reform: Lessons from Other Countries   Martin Neil Baily and Jacob Funk Kirkegaard
February 2009   ISBN 978-0-88132-425-9
How Ukraine Became a Market Economy and Democracy   Anders Åslund
March 2009   ISBN 978-0-88132-427-3
Global Warming and the World Trading System
Gary Clyde Hufbauer, Steve Charnovitz, and Jisun Kim
March 2009   ISBN 978-0-88132-428-0
The Russia Balance Sheet   Anders Åslund and Andrew Kuchins
March 2009   ISBN 978-0-88132-424-2
The Euro at Ten: The Next Global Currency?
Jean Pisani-Ferry and Adam S. Posen, eds.
July 2009   ISBN 978-0-88132-430-3
Financial Globalization, Economic Growth, and the Crisis of 2007–09   William R. Cline
May 2010   ISBN 978-0-88132-4990-0
Russia after the Global Economic Crisis
Anders Åslund, Sergei Guriev, and Andrew Kuchins, eds.
June 2010   ISBN 978-0-88132-497-6

Sovereign Wealth Funds: Threat or Salvation?
Edwin M. Truman
September 2010   ISBN 978-0-88132-498-3
The Last Shall Be the First: The East European
Financial Crisis, 2008–10   Anders Åslund
October 2010   ISBN 978-0-88132-521-8
Witness to Transformation: Refugee Insights
into North Korea   Stephan Haggard and
Marcus Noland
January 2011   ISBN 978-0-88132-438-9
Foreign Direct Investment and Development:
Launching a Second Generation of Policy
Research, Avoiding the Mistakes of the First,
Reevaluating Policies for Developed and
Developing Countries   Theodore H. Moran
April 2011   ISBN 978-0-88132-600-0
How Latvia Came through the Financial Crisis
Anders Åslund and Valdis Dombrovskis
May 2011   ISBN 978-0-88132-602-4
Global Trade in Services: Fear, Facts, and
Offshoring   J. Bradford Jensen
August 2011   ISBN 978-0-88132-601-7
NAFTA and Climate Change Meera Fickling and
Jeffrey J. Schott
September 2011   ISBN 978-0-88132-436-5
Eclipse: Living in the Shadow of China's
Economic Dominance   Arvind Subramanian
September 2011   ISBN 978-0-88132-606-2
Flexible Exchange Rates for a Stable World
Economy   Joseph E. Gagnon with
Marc Hinterschweiger
September 2011   ISBN 978-0-88132-627-7
The Arab Economies in a Changing World,
2d ed.   Marcus Noland and Howard Pack
November 2011   ISBN 978-0-88132-628-4
Sustaining China's Economic Growth After the
Global Financial Crisis   Nicholas R. Lardy
January 2012   ISBN 978-0-88132-626-0
Who Needs to Open the Capital Account?
Olivier Jeanne, Arvind Subramanian, and John
Williamson
April 2012   ISBN 978-0-88132-511-9
Devaluing to Prosperity: Misaligned Currencies
and Their Growth Consequences Surjit S. Bhalla
August 2012   ISBN 978-0-88132-623-9
Private Rights and Public Problems: The Global
Economics of Intellectual Property in the 21st
Century   Keith E. Maskus
September 2012   ISBN 978-0-88132-507-2
Global Economics in Extraordinary Times:
Essays in Honor of John Williamson
C. Fred Bergsten and C. Randall Henning, eds.
November 2012   ISBN 978-0-88132-662-8
Rising Tide: Is Growth in Emerging Economies
Good for the United States?   Lawrence Edwards
and Robert Z. Lawrence
February 2013   ISBN 978-0-88132-500-3
Responding to Financial Crisis: Lessons from
Asia Then, the United States and Europe Now
Changyong Rhee and Adam S. Posen, eds
October 2013   ISBN 978-0-88132-674-1
Fueling Up: The Economic Implications of
America's Oil and Gas Boom
Trevor Houser and Shashank Mohan
January 2014   ISBN 978-0-88132-656-7

How Latin America Weathered the Global
Financial Crisis   José De Gregorio
January 2014   ISBN 978-0-88132-678-9
Confronting the Curse: The Economics and
Geopolitics of Natural Resource Governance
Cullen S. Hendrix and Marcus Noland
May 2014   ISBN 978-0-88132-676-5

SPECIAL REPORTS

1   Promoting World Recovery: A Statement on
    Global Economic Strategy*
    by 26 Economists from Fourteen Countries
    December 1982   ISBN 0-88132-013-7
2   Prospects for Adjustment in Argentina,
    Brazil, and Mexico: Responding to the Debt
    Crisis*   John Williamson, ed.
    June 1983   ISBN 0-88132-016-1
3   Inflation and Indexation: Argentina, Brazil,
    and Israel*   John Williamson, ed.
    March 1985   ISBN 0-88132-037-4
4   Global Economic Imb alances*
    C. Fred Bergsten, ed.
    March 1986   ISBN 0-88132-042-0
5   African Debt and Financing*   Carol
    Lancaster and John Williamson, eds.
    May 1986   ISBN 0-88132-044-7
6   Resolving the Global Economic Crisis:
    After Wall Street*   by Thirty-three
    Economists from Thirteen Countries
    December 1987   ISBN 0-88132-070-6
7   World Economic Problems*   Kimberly Ann
    Elliott and John Williamson, eds.
    April 1988   ISBN 0-88132-055-2
    Reforming World Agricultural Trade*
    by Twenty-nine Professionals from
    Seventeen Countries
    1988   ISBN 0-88132-088-9
8   Economic Relations Between the United
    States and Korea: Conflict or Cooperation?*
    Thomas O. Bayard and Soogil Young, eds.
    January 1989   ISBN 0-88132-068-4
9   Whither APEC? The Progress to Date and
    Agenda for the Future* C. Fred Bergsten, ed.
    October 1997   ISBN 0-88132-248-2
10 Economic Integration of the Korean
    Peninsula   Marcus Noland, ed.
    January 1998   ISBN 0-88132-255-5
11 Restarting Fast Track*   Jeffrey J. Schott, ed.
    April 1998   ISBN 0-88132-259-8
12 Launching New Global Trade Talks: An
    Action Agenda   Jeffrey J. Schott, ed.
    September 1998   ISBN 0-88132-266-0
13 Japan's Financial Crisis and Its Parallels to
    US Experience   Ryoichi Mikitani and
    Adam S. Posen, eds.
    September 2000   ISBN 0-88132-289-X
14 The Ex-Im Bank in the 21st Century: A New
    Approach   Gary Clyde Hufbauer and
    Rita M. Rodriguez, eds.
    January 2001   ISBN 0-88132-300-4
15 The Korean Diaspora in the World
    Economy   C. Fred Bergsten and
    Inbom Choi, eds.
    January 2003   ISBN 0-88132-358-6

WORKS IN PROGRESS

DISTRIBUTORS OUTSIDE THE UNITED STATES

**Australia, New Zealand,
and Papua New Guinea**
Co Info Pty Ltd
648 Whitehorse Road Mitcham VIC 3132
Australia
Tel: +61 3 9210 77567
Fax: +61 3 9210 7788
Email: babadilla@coinfo.com.au
www.coinfo.com.au

India, Bangladesh, Nepal, and Sri Lanka
Viva Books Private Limited
Mr. Vinod Vasishtha
4737/23 Ansari Road
Daryaganj, New Delhi 110002
India
Tel: 91-11-4224-2200
Fax: 91-11-4224-2240
Email: viva@vivagroupindia.net
www.vivagroupindia.com

**Mexico, Central America, South America,
and Puerto Rico**
US PubRep, Inc.
311 Dean Drive
Rockville, MD 20851
Tel: 301-838-9276
Fax: 301-838-9278
Email: c.falk@ieee.org

Asia (*Brunei, Burma, Cambodia, China,
Hong Kong, Indonesia, Korea, Laos, Malaysia,
Philippines, Singapore, Taiwan, Thailand,
and Vietnam*)
East-West Export Books (EWEB)
University of Hawaii Press
2840 Kolowalu Street
Honolulu, Hawaii 96822-1888
Tel: 808-956-8830
Fax: 808-988-6052
Email: eweb@hawaii.edu

Canada
Renouf Bookstore
5369 Canotek Road, Unit 1
Ottawa, Ontario KlJ 9J3, Canada
Tel: 613-745-2665
Fax: 613-745-7660
www.renoufbooks.com

Japan
United Publishers Services Ltd.
1-32-5, Higashi-shinagawa
Shinagawa-ku, Tokyo 140-0002
Japan
Tel: 81-3-5479-7251
Fax: 81-3-5479-7307
Email: purchasing@ups.co.jp
*For trade accounts only. Individuals will find
Institute books in leading Tokyo bookstores.*

Middle East
MERIC
2 Bahgat Ali Street, El Masry Towers
Tower D, Apt. 24
Zamalek, Cairo
Egypt
Tel. 20-2-7633824
Fax: 20-2-7369355
Email: mahmoud_fouda@mericonline.com
www.mericonline.com

United Kingdom, Europe
(*including Russia and Turkey*)**, Africa,
and Israel**
The Eurospan Group
c/o Turpin Distribution
Pegasus Drive
Stratton Business Park
Biggleswade, Bedfordshire
SG18 8TQ
United Kingdom
Tel: 44 (0) 1767-604972
Fax: 44 (0) 1767-601640
Email: eurospan@turpin-distribution.com
www.eurospangroup.com/bookstore

**Visit our website at:
www.piie.com
E-mail orders to:
petersonmail@presswarehouse.com**